Conservation Criminology

Conservation Criminology

Edited by Meredith L. Gore

Michigan State University
USA

Registered Office
John Wiley & Sons Ltd, The Atrium, Southern Gate, Chichester, West Sussex, PO19 8SQ, UK

Editorial Offices
111 River Street, Hoboken, NJ 07030, USA
9600 Garsington Road, Oxford, OX4 2DQ, UK
The Atrium, Southern Gate, Chichester, West Sussex, PO19 8SQ, UK
Boschstr. 12, 69469 Weinheim, Germany

For details of our global editorial offices, customer services, and more information about Wiley products visit us at www.wiley.com.

Wiley also publishes its books in a variety of electronic formats and by print-on-demand. Some content that appears in standard print versions of this book may not be available in other formats.

Library of Congress Cataloging-in-Publication data applied for

ISBN: 9781118935484 (Hardback)

Cover Design: Wiley
Cover Image: (Right Images: Top to bottom) © somnuk krobkum/Gettyimages; © Kate Capture/Shutterstock; (Left Images: Top to bottom) david pearson/Alamy Stock Photo; © bluefern/Gettyimages; (Background) © Przemyslaw Wasilewski/Shutterstock

Set in 10/12pt Warnock by SPi Global, Pondicherry, India

10 9 8 7 6 5 4 3 2 1

To Mike, Claire, and Rachel, for your patience, support, and feedback. To Joel and Wendy, for never questioning my path. To Jonah, for teaching me what urgency with optimism can look like.

Contents

Notes on Contributors

Dr. Mark A. Axelrod is Associate Professor in Michigan State University's James Madison College and Department of Fisheries and Wildlife. His teaching and research center around comparative and international environmental law and politics, with a particular focus on India. His recent work is published in *The Journal of Environment & Development*, *Environmental Policy & Governance*, and the *European Journal of International Relations*. Mark is also active with the United Planet Faith & Science Initiative, and serves on the editorial board of the journal *Global Environmental Politics*.

Dr. Christine Browne-Nuñez received her Ph.D. in Wildlife Ecology and Conservation from the University of Florida, MS in Human Dimensions of Natural Resources from Colorado State University, and BA in Education from the University of Missouri. As a post-doctoral research associate at the University of Wisconsin-Madison Nelson Institute for Environmental Studies, she applied social science theory and methods to identify predictors of social tolerance of wolves. Christine served the Associate Director of Community Based Conservation at the San Diego Zoo Institute for Conservation Research. Currently, as a conservation social scientist with the U.S. Fish and Wildlife Service, Christine works to build human dimensions capacity in the agency through training, research, and technical support.

Dr. Julia Novak Colwell earned her Ph.D. in Fisheries & Wildlife at Michigan State University (2016) where she also earned her MSc (2013). She is currently Visiting Assistant Professor in the Pennoni Honors College at Drexel University. Her research has focused on the unintended impacts of resource management regulations, particularly pertaining to the fisheries sector in Tamil Nadu, India. Her current research aims to identify how underrepresented segments of the fisherfolk population, particularly women, are affected by management hierarchies and fisheries regulations and how those impacts feedback to influence resource use and resource health.

Dr. Fei Fang received her Ph.D. from the Department of Computer Science at the University of Southern California. She received her bachelor degree from the Department of Electronic Engineering, Tsinghua University in July 2011. Her research lies in the field of artificial intelligence and multi-agent systems, focusing on computational game theory with applications to security and sustainability domains. Her work has won the Deployed Application Award at

Innovative Applications of Artificial Intelligence, the Outstanding Paper Award in Computational Sustainability Track at the International Joint Conferences on Artificial Intelligence. She is the recipient of WiSE Merit Fellowship, and she has been awarded the Meritorious Team Commendation from Commandant of the US Coast Guard and Flag Letter of Appreciation from Vice Admiral. Her work has led to real-world applications that have fundamentally altered current practices of security resource allocation. Her work on "Protecting Moving Targets with Mobile Resources" has been deployed by the US Coast Guard for protecting the Staten Island Ferry in New York City since April 2013. Her work on designing patrol strategies to combat illegal poaching has lead to the deployment of PAWS application in a conservation area in Southeast Asia for protecting tigers.

Austin Flowers received his B.A. in International Relations from James Madison College at Michigan State University. His research focuses on criminal exploitation growth in the electronic waste trade to find possible deterrence strategies through legislating financial and criminal penalties. He is preparing for law school in the fall of 2017 while investigating entrepreneurial opportunities in electronic waste recycling.

Dr. David Foran is the Director of the Forensic Science Graduate Program at Michigan State University, which was founded in 1947. He is a Fellow of the American Academy of Forensic Sciences, is on the Editorial Board of The Journal of Forensic Sciences, and is court qualified as an expert on both nuclear and mitochondrial DNA profiling. He obtained his PhD in molecular genetics from the University of Michigan, was a post-doctoral fellow at McGill University in Montreal, and was a research associate at the University of California at Santa Cruz. Dr. Foran's area of expertise is forensic biology, focusing on human and animal identification using both nuclear and mitochondrial DNA. His research has been funded by the National Institutes of Justice, the Technical Support Working Group, the Department of Defense, and other agencies. He and his graduate students aid a variety of local, state, and federal agencies with specialized casework, are advisors to the Michigan Innocence Project, and conduct research on historical cases of broad interest.

Benjamin Ford is a fourth year Ph.D. student of Computer Science at the University of Southern California's Viterbi School of Engineering. He joined the Teamcore research group in August 2013 and is advised by Professor Milind Tambe. Previously, he completed his B.S. and M.S. in Computer Science at the University of Massachusetts Dartmouth in 2008 and 2010, respectively. After graduation and prior to joining Teamcore, he worked at the Naval Undersea Warfare Center in Newport, RI as a Software Engineer. Ben's primary research interests are in the application of concepts from the social sciences of Psychology, Criminology, Sociology, and Anthropology to improve the algorithms and solutions of Computer Science. Specifically, he is interested in applying human behavioral models to multi-agent systems with a large focus on human decision making. Since joining Teamcore, he has also developed an interest in applying Behavioral Game Theory to the Wildlife Conservation domain.

Dr. Jacinta M. Gau is an associate professor in the Department of Criminal Justice at the University of Central Florida. Her research is primarily in policing, with an emphasis on racial issues, police–community relations, procedural justice, and police legitimacy. Her work has appeared in journals such as Justice Quarterly, Criminal Justice and Behavior, Crime and Delinquency, and Journal of Criminal Justice.

Mark C. G. Gibson is a doctoral student at the School of Criminal Justice, Michigan State University. He has an MA in Economics and Environmental Policy from the School of Advanced International Studies, Johns Hopkins, and a BA in International Relations from the University of Pennsylvania. Prior to starting his PhD program, Mark supported World Wildlife Fund's on-the-ground work to reform Latin American fisheries management, and the Pew Charitable Trusts to advocate for conservation of vulnerable deep-sea ecosystems globally. His research interests include wildlife and fisheries crime, data-poor compliance assessment, organizational theory of conservation enforcement, and voluntary compliance drivers.

Dr. Meredith L. Gore is a conservation social scientist whose interdisciplinary research explores relationships between human behavior and the environment. She is an Associate Professor in the Department of Fisheries & Wildlife and School of Criminal Justice at Michigan State University (MSU). She is a National Academies of Science Jefferson Science Fellow serving as a Senior Science Advisor in the Office of the Geographer and Global Issues at the U.S. Department of State. Dr. Gore is a MSU Global Research Fellow and President of the Society for Conservation Biology's Social Science Working Group. Her research interests focus on community-based natural resource management and enhancing understanding of risk concepts and their application to biodiversity conservation. Dr. Gore co-developed the Conservation Criminology research framework and teaching certificate program at MSU; the interdisciplinary approach synthesizes natural resource policy, risk and decision analysis, and crime science. Her leadership in this field has resulted in new scientific insight regarding conservation of species such as white sharks, lemurs, cranes, sea turtles, rhinos, elephants, ploughshare tortoises, double-crested cormorants, black bears and gray wolves. Dr. Gore received her PhD in Natural Resource Policy and Management from Cornell University, MA in Environment and Resource Policy from George Washington University, and BA in Anthropology and Environmental Studies from Brandeis University. Phi Kappa Phi has recognized Dr. Gore's leadership in interdisciplinary research.

Katherine Groff received her MS from the Department of Fisheries and Wildlife at Michigan State University. Under the advisement of Dr. Mark Axelrod, she studied the conflicts between community development and conservation goals in resource management across national borders. Her interests lie in science policy and animal protection, and she currently applies.

Jamie Hogberg earned her MS in Conservation Biology at UW Madison, and is academic staff for the Nelson Institute for Environmental Studies' Environmental Conservation Professional Masters Program. She also directs the Society for

Conservation Biology – North America's biennial North American congress (2016). Her research focuses on human–wolf conflict, management, and policy in the mid western U.S. Her prior work includes avian and tropical conservation in the Western U.S. and South America.

Jessica S. Kahler is a PhD candidate at Michigan State University, researching applied conservation criminology, and an independent consultant currently working to develop community-based wildlife crime prevention approaches. She has conducted applied, interdisciplinary social science research on wildlife crimes, such as poaching, and facilitated training related to wildlife crime prevention in Cameroon, Indonesia, Madagascar, and Namibia. In 2010 she received a MS in Fisheries and Wildlife from Michigan State University with a focus on the human dimensions of human-wildlife conflict in community conservation areas in the Zambezi, Namibia. Attending The Ohio State University she received a BA in Anthropology and a BS in Natural Resources Management, with distinction in Wildlife Management. Prior to attending MSU, she served in the US Peace Corps for three years as a Community Coastal Resources Advisor and National ReefCheck Coordinator in the island country of Vanuatu.

Dr. Jens Karlsson Frank is a Researcher at the Department of Ecology and Wildlife Damage Center at the Swedish Agricultural University. He works extensively with applied research on problem situations with large predators. His research primarily focuses on damage to domestic animals and various measures to prevent these but is also interdisciplinary and explores connections with people's fear of bears and wolves.

Dr. Heidi Kretser is the Deputy Director, Conservation and Communities, for the Wildlife Conservation Society's North America Program. She has worked with WCS for 18 years in numerous capacities, her current interests include addressing complex conservation questions by creating effective communication that generates action on topics as varied as wildlife trafficking and white-nose syndrome, devising strategies for reducing the impacts of low-density rural development on wildlife, and building collaborative approaches for increasing capacity and achieving conservation outcomes across diverse constituents. She completed her Ph.D. in the Human Dimensions Research Unit at Cornell University and holds a master's degree from the Yale School of Forestry. She also serves as Adjunct Associate Professor at Cornell University's Department of Natural Resources.

Dr. Andrew M. Lemieux is a Researcher at the Netherlands Institute for the Study of Crime and Law Enforcement. His main areas of interest are the spatial and temporal distribution of crime, the use of technology to improve law enforcement operations, and anti-poaching operations in Africa.

Alexa Montefiore is a Program Manager for the Wildlife Conservation Society's (WCS) Americas Program. Prior to this position, she served as the Program Manager for the SMART Partnership, a collaboration of nine global conservation organizations, addressing a pressing conservation need by creating a proven, simple to deploy, free solution to strengthen conservation management. She worked across the Partnership to encourage adoption of SMART worldwide and to establish greater support for the implementing partners. Prior to joining SMART, she worked at Ogilvy Public Relations Worldwide, focusing on a range of initiatives for social good, with the ultimate goal of helping people live happier, healthier, and safer lives. Alexa is interested in cultivating innovative programs that help people think and act differently. Alexa received a master's degree from NYU in Environmental Conservation.

Dr. William D. Moreto is an assistant professor in the Department of Criminal Justice at the University of Central Florida and a visiting scholar at the Netherlands Institute for the Study of Crime and Law Enforcement. He received his doctorate from the Rutgers School of Criminal Justice. His research focuses on environmental criminology and crime prevention, wildlife crime, and wildlife law enforcement. His research has been published in The British Journal of Criminology, Justice Quarterly, Deviant Behavior, European Journal on Criminal Policy and Research, Crime Science and Oryx: The International Journal of Conservation.

Dr. Lisa Naughton-Treves is a Geography professor at the University of Wisconsin-Madison, USA. Her research concerns the social dimensions of biodiversity conservation, with particular emphasis on protected areas and land use conflicts in the tropics. She has long-term field studies in Uganda, Ecuador, and Peru. She directed UW-Madison's Land Tenure Center, chaired the graduate program in Conservation Biology and Sustainable Development, and now chairs the Geography Department.

Jessica Bell Rizzolo is a Ph.D. student in Sociology at Michigan State University who holds specializations in Animal Studies, Environmental Science and Policy, and Conservation Criminology, and an affiliate of the Kerulos Center. Jessica's research areas include trans-species psychology, discursive representations of wildlife, the sociopolitical dynamics of conservation initiatives, wildlife tourism, and the illegal wildlife trade. Her current work focuses on mahout cultures and psychological indicators of elephant trauma and wellbeing in Thailand.

Dr. Shawn J. Riley is the Parrish Storrs Lovejoy Professor of Wildlife Management in the Department of Fisheries and Wildlife at Michigan State University, and a scientist in the Partnership for Ecosystem Research and Management. He is a Fellow in The Wildlife Society, and was a Senior Fulbright Fellow at the Swedish Agricultural University. His research focuses mostly on human-wildlife interactions, how those interactions affect human attitudes and behaviors toward wildlife, and how to more effectively integrate social science insights in decisions about wildlife management. Shawn teaches a senior-level course, Human Dimensions of Fisheries and Wildlife, at MSU for which he was awarded his college's Excellence in Teaching Award.

Dr. Brent A. Rudolph is a Wildlife Research Specialist and serves as the Social Science Coordinator for the Michigan Department of Natural Resources, Wildlife Division. Brent earned his Ph.D. in Fisheries and Wildlife (working in the human dimensions focus area and with the conservation criminology program) from Michigan State University, his M.S. in Environmental and Forest Biology (with a wildlife biology concentration) from the SUNY College of Environmental Science and Forestry, and his B.S. in Biology (with a field studies concentration) from Ohio Northern University. Brent is involved in a wide variety of multidisciplinary and interdisciplinary research projects. He has enjoyed collaborating with numerous agency, university, and nongovernmental organization partners to comprehensively inform natural resource management and public policy over more than 17 years of public service. His current focus is on improving wildlife governance through gaining greater understanding of how the public forms judgments of trust in wildlife agencies, and the effects of that trust and other factors on compliance and cooperation with management programs.

Dr. Niki Rust is a wildlife conservationist with a special interest in using social science to better understand conservation problems. She focuses on bridging qualitative ethnographic studies with quantitative methods and is particularly keen on devising participatory decision-making tools. Her research topics include community-based conservation, human-wildlife interactions and African carnivores. Niki recently completed a PhD at the University of Kent, UK, where she studied the interaction between farmers, farm workers, livestock and wildlife on Namibia's commercial farms. She is now working as a Wildlife Technical Adviser for WWF-UK. In her spare time, Niki a journalist and is keen on furthering science communication to benefit society.

Dr. Emma Stokes is the Director of Conservation Science for the Wildlife Conservation Society's Africa Program. She has 20 years' experience of conservation science and management in tropical forests, with a focus on large mammal ecology and population status. She has conducted fieldwork on apes in Indonesia, Uganda and Republic of Congo, and coordinated landscape-scale implementation of conservation assessment and wildlife monitoring programs for apes and elephants in Northern Congo and for tigers across South-East Asia. Her skills include scientific design and application of management-focused biodiversity monitoring programs and strategic evaluation of conservation outcomes, with a focus on law enforcement effectiveness. She holds a degree in Natural Sciences from Cambridge University and a PhD in cognitive ecology from the University of St Andrews. She has worked for the Wildlife Conservation Society since 1999.

Dr. Aksel Sundström is a postdoctoral researcher affiliated to the Quality of Government (QoG) Institute, University of Gothenburg, Sweden. His research agenda focuses on public administration and political institutions. He is also working on women's political representation. Sundström has published in peer-reviewed outlets such as Biological Conservation, Electoral Studies, Energy Policy, Environmental Politics, Global Environmental Change, Party Politics and Public Administration.

Dr. Milind Tambe is Helen N. and Emmett H. Jones Professor in Engineering at the University of Southern California(USC). He is a fellow of AAAI and ACM, as well as recipient of the ACM/SIGART Autonomous Agents Research Award, Christopher Columbus Fellowship Foundation Homeland security award, INFORMS Wagner prize for excellence in Operations Research practice, Rist Prize of the Military Operations Research Society, IBM Faculty Award, Okawa foundation faculty research award, RoboCup scientific challenge award, and other local awards such as the Orange County Engineering Council Outstanding Project Achievement Award, USC Associates award for creativity in research and USC Viterbi use-inspired research award. Prof. Tambe has contributed several foundational papers in AI in areas such as multiagent teamwork, distributed constraint optimization (DCOP) and security games. For this research, he has received the "influential paper award" and a number of best paper awards at conferences such as AAMAS, IJCAI, IAAI, and IVA. In addition, Prof. Tambe pioneering real-world deployments of "security games" has led him and his team to receive the US Coast Guard Meritorious Team Commendation from the Commandant, US Coast Guard First District's Operational Excellence Award, Certificate of Appreciation from the US Federal Air Marshals Service and special commendation given by LA Airport police from the city of Los Angeles. For his teaching and service, Prof. Tambe has received the USC Steven B. Sample Teaching and Mentoring award and the ACM recognition of service award. He has also co-founded a company based on his research, ARMORWAY, where he serves as the director of research. Prof. Tambe received his Ph.D. from the School of Computer Science at Carnegie Mellon University.

Dr. Adrian Treves earned his PhD at Harvard University in 1997 and is now an associate professor of Environmental Studies at the University of Wisconsin–Madison. His research focuses on ecology, law, the public trust, and agroecosystems where crop and livestock production overlap carnivore habitat. He and his students work to understand and manage the balance between human needs and carnivore conservation. He has authored more than 100 scientific papers on predator-prey ecology or conservation. Most recently Dr. Treves has been writing and speaking on the public trust doctrine.

Dr. Serge Wich started his biology study at the University of Amsterdam and obtained his PhD in 2002 at Utrecht University. He joined Liverpool John Moores University (Liverpool, UK) as a professor in primate biology in 2012. In 2014 he joined the UvA as an honorary professor for the conservation of the great apes. Serge is also a Founding Director of the non-profit, ConservationDrones.org. His research focuses on primate behavioral ecology, tropical rain forest ecology and conservation of primates and their habitats. Together with Dr. Lian Pin Koh he founded ConservationDrones.org and uses drones for conservation applications.

Dr. Tanya Wyatt is a Reader in Criminology at Northumbria University in Newcastle, UK. She is a green criminologist specializing in wildlife trafficking and the role of corruption, terrorism and organized crime in committing this crime. Her publications include Wildlife Trafficking: A deconstruction of the crime, the victims and the offenders as well as numerous peer reviewed publications in journals such as Deviant Behavior, Crime, Law and Social Change and Contemporary Justice Review.

Dr. Rong Yang received her Ph.D. from the Computer Science Department at the University of Southern California. She worked with Dr. Milind Tambe on problems related to addressing the unrealistic perfect rationality assumption of the human adversary in Stackelberg Security Games for real-world security problems. Dr. Yang is currently at Google Inc. She is working on improving YouTube user experience using machine learning technologies.

Zachary Voyles earned degrees in Wildlife Biology (B.S., 2008), Communication Studies (B.A. 2008), and Conservation Biology (M.S. 2013) and has worked in the private, government and non-profit sectors. His professional work experience and research have focused on human–bear and human–wolf conflicts in the Upper Midwest and Central Rocky Mountain regions. He is currently a Farm Bill Wildlife Biologist for Pheasants Forever, Inc.

Preface

Certain questions have always puzzled me. Why doesn't science work to answer conservation policy questions in a systematic, reliable, and holistic way? Why isn't science easily translated into science-based policy? Why don't scientists listen to policymakers' questions about evaluation, assessment, and feasibility estimates and better advance the scientific knowledge base needed to answer policy questions?

I pursued a conservation social science PhD under Barbara Knuth at Cornell University in order to position myself to answer these questions through the process and products of doctoral research. My dissertation explored the human dimensions of black bear management. In many ways the context was ubiquitous to human–wildlife conflict around the world. Humans and black bear populations were increasingly overlapping and coming into contact with each other. When a black bear attacked an infant who later died from her injuries, there was widespread agreement among stakeholders that social science, along with ecology, was needed for decision-making. My research explored how to foster voluntary behavior change and compliance with rules among humans so as to reduce human–black bear conflict. I will never forget the last question I received during my dissertation defense. Lou Berchelli, the New York State Department of Environmental Conservation bear biologist, asked me why the behavior change program I designed, implemented, and evaluated did not generate intended outcomes and what I would change if I could do it all over again. My answer was automatic: I would focus more on non-compliance and enforcement. It was at that moment that I started to think deeply about why a marriage between conservation and criminology would be a good idea and what it might look like. I also considered what such an interdisciplinary perspective might bring to the conservation policy arena.

Fast forward to today, and human-wildlife conflicts are globally distributed and pose risks to people and wildlife. There is agreement that a scientific understanding of human behavior is critical for effective environmental policy and to improve humans' ability to predict and adapt to environmental change emerging as a cause and/or consequence of natural resource declines. The volume that follows is the product of many hours of hard work by the contributors and myself to produce new and innovative boundary science—that is, science that connects the knowledge base to practice associated with the risks from natural resource declines. Chapters reflect agreement that scientists and policymakers can work together and better address the issue of extra-legal exploitation of natural resources. One way this can occur is by increasing interdisciplinary collaborations among and between sectors. Policymakers can delineate for scientists the practical gaps in knowledge needed to inform development or implementation of policy, context specificity, and evaluation. Scientists can work to present their results in ways that help policymakers scale implications. Along with broadening opportunities for interdisciplinary cooperation, it is worthwhile to provide ample space for disciplinary specialists to contribute when needed.

A second parallel opportunity for scientists and policymakers to pursue is engaging the public. Both may engage publics to assist in surveillance and monitoring of natural resource exploitation. Considering publics as informants rather than suspects in natural resource exploitation can help build datasets to help study change over time, enhance capacity of civil society regarding natural resource management, and broaden the network of defenders against extra-legal exploitation. In practice, public participation is challenging but worth pursuing because broadening the quality of the intelligence base can help policy-makers craft policy that is as effective, efficient, and feasible as possible.

I'm indebted to the authors for their time and perspective. I believe there is a valid sense of urgency for us to collaborate and address the negative effects of natural resource declines, but I also have a sense of optimism about what can be resolved. It is my hope that this volume contributes to solutions both on the ground, in the policy arena, and for science diplomacy.

Meredith L. Gore
East Lansing, Michigan
January 2017

Acknowledgments

Marcia Baar, Rachel Boratto, Tamara Dempsey, Mark Gibson, Molly Good, Joe Hamm, Michelle Lute, Mike Mascia, Jen Owen, Ethan Shirley, Bill Siemer, Do Mi Stauber, Heather Triezenberg, Lee Schwartz. Thank you for your support, critique, inspiration, and feedback.

1

Global Risks, Conservation, and Criminology

Meredith L. Gore

1.1 Conservation Crimes Are a Global Problem

In recent years, levels of unsustainable and illegal natural resource exploitation have escalated in scope, scale, and severity such that the issue is now firmly in the crosshairs of high-level policymakers. Exploitation is now the dominant cause of global wildlife decline, surpassing habitat degradation, climate change, and habitat loss (McLellan, 2014). The World Wildlife Fund's 2014 Living Planet Index, which measures trends in thousands of vertebrate species, showed a 52% decline in size of populations between 1970 and 2010. Populations of freshwater species fell by a staggering 76% during this time period; marine populations dropped 39% (McLellan, 2014). Today, a wide array of government, civil society, nongovernmental, and private sector partners are collaborating and coordinating to address this problem at multiple scales.

Wildlife-related problems were once considered boutique issues fitting squarely within the purview of the conservation community. Due to their widening range of impacts, these issues are now considered a global scourge in a swath of sectors. The problem is no longer viewed as solely limited to the ecological impacts or moral implications of species extinction, although these consequences are profound (e.g., Valiente-Banuet *et al.*, 2015; Vucetich, Bruskotter, & Nelson, 2015). Wildlife trafficking threatens the security and prosperity of people, poor inspection processes of at border crossings allow the spread of zoonotic diseases, park rangers are being killed, and rebel militias are players in global ivory markets (Clinton, 2012). Reductions in biodiversity or the population sizes of species can have other substantial negative human health impacts unrelated to these risks, including loss of potential sources of pharmaceuticals, experimental models for studying disease, crop pollination, and both micro- and macronutrients for humans lacking alternative sources of protein (Meyers *et al.*, 2013). Recent recognition of these risks by policymakers has led to calls for inclusive approaches to create a comprehensive picture of the problem to inform on-the-ground programs and high-level policies. Diverse sectors with equities in wildlife policy generation commonly

Conservation Criminology, First Edition. Edited by Meredith L. Gore.

acknowledge proactive solutions require holistic, integrative, and innovative perspectives. For example:

- Secretary of State Hillary Clinton, in her 2012 remarks to the Partnership Meeting on Wildlife Trafficking stated there is a need to look at the problem of wildlife trafficking in a comprehensive, holistic way (Clinton, 2012).
- In July 2013, U.S. President Barack Obama signed Executive Order (EO) 13648 on Combatting Wildlife Trafficking. The EO established a Presidential Task Force on Wildlife Trafficking and Interagency Advisory Council on Wildlife Trafficking, both of which were charged with incorporating knowledge from multiple sectors and diverse agencies (Obama, 2013).
- The United Nations Environment Programme published an Environmental Crime Crisis report, discussing far reaching societal consequences of the illegal wildlife trade; the report called for a global and holistic response to be implemented at all levels and with all means possible (Nellemann, Henreiksen, Raxter, Ash, & Mrema, 2014).
- HRH The Prince of Wales and HRH The Duke of Cambridge hosted the End Wildlife Crime Conference; during his speech the Prince acknowledged finding a solution to illegal wildlife trade will require people from many different sectors to work together (Prince of Wales, 2013).
- In 2015, 41 governments signed the Kasane Statement at the Kasane Conference on Wildlife Trafficking, committing to engaging with the transport sector to raise awareness of the role they can play and support development of industry-wide practices that eliminate the illegal wildlife trade (Kasane Statement, 2015).

These policy statements and new funding lines indicate conservation crimes are a high political priority at this time; they also underlay new interdisciplinary collaborations, multi-sectoral partnerships, and renewed scientific attention to the global problem. Across these initiatives, programs, and speeches there is widespread agreement that the convergence of threats—to ecosystems, geopolitical stability, national security, human health and well-being, and future generations—requires multidisciplinary and multidimensional approaches to resolve negative effects. However, policymakers are often uncertain about what data are needed, available, and attainable to inform the most effective solution architecture.

This book is intended to complement the work being done by government actors, private sector partners, civil society and nongovernmental organizations, development institutions, and others to reduce the negative effects of conservation crimes on people and the environment. The academic community has much to contribute, particularly in terms of evidence for evaluating the efficacy, efficiency, and feasibility of policy alternatives. Academic inquiry can help document the voice of local people and other publics who are necessary players for meaningful outcomes. The science of conservation crime, also referred to as conservation criminology, is particularly relevant (Gore, 2011). This paradigm offers an integrative means for addressing the natural and societal domains inherent in wildlife trafficking. Comprised of three primary disciplines—natural resources management, risk and decision science, and criminology—conservation criminology seeks to overcome limitations inherent to single-discipline science and provide practical guidance about on-the-ground practice (Figure 1.1). It is not a rigid, prescriptive dogma and it is not confined to the walls of the ivory tower. Rather, it is a lens that different stakeholders can use to view the risks associated with human-environment relationships. As an interdisciplinary paradigm, the fundamental goal of conservation criminology is to provide a platform for conversations and connections that lead to new knowledge. The paradigm incorporates the principle of holism—the whole is not only greater than the sum of the parts but the parts are related in such a way that their functioning is conditioned by their relationship to each other.

This chapter profiles conservation criminology in its current form, as well as its key strengths and limitations. Additional chapters in this volume elaborate and build upon many of the concepts described in this chapter. Ideally, current and future practitioners will adapt principles discussed in this and other chapters,

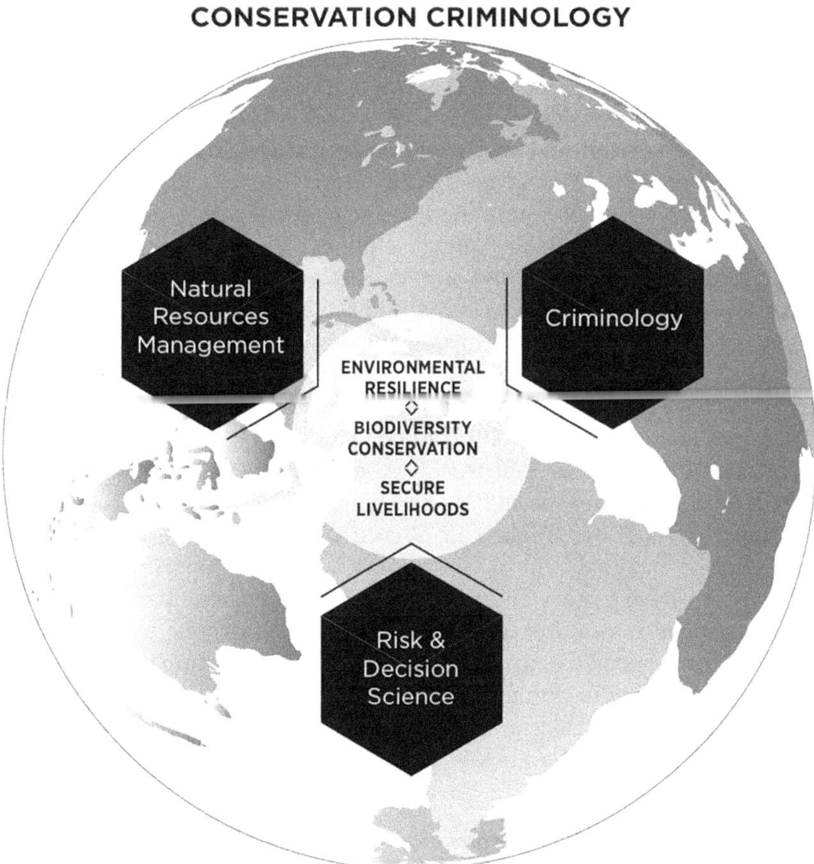

Figure 1.1 Conservation criminology is an interdisciplinary and applied paradigm for understanding programs and policies associated with global conservation risks. By integrating natural resources management, risk and decision science, and criminology, conservation criminology-based approaches ideally result in improved environmental resilience, biodiversity conservation, and secure human livelihoods.

allowing for the evolution of applied conservation criminology. This chapter first discusses the three foundational disciplines of conservation criminology, paying particular attention to key theories and principles. Reviewing the attributes of the three different disciplines enables readers to have a common foundation upon which they can consider the solution architecture of conservation criminology as a concept. The chapter details strengths and weaknesses with the approach and identifies gaps in the knowledge base. It concludes with a roadmap for the book, highlighting important landmarks and a vision for the future of conservation criminology.

1.2 Three Foundational Fields of Conservation Criminology

1.3 Foundation 1: Natural Resource Management and Policy

Science surrounding Earth's natural biophysical systems—climate, stratospheric ozone, terrestrial and marine ecosystems, and the cycles of water, nitrogen, and carbon—is the purview of the natural sciences. Of specific interest to conservation criminology are the sister sciences of natural resource management and conservation biology. Both disciplines include a focus on exploring and understanding direct and indirect threats to biodiversity and natural resources including trees, water, animals, and minerals. They consider natural systems as well as the different anthropogenic processes, including deforestation, desertification, pollution, agricultural expansion, or urban sprawl that can drive species extinction, habitat loss, introduced species, or overexploitation of species (Mulder & Coppolillo, 2005). The natural biophysical systems disciplines that are most relevant to conservation crimes diverge by context. Problem definition dictates the extent to which geography, ecology, zoology, or other natural sciences are applied in pursuit of attaining the answers that achieve desirable end goals. In many ways and in contrast to criminology, the natural sciences have historically prioritized thinking about harm as something humans have caused instead of suffer from (e.g., driving the Mauritius dodo or passenger pigeon to extinction was harmful to non-human species and did not functionally cause humans harm). Select themes recurrent in natural resource management and conservation biology that clearly connect to conservation criminology are profiled below.

1.3.1 Different Values Underlie Natural Resource Management and Conservation

Fundamentally, natural resource management and conservation biology exist because society values natural systems, although our values can, and do, differ. Here, a value is a stable, superordinate cognitive structure. Values form the root of attitudes and behaviors associated with conservation, are important elements of cultural transmission, and are linked to prevailing human needs. One example in conservation biology is the "no use" value of preservation, which aims to protect species, ecosystems, or landscapes without reference to natural changes in living systems or human requirements. Alternatively, "wise use" values of natural resource management involve the maintenance of environmental quality and resources, or a particular balance among species, including people, of a particular area (Callicott & Nelson, 1998). Value typologies from psychology compliment social norm theories and attitude frameworks describing different stakeholders' motivations, satisfaction, and participation in conservation action (e.g., Decker, Brown, & Seimer, 2001).

Values underlie a number of tensions that are often found within natural resource management and conservation biology. A well-known example is the tension between conservation (i.e., wise use) and preservation (i.e., no use). Both terms define human relationships with the environment, but invoke fundamentally different approaches for governance and reform (see Callicott & Nelson, 1998). Friction between integrated conservation and development projects (ICDPs) and sustainable development is another example (see Tisdell, 1999). On the one hand, ICDPs aim to promote voluntary compliance with conservation rules, ideally providing livelihood alternatives so as to simultaneously conserve biodiversity and preserve livelihoods. ICDP-based strategies have met mixed results in the field (see Barrett & Arcese, 1995; Gandiwa, Heitkönig, Lokhorst, Prins, & Leeuwis, 2013). On the other hand, sustainable development activities may be implemented in a top-down manner that promotes exclusion of people from geographic spaces, generally locals, in order to achieve compliance with conservation rules. This fences and fines approach ideally results in high deterrence rates and thus compliance with conservation rules but the conditional technique and lack of local involvement in decision-making commonly backfires (Kubo & Supriyanto, 2010).

There is an inherent set of assumptions about the value of social sciences in natural resource management and conservation or more specifically how, when, and in what contexts social science can contribute to conservation science policy (Mascia, 2006). Here, value, the verb, is applied as an assignment of importance in terms of whose science is privileged and whose is marginalized within the conservation domain (e.g., setting research agendas, the weight of results in decision-making and authoritativeness of the science). These assumptions remind us there are many different stakeholders with equity in conservation (e.g., states, corporations, donors, organized crime cartels). Stakeholders operate within the context of institutional settings such as family, friends, tribes, communities, health systems, policy, and schools. At a micro level, individuals can play different roles within the natural resource management process being investigated; people hold diverse social roles and are not in fact homogenous, although sometimes during stakeholder engagement processes, we assume they only hold one identity! These factors add to the complexity of the networks engaged in the problem. Because of values, human-human relationships are often as important to consider as human-natural resource relationships (Lute & Gore, 2014).

1.3.2 The Precautionary Principle and Prevention

The precautionary principle is a regulatory instrument developed in response to situations of environmental risk, such as those associated with biodiversity conservation (Myers, 1993). Applied in different forms around the world, it is relevant to issues such as hazardous substances and toxic chemicals. It is considered a multidisciplinary concept embedded in legal, economic, and scientific policies. The precautionary principle reflects the idea that uncertainty about environmental risks should not preclude preventative action (Cooney & Dickson, 2005). Further, preventative actions can be taken in the face of uncertainty about outcomes and the burden of proof is reversed (e.g., guilty until proven innocent). The precautionary principle is widely applied, for example, in guiding decisions about which species should be included in the Convention on International Trade of Endangered Species of Wild Fauna and Flora Appendices, and thus subject to international trade controls. Precautionary approaches also appear in many multilateral fisheries agreements on management and conservation such as the North Atlantic Salmon Conservation Organization. Perhaps the most well-known global application of the precautionary principle relates to protected area sites for biodiversity conservation. These mechanisms link indicators of biological risk such as species status to management responses such as prohibition on use (Cooney & Dickson, 2005). In reality, some conservation decisions simultaneously pose threats and benefits to humans and the environment. Many biodiversity conservation contexts do not adhere to a decision-making model where there is only one clearly risky strategy and a precautious one. Often, decisions are between risk to and from different sources and over different timescales. A widely known example of this phenomenon would be wildlife harvest (i.e., hunting) bans. The tradeoffs of this approach involve, in a highly simplified form, the risk of overexploitation of a species on the one hand and the risk of illegal trade on the other. Decision-making regarding wildlife harvest bans involves a complex array of dimensions, including ethics associated with the method of take, sustainable livelihoods, allocation of benefits associated with wildlife trophies, and economics of wildlife trade (see Challender & Cooney, 2016).

The precautionary principle can be considered a source of friction in an increasingly connected world; frictions provide barriers and obstacles to risks. When effective, friction counteracts the flows (e.g., how we distribute natural resources and energy) that create risks (Khanna, 2016). Ultimately, conservationists are propelled by a sense of urgency to increase friction (e.g., retard extinction) and so the precautionary principle accommodates, and is used to justify, the need for preventative action (Cooney, 2004). Such actions, designed to control flow, can be the result of conservation for the purpose of moral duty for future generations or utilitarian values and ecosystem services (Hance, 2016).

1.3.3 Community-Based Conservation

Community-based conservation (CBC) involves the devolution of authority to local communities to manage natural resources (Bergh, 2004). The approach stands in contrast to top-down approaches in which decision-makers make and take actions unilaterally based on their professional knowledge, training, and expertise. CBC accounts for the fact that local people cannot undertake conservation (i.e., a long-term strategy) when their short-term needs are not met. One broad appeal of CBC is that it theoretically ensures benefits for local people and recognizes indigenous people's rights to land and resources. Ideally, this model attends to the increase in public expectations for conservation solutions tailored to the local context and decrease in agency funds and personnel to effectively conserve all natural resources across time (Raik & Decker, 2007). CBC is intended to bridge the conservation-development divide and can take different forms. ICPD projects are a subset of CBC; all are implemented at the community level but not all CBC projects involve the scale of economic development entailed in ICDP. Community-based natural resource management tends to refer to rural programs concerned more with utilization of natural resources than protected area management (Mulder & Coppolillo, 2004). One reason CBC is widely applied is that it can enable citizen participation in natural resource and conservation decisions. Citizens can be involved in making, understanding, implementing, or evaluating decisions for improved outcomes (Decker *et al.*, 2001). The overall conservation climate is enhanced through improved relationships among relevant stakeholders and increased capacity of different stakeholders to contribute to conservation in practice. Challenges to citizen participation abound and can include lack of time and money, resistance among decision-makers, complexity of weighting the input of different opinions, and poor relationships with certain stakeholders (Decker *et al.*, 2001). Precaution may be aligned with the long-term interest of those people whose actions threaten biodiversity (Cooney, 2004).

1.3.4 Protected Areas

Protected areas (PAs) are one of the most widely used and flexible policy instruments in biodiversity conservation, even more so than market mechanisms such as direct land acquisitions, supply chain mechanisms such as green certification, or ICDP projects such as community forestry. In 2011, there were an estimated 160,000 terrestrial and marine PA established globally and the 193 Parties to the Convention on Biological Diversity committed to increasing the global extent of PAs to 17% of national lands (up from 12.7%) and 10% of marine areas under national jurisdiction (up from 4.0%) (Mascia *et al.*, 2014). They are geographically defined areas designated or regulated to achieve specific conservation objectives; they are a common mechanism for implementing a precautionary approach for conservation threats. PA management categories include strict nature reserve, species management area, national park, or managed resource PA. And, they can have different management objectives including science, sustainable use of natural ecosystems, or conservation through intervention. These categories acknowledge PAs are socially defined and involve socially constructed governance regimes. These human dimensions of PA management have long been recognized, and given PAs' regulatory dependence, the enforcement community has been and will likely continue to be a key player in their use as a conservation tool. The fences and fines approach to PA management necessitates engagement of the enforcement community. Police or rangers are key players in resolving deviant human behavior within the geographic boundaries of PAs through both enforcement and relationship building with local peoples, however, there are other relevant authorities that can be involved in rule setting (see Ratsimbazafy, Gore, & Rakotoniaina, 2013).

Debate exists about the requirements for successful PAs; they are often restrictive and top-down in their regulatory composition and local communities relying on natural resources for their livelihoods often experience significant adverse impacts. PAs are generally considered to be permanent fixtures on the landscape but that is not always the case. PAs are regularly downgraded, downsized, and degazetted (i.e., PADDD); indeed there is evidence of PADDD from as long ago as 1902. PADDD decreases the legal restrictions imposed on human activities within a protected area by a relevant authority. PAs may also experience a total functional loss of legal protection (Mascia & Pailler, 2011). PADDD demonstrates one way that PAs are responsive to social pressures involving tradeoffs between conservation goals and other objectives such as industrial scale activities, local land pressures, or land claims (Mascia *et al.*, 2014). At a broader level, devolution is a manifestation of local control over geography and autonomy to pursue one's own interests; some argue greater autonomy will bring greater stability (Khanna, 2016).

1.4 Foundation 2: Criminology, Crime Science, and Criminal Justice

Criminology is a well-established social science, for hundreds of years its aim has been to study, understand, and prevent crime. As criminologists work to understand the various causes of crime, its distribution and control, explanations for how crimes occur are produced alongside insight about why some people commit crime. Many models have emerged to explain crime, including learning, biological, and psychological theories of crime. The explanation of crime is theoretically competitive. In some cases the explanations involve references to rule or law, law making, or role of law enforcement agencies. Other views refer to culture or the postmodern conditions of life that result in crime. Generally, criminological theories share a focus on criminal behavior, study crime defined by law, and consider victimization of non-humans peripheral. Harm emerges from crime and is commonly viewed as something that affects humans. In this regard much of what natural scientists know has had little impact on criminology. The field implies human control in the legalistic or normative sense is possible, effectual, warranted, and justified. It is known for being highly theoretical and sometimes critiqued as being peripheral from policy and practice.

Only recently has criminology thought about crimes against nature as a distinguishable type of crime, versus, for example, street crime or white-collar crime. These experts are often called green criminologists. For example, theories of green behaviorism tell us that crime, if the result of an individual's biological response to environmental toxins such as high levels of lead in drinking water, cannot be eradicated or controlled. By exploring effects of lead exposure on criminal behavior, green criminologists explain the negative public and environmental health outcomes related to lead exposure as a functional response to environmental conditions; the causes of an individual's behavior are thus external rather than internal. Green criminologists offer a provocative perspective, within their discipline, by proposing green harms are more widespread than criminal harms. They are the most important concerns in society because they cause the most injury, violence, damage, or loss to both people and ecosystems as a single green harm may result in widespread exposure to a toxin. Some behaviors not legally defined as criminal also cause harm. The legality of a behavior is not predictive of the harm's magnitude or whether that harm is adequately defined in law. They argue harmful outcomes, not the behavior as defined by the rule of law, should be examined and become the subject matter of criminology. Environmental problems—pollution, global warming, resource depletion—cannot be fully understood or analyzed when the frame of reference emphasizes the importance of problems only for humans. Often, nature is viewed as a benign actor who is victimized itself at times. Although academically interesting, this book does not offer a substantial critique of green criminology or invest heavily in theoretically comparing conservation, green, and environmental crime. Lynch and Stretesky (2014), White (2008), and to some extent Gibbs, Gore, McGarrell, and Rivers (2010) and Gibbs *et al.* (2016), offer such insight. Next, select theories, patterns, and typologies from criminology, crime science, and criminal justice that relate to real world problems of conservation are discussed.

1.4.1 Opportunity Structures of Crime

Many theories of crime come from a dispositional point of view; certain discrete tendencies exist among those who commit crime compared to those that do not. Deviant behavior is explained as the product of differential socialization processes that result in individual proclivities to commit crime. Alternatively, the opportunity perspective extended by Cohen and Felson (1979) recognized the broader role that a situational landscape plays in producing crime. Context matters and is central to the axiom that opportunity has a causal role in crime. This approach considers wildlife poaching to be like other crime in that it is the result of motivated offenders seizing criminal opportunities they encounter. The existence of criminal opportunity is a requirement for a crime to occur. This perspective facilitates thinking about how criminal opportunity structure(s) for poaching develop and are exploited by poachers.

Drawing on the routine activity theory of crime (Clarke & Felson, 1993), poaching can be viewed as a criminal opportunity involving three groups: offenders, victims, and guardians. Crime opportunities are highest when victims and offenders meet in the absence of capable guardians. Opportunity structure theories of crime offer exciting tools for conservationists because policies and programs can work to reduce crime by focusing on how to dismantle opportunity structures for poaching as well as address who is committing the crime. Guardians stand out as a direct way to protect victims, which is one reason why we focus so much on improved enforcement in conservation in policies such as the U.S. Strategy Against Wildlife Trafficking. Strategies aim to improve the capacity of guardians to deter offenders with their presence or intervene during commission of a crime. Understandably, conservation resources are regularly focused on increased enforcement efforts. For example, patrols can be directed into areas preferred by poachers to increase apprehension or guardians can decrease response times to poaching reports. Criminology prods the conservation movement to think about poaching prevention as well as enforcement.

1.4.2 Crime Prevention

Criminologists excel at building knowledge about who commits crime and why, and crime scientists explore the opportunity structures that make crime possible. Crime scientists know effective crime prevention strategies are ideally tailored to the criminal opportunity structure as well as the motivations of the offender. They think about ways to engage in preventative interventions for a specific poaching problem. They do this by designing interventions that work to increase the effort, increase the risk, decrease the reward, remove excuses, and remove provocations for committing crime. These five intervention targets comprise the increasingly popular and prescriptive situational crime prevention techniques (SCP) (see Lemieux, 2014). Thinking about these basic elements of a poaching problem identifies entry points for intervention using SCP. Along these lines, crime scientists ask:

- What is the specific problem? Is the problem triggered by prompting, provocation, pressure, or permission?
- Who are the offenders? Are they repeat offenders? What are their motives? What do they need to be effective? Are they provoked, mundane, or anti-social?
- What tools do offenders use? Can tool procurement be disallowed? How do the tools get to the target?
- Who are the victims/what are the targets? Are some repeatedly involved? Why are targets at locations where problems take place? Can they relocate? Can targets be made less attractive?

Answering these questions inform the appropriateness of SCP activities. Importantly, evaluating the efficacy of SCP to prevent wildlife poaching problems can be complicated. This complication stems in part from the nature of crime-related data: no matter what the outcome of prevention efforts, not all results will appear in official data sources; rangers are not always there to detect illegal activity and victims cannot file reports. This differs from traditional police data, which typically entails a combination of law enforcement observations and victim reports. Using multiple sources of intelligence (e.g., local sources, expert sources) to improve the size, scope, and level of detail in databases may help overcome this deficiency. The U.S. Office of the Director of National Intelligence recently formed a Counter Wildlife Trafficking Community of Interest in response to this need (Quinn, 2016).

1.4.3 Criminological Typologies

Criminologists excel at producing typologies of crime, for example green criminological typologies of wildlife trade (Wyatt, 2013). These typologies help guide strategies and tactics to reduce negative effects of crime. One typology identifies at least four opportunities for involvement in wildlife crime: pseudo conservation, pseudo hunting, theft, and poaching (Lemieux, 2014). Pseudo conservation involves networks of conservation professionals that cooperatively evade laws and covertly acquire products destined for market. Pseudo hunting entails someone with no hunting experience who applies for permits to hunt legally and supplies parts to market. Markets may be supplied though theft or robberies of wildlife parts from warehouses, museums, game reserves, safari lodges, or taxidermies. Poaching, a fourth opportunity type of wildlife crime, may be considered separately from other sources of wildlife crime because the criminal opportunity structure for the crime is vastly different than pseudo conservation or pseudo hunting. Successful poaching favors individuals with knowledge of animal and ranger movement patterns, access to weapons, and hunting experience. Also, the risk they face while poaching is different than other groups who conceal their actions from enforcement agencies through collusion and legal loopholes.

Another typology for thinking about wildlife crime involves markets for criminally derived goods or products (Lemiuex, 2014). This typology proposes at least three types of crime markets; each can be targeted using different strategies and tactics (e.g., policy, regulation). Markets are often in places where other goods such as textiles and produce are being sold. Local markets capture many of the products derived from a local area. For example, the Guangzhou market in southern China is close to Nankunshan National Park; a common activity in the market for tourists is to knowingly purchase wildlife for food consumption (Chow, Cheung, & Yip, 2014). Exclusively local markets have low human population, high locally available species, low amounts of rare species, low sources of distribution and low total product. Regional markets are able to acquire products from far off distances because they attract middlemen who traffic species from city to city. The bird markets in Medan, Indonesia are known as being primary hubs for wildlife trade in Asia and have been estimated to sell at any given time up to 200 species of wild birds as pets. Regional markets tend to have relatively high human populations, low species availability, high rare species, low distribution and medium number of product. Feeder markets are local markets that distribute product to other cities and distribute produce for local demand. These markets have variable human populations, high species available, high rare species, high sources of distribution, and high number of product. Until it was recently bulldozed by authorities, the Bellavista local market was known as one of Peru's main hubs of illegal wildlife trade, selling up to 1,100 animals a week (Brenna, 2016).

1.5 Foundation 3: Risk and Decision Science

The third foundational field of conservation criminology is risk and decision science. The field explores human judgment, the processes and outcomes of decision-making, and risk assessment. In many ways, the field is concerned more with the decision itself and decision process than it is concerned with the consequence of decisions. Some sociologists theorize risk is the dominant paradigm through which contemporary society operates—we live in a risk society (Beck, 1992). Risk and its management pose existential concerns on a global level; threats are a function of civilization's success, and chance and danger evolve from industrialization. These scholars posit that categories of risk reflect a response to uncertainty, which today is unable to be overcome by more knowledge. This view promotes thinking about the multidisciplinary dimensions of risk and its management in that it links the natural, technical and social sciences and can be applied to highly diverse phenomena. Risk remains foundational to technology, economics, natural science, and politics. Crosscutting themes from the idea of the risk society include:

- Threats are contagious and can transform social inequality by dividing, excluding, and stigmatizing risk persons or groups.
- Threats enable a global community.
- Science enhances the acuteness of risk perception and makes risks collectively visible.
- Fear is transforming security into a consumer good such as electricity.

These themes of the risk society carry assumptions. First, because risks address future events that may occur and that threaten us, we are obliged to take preventative action (i.e., precautionary principle). Second, knowledge is hierarchical such that knowing and not knowing can be distinguished and those with knowledge (i.e., experts) are superior over those without knowledge (i.e., laypersons). Environmental risks in particular fall into this category as they are hidden risks that for the most part escape everyday perception and often rest on esoteric scientific models and calculations that can be controversial. Third, old threats pose new risks. Indeed, wildlife poaching and trade has occurred since the time Venetian merchant Marco Polo traversed Europe and Asia but today is considered to be at a crisis level by the United Nations and many others. Fourth, risks cannot be locally circumscribed. The globalization of environmental problems, in particular, such as wildlife poaching, equates threats to the environment with social threats. Wildlife poaching, as one of many global risks, decouples social location and social decision-making responsibility from the places and times at which other people become the object of possible physical and social injury. Finally, global environmental risks such as wildlife poaching have distinctive qualities. They are delocalized such that the causes and consequences are not limited to one geographic location or space. Global risks are, in principle, omnipresent and vary across spatial, temporal, and social scales. The consequences are incalculable. For example, beyond the extinction of a species through wildlife poaching, there is a universe of collateral effects on local and regional economies, ecosystem function, or cultural and religious traditions. The principles of precaution through prevention dominates because global risks are considered to be irreversible and losses irreplaceable. For example, Madagascar's endemic lemurs are found nowhere else on earth. Thus, if they go extinct as a result of deforestation, hunting, or disease, they are gone forever. Critiques of the risk society provoke thinking about, among other issues, the extent to which its ideas do or do not apply to the global south, promote discourse among different people who engage with risks, and the extent to which they perceive those encounters as risky (see Gore, Lute, Ratsimbazafy, & Rajaonson, 2016). It is also worthwhile to consider the extent to which the risk society leaves room for non-technical solutions to problems; for example, is there room for environmental ethics or religion in the conversation.

1.5.1 Risk Assessment and Perception

Definitions of risk generally include a technical component that examines the probability of occurrence and severity of consequences as well as a value-based component that examines the level of dread or outrage associated with an event (Gore *et al.*, 2009). Technical risk assessments typically involve expert-based quantitative approaches that estimate probabilities. Risk assessment informs decision-making under uncertainty and is widely applied across conservation and criminological contexts (Gore *et al.*, 2009). For example, the International Union for Conservation of Nature uses various criteria to assess the extinction risk to various species (e.g., vulnerable, threatened, critically endangered) on their Red List. The 1992 Preamble for the Convention on Biological Diversity notes the high risk of loss of biodiversity as an insufficient reason for postponing action to minimize risk. Hotspot maps illustrate geographic regions at greatest risk from a particular threat (e.g., car theft, commercial wildlife poaching), which can then inform risk management activities.

Risk perception, on the other hand, is a risk judgment; this social psychological concept is complementary to risk assessment in that risk perception is relevant for understanding individuals' attitudes about risk-related policy as well as behavior toward policy (e.g., support or opposition). It is common for environmental risk perceptions and assessments to not mirror one another (Gore, Knuth, Scherer, & Curtis, 2008). For example, it is perceptually easy to underestimate risks presented by policy advocates and overestimate risks presented by people faced with dealing with the consequences. Additionally, many people anchor their risk perceptions on initial risk estimates. Because of these and other reasons (see Gore, Knuth, Curtis, & Shanahan, 2007 for a discussion of factors influencing risk perception), risk perception affects regulatory design and compliance. Risk and decision science is valuable for understanding local people's perception of risk, their associated behavior (or lack thereof), as well as the social and physical space within which risks occur.

Environmental risk is commonly described as any source of hazard that resides in the natural or built environment and poses some degree of threat to humans (Keller *et al.*, 2012), versus a risk associated with technology such as nanotechnology. Some chapters in this book illustrate a more inclusive scope of the term. Environmental risk management, then, makes use of the results and insights from risk assessment to reduce negative effects on people and the environment they interact with. Environmental risk perception scholars build understanding about environmentally relevant behaviors and methods to change behavior including decision-making processes, risk and benefit judgments, acceptance, information seeking, risk reducing behavior, pro-environmental behavior, political actions, and collective action to ameliorate risks. These studies improve how we address emotional, perceptual, and behavioral components of environmental risk perception using tools and techniques from, for example, risk communication.

1.5.2 Risk Communication

Risk communication is the interactive exchange among individuals, groups, and institutions related to the characterization, assessment, and management of risk. Risk communication often contains contextual messages regarding facts or hypotheses about the level of risk and the significance of the risk relative to other issues or actions that are undertaken to manage risk. The format and content of risk communication materials can affect how an individual responds to risk messages. For example, statistical presentations of risk are frequently difficult to interpret and fail to motivate risk-reducing behavior. Risk communication activities can have several design advantages over other interventions (e.g., regulations, incentive programs) because they are flexible; they can target multiple human audiences and management of diverse wildlife species, address numerous issues, involve different stakeholders, achieve multiple objectives, and use assorted evaluation frameworks (Gore *et al.*, 2009).

Risk communication can facilitate decision-making by identifying and incorporating both public risk perceptions and expert assessments into the decision process. Decision-makers might use a persuasive communication approach to induce a change in attitudes, beliefs, or behaviors associated with decision alternatives, achieve acceptance of a preferred management strategy, or motivate action in response to a problem (e.g., use synthetic substitutes rather than real bear bile when practicing Traditional Chinese Medicine). A participatory communication approach might be used to facilitate decision-making processes, resolve stakeholder conflict through participation, or communicate how decisions could be and are made. This latter approach relies on a two-way flow of information and values the importance of knowledge from diverse stakeholders. It also recognizes that messages by themselves are not always effective and acknowledges that poor communication can lead to stakeholder backlash.

1.5.3 Risk Governance

Regardless of how or from whose perspective risk is investigated, its causes and consequences do not usually go ignored: decision-making is an essential task of environmental risk management. Risk governance describes the diversity of structures and processes available for decision-making; it often involves diverse stakeholders, governmental, and non-governmental actors who interact horizontally through multilateral agreements or vertically through community-based management (Renn, 2002). Although decision-makers cannot control all the outcomes of a decision, they may employ high-quality decision-making processes, which can increase the likelihood of good decision outcomes. Quality processes increase the likelihood that decisions are consistent with management objectives, based on the best available information, and responsive to stakeholders' needs. Developing and maintaining high quality processes is a significant challenge in conservation. Policy-makers typically must decide among risk-reduction options and usually do not (or cannot) attempt to maximize net benefits. Risk governance reminds us that focusing on effects and likelihood alone can be of limited use for decision-making, particularly for the context of conservation crime.

Procedure and due process are similarly important considerations for making decisions. This is because people are not only concerned about the risks that are imposed on them but also about the processes by which the decision has been made; thus, the relationship between stakeholders is an integral piece of governance. Social science contributes to risk governance by providing different explanations for how results of technical risk assessment are mediated by context or social and mental processes. For example, the rational choice approach for explaining decision-making proposes people have knowledge about potential outcomes, can distinguish between ends and means to achieve ends, and have preferences based on values. Another framework for thinking about risk and decision-making is social amplification of risk, which links psychological, social and cultural risk theories influence decision-making. Systems theory defines risk as a fundamental social construct that is closely linked to the particular rationality of society's subsystems. In sum, social science perspectives on risk include a range of perspectives about how individuals and cultures think about and respond to risk; networked perspectives offer insight about the structural effects of individuals behaving within a broader societal context.

1.6 Combining the Three Foundations: Conservation Criminology

Interdisciplinary research is "a mode of research by teams or individuals that integrates information, data, techniques, tools, perspectives, concepts, and/or theories from two or more disciplines or bodies of specialized knowledge to advance fundamental understanding or to solve problems whose solutions are beyond the scope of a single discipline or area of research practice" [National Academies of Science Committee on Facilitating Interdisciplinary Research Report (2004, p. 2)]. The current conceptualization of conservation criminology fits this definition (Figure 1.1). Synthesizing theories, methods, and analytic approaches from the three foundational disciplines provokes interdisciplinary thinking about many of the conservation-related problems facing contemporary society. Often, synthetic thinking about problems is beneficial in its capacity to compensate for weaknesses of individual perspectives. Interdisciplinary problem definition broadens the suite of possible solutions and pushes the boundary of innovation. Conservation criminology creates a safe space for testing new approaches for resolving environmental risks and discarding ineffective ones. In order to leverage the benefits of the paradigm, it is not sufficient to simply take a conservation biology issue, "add" decision science and criminology to the recipe, and "stir." As an interdisciplinary science, conservation criminology requires the constant and creative combination of theories, methods, and techniques from diverse disciplines throughout the entire processes of research, practice, education, and policy. Thinking about the interdisciplinary nature of conservation criminology can be quite exciting but does require patience and understanding of the different languages, epistemologies and ontologies of the core disciplines. The National Science Foundation noted interdisciplinary research is continuously emerging, melding, and transforming. And, what is considered interdisciplinary today might be considered disciplinary tomorrow!

1.6.1 Strengths

In many ways the interdisciplinary thinking facilitated by conservation criminology is its greatest strength. Using reductionist or unidirectional models of a single discipline to study relationships between people and environments can result in critical interactions being overlooked across system components (Milner-Gulland, 2012). Attending to one aspect of the problem will not make much of a difference unless all parts of the continuum are addressed at the same time. No single discipline can accomplish the feat of producing evidence that resolves all negative effects of human-environment relationships. Situating conservation problems inside the broader socio-ecological systems (SES) within which they occur helps transcend reductionist limitations. SES are multi-actor systems whose connectivity is the root cause of complexity (Khanna, 2016). Conservation criminology may be thought of as a skeleton for SES, providing the structural support needed to link individual, social, and landscape factors, as well as feedbacks from within the system that influence conservation crimes. For example, although law enforcement is seen as a critical element in combatting illegal wildlife trade, an exclusive focus on top-down enforcement-led approaches can create new risks to communities, governance, and conservation (Cooney, 2016). Conservation criminology concomitantly engages the knowledge base from multiple disciplines to consider communities as powerful and positive agents of change, the risks that communities bear when living with wildlife, the ecological importance of wildlife in maintaining healthy ecosystems, the contribution of wild meat to food security and human nutrition, and the connection between killing and eating wildlife with increased risk exposure of contracting infectious diseases that animals transmit. Beyond delineating a space for building theoretical understanding about the nature of the problem and characterizing the on-the-ground context, conservation criminology offers a broad and evolving suite of tools for reform such as those discussed in Chapter 9. These tools are not necessarily limited in scope to single disciplines (e.g., technological fixes are a common solution in risk analysis). Conservation criminology helps mainstream traditionally disparate disciplines into current narratives about global environmental risks, including those related to illegal wildlife trade or environmental security (Gore *et al.*, 2016).

1.6.2 Shortcomings

Conservation criminology is not without its weaknesses. To date, the paradigm appears to be applied to problems, harms, and crimes very relevant the global north, meaning discourse is dominated by northern problem definitions, research themes, and crime priorities. Discourses are typically framed using global north language, both politically and scientifically. The north/south divide debate invites additional consideration about the nature of human-environment interactions. More specifically, do people view themselves as part of or distinct from their environment? What is considered to be natural? The value and potential of a using a conservation crime perspective may be misestimated when one considers the on-the-ground context or scope of policy. For example, illegal exploitation of natural resources is often related to a variety of other illegal acts, varying from corruption to systemic violence. Exploitation is also legal in a wide array of domains and is regulated as such. Not all harms are or should be considered illegal and laws may not be the default form of social control in all regions of the world. It is also unclear what the endgame is; what are we as a society trying to accomplish—a restored ecosystem? A minimum viable population of species? A return to Eden? Risks that are as low as reasonably allowable? Who decides?

Many of conservation criminology's shortcomings may be underlain by unanswered questions associated with a lack of testing and application. For example, criminological definitions of actors may not hold in a conservation context. Does conservation criminology sufficiently account for the complexity and dynamism of global environmental risks? Is something missing? Does conservation criminology offer sufficient space to consider the multiple factors of social change and examine the extent to which these factors interact? Perhaps most importantly, are we really facing a crisis? Is it really new? What really makes the current environmental situation truly different than what we have previously experienced over time? One of my graduate students recently summed up this reality by sharing an anecdote from his dissertation fieldwork in sub-Saharan Africa. During a focus group, a participant responded to his question about the morality of trafficking children for pastoral labor: "You see danger. I see bread."

1.7 How to "Do" Conservation Criminology

Students, conservation practitioners, agency personnel, and other faculty have asked me how to "do" conservation criminology. I do not believe there is any single way to "do" conservation criminology. However, I like to think of conservation criminology as a minimum viable concept (MVC) (Reiss, 2011). Rather than seek perfect information to predict the future, I can ask, "What is the basic information I need to know to get out in the field and start doing?" The idea of the MVC resonates with conservation criminology because it enables action in the face of imperfect and incomplete information so that we can put forward concepts to empirically investigate. The three foundational fields of conservation criminology offer the most basic framework for understanding and generating actionable intelligence that can help resolve the negative aspects of human-environment relationships. Employing the idea of the MVC, conservation criminologists can subscribe to Reiss's (2011) Principles of Agility. As a group, collaborators can focus on problems before specific solutions, value relationships over processes, and integrate with existing efforts instead of creating isolated programs (Reiss, 2011).

Conservation criminology may be accomplished using design thinking strategies. These tactics puts a potential beneficiary (i.e., user of scientific information) at the center of design and calls for interacting with them and all the stakeholders involved in the system throughout the scientific process of framing the problem, working with them to frame the right questions about their collective needs, and creating multiple ideas to test and see what works and learn from what doesn't. Conservation criminology is an approach that relies on the broad cross-sector coordination permitted by design thinking. This means abandoning individual agendas in favor of a collective approach to engaging in scientific inquiry in response to a real world societal problem. Design thinkers (e.g., Kolko, 2015) call this a form of collective impact, or the commitment of a group of actors from different sectors to a common agenda for solving a specific social problem. Collective impact involves a centralized infrastructure and mutually reinforcing activities among all participants. Collective impact initiatives have defining characteristics. Their actions are supported by a shared measurement system, mutually reinforcing activities, and ongoing communication, and are staffed by an independent backbone organization (Kolko, 2015). The foundational fields of conservation criminology offer a shared measurement system (Gibbs *et al.*, 2010).

Kolko (2015) acknowledged large-scale social change comes from better cross sector coordination rather than from attention from individual disciplines. Cross sector coordination, which is what conservation criminology entails, does not happen often— not because it is impossible but because it is rarely attempted. Stakeholders are used to focusing on independent action as the primary vehicle for social change. The norm is for disciplines to make isolated impacts. There is a traditional orientation toward finding a solution embodied within a single discipline coupled with the hope that others will grow or replicate findings to extend impact more widely. By relying on multiple disciplines, conservation criminology leapfrogs this ideal; it promotes thinking about second- and third-order consequences of risks, not just isolated trends (Khanna, 2016).

1.8 Roadmap

The following chapters include and build upon the foundational fields of conservation criminology to highlight the benefits of thinking about conservation issues from an interdisciplinary perspective. Ideally, these chapters offer insight about how we might effectively navigate the road ahead. There are some considerations that the chapters in this book do not tend to, but are likely relevant for conservation criminology to incorporate in the future. Perspectives from environmental justice, gender, history, journalism, public health, religion and ethics, human geography, or urban studies are mostly missing from the book. Ideally, future scholars and volumes can help build the knowledge base so as to bring these perspectives, and others, into the fold.

In the first section, Chapters 2 and 3 conceptually elaborate on a number of suppositions from the foundational fields. Chapter 2 investigates the application of crime science to conservation. Chapter 3 identifies limitations in current thinking about deterrence and how those limitations bear acute implications for conservation and around PAs. These chapters challenge assumptions, offer recalibrated ways of thinking, and propose a remapping of ideas so as to improve the ability of the foundational fields to contribute to conservation criminology.

In the second section, Chapters 4 through 8 provide a suite of case studies illustrating breadth and depth of global risks, crime, and conservation as well as how conservation criminology applies to diverse ecosystems. Chapter 4 explores dominant forms of governance within three conservation contexts and compares implications for effective engagement of publics. Chapter 5 uses wildlife harvest as a context with which to consider compliance and cooperation with conservation rules. Chapter 6 unpacks the role of corruption and organized crime, as well as their linkages and potential policy-oriented solutions. Chapter 7 considers how current thinking in policing might be mainstreamed to improve outcomes for conservation, including enforcement and compliance. Chapter 8 describes how sociological work on power relations and authenticity can inform understanding about markets for wildlife tourism. These chapters summarize discrete contexts and integrate different disciplinary principles into conservation criminology to explore practical implications for conservation.

In the final section, Chapters 9 through 11 profile innovations and models within the conservation criminology sphere. Chapter 9 reviews the strengths and weaknesses of mobile applications, forensic science, conservation drones, and open-source software for enhancing detection, deterrence and enforcement. Chapter 10 presents a game theoretic model of human behavior for designing enforcement patrols to protect wildlife and interdict potential poachers. Chapter 11 utilizes social psychology to predict individual's potential to poach. These chapters illustrate the fantastic potential of innovation and boundary advancement that is possible with interdisciplinary thinking.

Global strategist Parag Khanna (2016) offered a characterization of an increasingly connected world. He argued connectivity is a meta-pattern of our age, and infrastructure is the mechanism by which people connect. In this way, functional geography is becoming more important than political geography. Tensions that arise over illicit movements of wildlife or other natural resources are fundamentally about who gains the most from connectivity. Mapping functional geography (e.g., transportation routes, energy grids, forward operating bases, financial networks, internet servers) concomitantly maps the pathways by which power is projected and leverage exercised. These pathways also distribute risks and benefits across time and space. Infrastructure enables connectivity, which in turn enables supply chains. Supply chains do not acknowledge geopolitical borders and they are increasing in size and global distribution. Khanna (2016) proposed supply chains are how the market exploits the earth and provide a conduit for marauding rainforests, oceans, and other natural resources. Supply chains are the channels for transnational organized crime syndicates (e.g., Russian Bratava, Mexican Sinaloa, Italian Camorra and 'Ndrangheta, Japanese Yakuza) to bridge supply and demand for rhino horns, illegal timber, drugs, people, counterfeit goods, and synthetic drugs. Connectivity makes exploiting nature easier and connectivity is going to increase. For individuals and groups working to reduce risks to people and biodiversity, the road ahead appears to have deep potholes.

References

Barrett, C. B., & Arcese, P. (1995) Are integrated conservation-development projects (ICDPs) sustainable? On the conservation of large mammals in sub-Saharan Africa. *World Development,* 23, 1073–1084.

Beck, U. (1992). *Risk society: Towards a new modernity.* United Kingdom: SAGE Publications.

Bergh, S. (2004). Democratic decentralization and local participation: A review of recent research. *Development in Practice*, 14, 780–790.

Brenna, L. (2016). Peru reduces to rubble one of the world's largest illegal wildlife markets. *Lifegate.* Retrieved from http://www.lifegate.com/people/news/peru-bellavista-illegal-wildlife-market-reduced-to-rubble

Chow, A. T., Cheung, S., & Yip, P. K. (2014). Wildlife markets in South China. *Human-Wildlife Interactions,* 8, 108–112.

Clarke, R. V., & Felson, M. (1993). *Routine activity and rational choice* (Vol. 5). New Brunswick: Transaction Publishers.

Clinton, H. (2012). Remarks at the partnership meeting on wildlife trafficking. Retrieved from http://www.state.gov/secretary/20092013clinton/rm/2012/11/200294.htm

Cohen, L. E., & Felson, M. (1979). Social change and crime rate trends: A routine activity approach. *American Sociological Review,* 44, 588–608.

Callicott, J. B., & Nelson, M. P. (Eds.). (1998). *The great new wilderness debate.* Athens, Georgia: University of Georgia Press.

Challender, D. W. S., & Cooney, R. (2016). *Informing decisions on trophy hunting: A briefing paper for European Union decision-makers regarding potential plans for restriction of imports of hunting trophies.* International Union for the Conservation of Nature, Gland, Switzerland.

Cooney, R. (2004). *The precautionary principle in biodiversity conservation and natural resource management: An issues paper for policy-makers, researchers, and practitioners.* International Union for the Conservation of Nature Policy and Global Change Series, Gland, Switzerland.

Cooney, R. (2016). *Poachers or protectors? Local communities at the frontline of conservation-what really drives wildlife trade, hunting, and trafficking.* European Parliament Intergroup CCBSD, Collaborative Partnership on Sustainable Wildlife Management Session, Brussels.

Cooney, R., & Dickson, B. (2005). *Biodiversity and the precautionary principle: risk, uncertainty and practice in conservation and sustainable use.* United Kingdom: Earthscan.

Decker, D. J., Brown, T. L., & Siemer, W. F. (2001). *Human Dimensions of Wildlife Management in North America.* Bethesda, Maryland: The Wildlife Society.

Gandiwa, E., Heitkönig, I. M. A., Lokhorst, A. M., Prins, H. H. T., & Leeuwis, C. (2013). CAMPFIRE and Human-Wildlife Conflicts in Local Communities Bordering Northern Gonarezhou National Park, Zimbabwe. *Ecology and Society*, 18, 7.

Gibbs, C., Gore, M. L., McGarrell, E. F., & Rivers, L. (2010). Introducing conservation criminology: Towards interdisciplinary scholarship on environmental crimes and risks. *British Journal of Criminology*, 50, 124–144.

Gibbs, C., Gore, M. L., Hamm, J., Rivers III, L., & Zwickl, A. (2016). Conservation Criminology. In A. Brisman, C. Eamonn, & N. South (Eds). *The Routledge Companion to Criminological Theory and Concepts*. London: Routledge.

Gore, M. L. (2011). The science of conservation crime. *Conservation Biology*, 25, 659–661.

Gore, M. L., Knuth, B. A., Curtis, P. D., & Shanahan, J. E. (2007). Factors influencing risk perception associated with human-black bear conflict. *Human Dimensions of Wildlife*, 12, 133–136.

Gore, M. L., Knuth, B. A., Scherer, C. W., & Curtis, P. D. (2008). Evaluating a conservation investment designed to reduce human-wildlife conflict. *Conservation Letters*, 1, 136–145.

Gore, M. L., Lute, M. L., Ratsimbazafy, J. H., & Rajaonson, A. (2016). Local perspectives on environmental security and its influence on illegal biodiversity exploitation. *PLoSONE*. DOI: 10.1371/journal.pone.0150337.

Gore, M. L., Nelson, M. P., Vucetich, J. A., Smith, A. M., & Clark, M. A. (2011). Exploring the ethical basis for conservation policy: The case of inbred wolves on Isle Royale, USA. *Conservation Letters*, 4, 394–401.

Gore, M. L., Wilson, R. S., Siemer, W. F., Hudenko, H. A., Clarke, C. E., Hart, S. P.,...Muter, B. A. (2009). Application of risk concepts to wildlife management: special issue introduction. *Human Dimensions of Wildlife*, 14, 301–313.

Hance, J. (2016). Has big conservation gone astray? *Mongabay*. Retrieved from https://news.mongabay.com/2016/04/big-conservation-gone-astray

Kasane Statement. (2015). Kasane Conference on Wildlife Trafficking. March 25 2015.

Keller, C., Bostrom, A., Kuttschreuter, M., Savadori, L., Spence, A., & White, M. (2012). Bringing appraisal theory to environmental risk perception: A review of conceptual approaches of the past 40 years and suggestions for future research. *Journal of Risk Research*, 15, 237–256.

Khanna, P. (2016). *Connectography: mapping the future of global civilization*. New York, New York: Random House.

Kolko, J. (2015). Design thinking comes of age. *Harvard Business Review*. Retrieved from https://hbr.org/2015/09/design-thinking-comes-of-age

Kubo, H., & Supriyanto, B. (2010). From fence-and-fine to participatory conservation: mechanisms of transformation in conservation governance at the Gunung Halimun-Salak National Park, Indonesia. *Biodiversity and Conservation*, 19, 1785–1803.

Lemieux, A. M. (Ed.) (2014). *Situational prevention of poaching*. United Kingdom: Routledge.

Lute, M. L., & Gore, M. L. (2014). Knowledge and power in wildlife management. *Journal of Wildlife Management*, 78, 1060–1068.

Lynch, M. J., & Stretesky, P. (2014). *Exploring green criminology: Toward a green criminological revolution*. Burlington: Ashgate Publishing Company.

Mascia, M. B. (2006). Conservation social science: What's in the black box. *Society for Conservation Biology Newsletter*, 13, 1.

Mascia, M. B., Pailler, S., Krithivasan, R., Roshchanka, V., Burns, D., Mlotha, M. J.,...Peng, N. (2014). Protected area downgrading, downsizing, and degazettement (PADDD) in Africa, Asia, and Latin America and the Caribbean, 1900–2010. *Biological Conservation*, 169, 355–361.

Mascia, M. B., & Pailler, S. (2011). Protected area downgrading, downsizing, and degazettement (PADDD) and its conservation implications. *Conservation Letters*, 4, 9–20.

McLellan, R. (2014). World Wildlife Fund 2014 Living Planet Report. World Wildlife Fund, Gland, Switzerland.

Meyers, S. S., Gaffikin, L., Golden, C. D., Ostfeld, R. S., Redford, K., Ricketts, T. H.,...Osofsky, S. A. (2013). Human health impacts of ecosystem alteration. *Proceeding of the National Academy of Science*, 110, 18753–18760.

Milner-Gulland, E. J. (2012). Interactions between human behavior and ecological systems. *Philosophical Transactions of the Royal Society B-Biological Sciences*, 376, 270–278.

Mulder, M. B., & Coppolillo, P. (2005). *Conservation: linking ecology, economics, and culture*. Princeton, New Jersey: Princeton University Press.

Myers, N. (1993). Biodiversity and the Precautionary Principle. *Ambio*, 22, 74–79.

National Academy of Sciences, National Academy of Engineering, Institute of Medicine. (2004). *Facilitating Interdisciplinary Research*. National Academies Press: Washington D.C..

Nellemann, C., Henreiksen, R., Raxter, P., Ash, N., & Mrema, E. (2014). *The environmental crisis-threats to sustainable development from illegal exploitation and trade in wildlife and forest resources*. United Nations Environment Programme: Gland Switzerland.

Obama, B. (2013). *Executive Order--Combating Wildlife Trafficking*. Retrieved from https://www.whitehouse.gov/the-press-office/2013/07/01/executive-order-combating-wildlife-trafficking

Prince of Wales. (2013). *A speech by The Prince of Wales at the Illegal Wildlife Trade Conference*. Retrieved from http://www.princeofwales.gov.uk/media/speeches/speech-the-prince-of-wales-the-illegal-wildlife-trade-conference

Quinn, K. (2016). *Intelligence and the illegal wildlife trade*. Retrieved from http://trajectorymagazine.com/got-geoint/item/2136-intelligence-and-the-illegal-wildlife-trade.html

Raik, D. B., & Decker, D. J. (2007). A multisector framework for assessing community-based forest management: Lessons from Madagascar. *Ecology and Society*, 12, 14.

Ratsimbazafy, J., Gore, M. L., & Rakotoniaina, L. J. (2013). Community policing in Madagascar. In M. Nalla (Ed.). *Community policing in indigenous communities*. Boca Raton, Florida: CRC Press.

Reiss, E. (2011). *The lean start up*. New York, New York: Crown Business.

Renn, O. (2008). *Risk governance: Coping with uncertainty in a complex world*. United Kingdom: Earthscan.

Tisdell, C. (1999). *Biodiversity conservation and sustainable development: Principles and practices with Asian examples*. Cheltenham, United Kingdom: Edward Elgar.

Valiente-Banuet, A., Aizen, M. A., Alcántara, J. M., Arroyo, J., Cocucci, A., Galetti, M.,...Zamora, R. (2015). Beyond species loss: the extinction of ecological interactions in a changing world. *Functional Ecology*, 29, 299–307.
Vucetich, J. A., J. T. Bruskotter, & Nelson, M. P. (2015). Evaluating whether nature's intrinsic value is an axiom of or anathema to conservation. *Conservation Biology*, 29, 321–332.
White, R. (2008). *Crimes against nature: Environmental criminology and ecological justice*. Portland, Oregon: Willan Publishing.
Wyatt, T. (2013). *Wildlife trafficking: A deconstruction of the crime, the victims, and the offenders*. United Kingdom: Palgrave Macmillan.

Part I

Conceptual Advancements in Conservation Criminology

2

Conservation Crime Science

Jessica S. Kahler and Meredith L. Gore

2.1 Exploitation of Natural Resources in a Globalized World

The use of wildlife and other natural resources for sustenance, clothing, trophies, and tools has historically been a fundamental part of the human cultural, economic, and ecological experience. Human populations have expanded, migrated, colonized each other, drawn and redrawn political boundaries, and built and destroyed economies. With all this political, cultural, and geographic change, the cultural views of people's relationship with nature, their societal norms, rules, and regulations surrounding wildlife have evolved. Rules and regulations regarding who can harvest wildlife, how many, and which species can be taken hasn't always been and in many instances still isn't, restricted to the biological characteristics of wildlife populations. Today, in many contexts, wildlife rules and regulations have criminalized local subsistence hunting in an effort to reduce the negative effects of violent, organized, and profit driven poaching (Challendar & Cooney, 2016; Duffy, 2010). Whether in reference to the "king's deer" (Eliason, 2012a) or a modern-day post-colonial African nation where big game hunting is reserved for affluent trophy hunters from foreign countries, many local people previously dependent on wildlife for food and economy are now criminalized as poachers because of revisions to local laws, national regulations, or multilateral treaties.

The growing human population and exploding global economy combine with other environmental harms (e.g., emerging infectious disease) to create legitimate concerns about the ability of plant and animals species to persist in the face of both legal and illegal harvest. Although not a new threat, poaching in a globalized world poses significant risk to species worldwide as well as the people that depend on them. The increasing involvement of transnational crime syndicates in trafficking wildlife and their parts as well as the use of violence and technology to exploit wildlife for large profits has helped elevate the issue to the high global policy arenas such that national governments have been compelled to respond. For example, the U.S. Wildlife Trafficking Enforcement Act of 2015 included wildlife trafficking under federal Racketeer Influenced and Corrupt Organizations Act; China's Standing Committee of the National People's Congress passed an interpretation of the Criminal Law in 2014 putting eaters of rare animals in jail.

Conservation Criminology, First Edition. Edited by Meredith L. Gore.

Exploitation is now the dominant cause of global wildlife decline, surpassing habitat degradation, climate change, and habitat loss (McLellan, 2014).

Illegal harvest of plant and animal species occurs around the world, poses risks to species, ecosystems, and people. The activity is often called poaching by conservation policy makers and practitioners. Estimating the economic scale of the trade is difficult, given its illicit nature. Contemporary estimates for the global illegal trade of wildlife ranges between $U.S. 7 and 23 billion (Nellemann, Henreiksen, Raxter, Ash, & Mrema, 2014) and rivals the size of the illicit market of arms and drugs (Clinton, 2012). Further, estimates of illegal, unreported, and unregulated harvest of fisheries resources and trade of products from illegal logging operations are $U.S. 11 to 30 billion and $U.S. 30 to 100 billion respectively (Nellemann *et al.*, 2014). Beyond the risk of irreversible species loss, these estimates represent stolen natural resources, human rights abuses, and regional destabilization in some of world's most vulnerable developing nations (Brashares *et al.*, 2014). These risks have been acknowledged beyond the conservation community in the global high policy arena; the United Nations Office on Drugs and Crime, Organization for Economic Co-operation and Development, United States Government, Prince of Wales, and others now publically acknowledge poaching is a substantial threat to human economies, security, and well-being (Nellemann *et al.*, 2014).

Finding sustainable and socially just solutions to the biodiversity exploitation crisis necessitates at least a better understanding of the illegal crimes and normative rule violations against non-human species and the environment. Further, what are the most efficient and effective ways to motivate diverse people to comply with conservation rules and regulations? Thus far, the overwhelming policy and programmatic response to this need has been to identify the key requisite of an approach should be interdisciplinary. Over four decades ago, wildlife biologists argued law enforcement was as important as research and management in administration of wildlife resources, but it has not received proportionate attention from administrators and researchers (e.g., Morse, 1973). This is problematic because without adequate law enforcement, the finest research and management will have little to no effect in protecting the resource (Morse, 1973). Morse (1973, p. 44) went on to specify that a gap needed to be filled by starting "comprehensive, interdisciplinary law enforcement research programs at once; including human attitudes and behavior as well as development of new enforcement techniques." Today, the call for multidisciplinary and multidimensional approaches continues. For example, speakers at the March 2016 U.S. Congressional Forum on Criminal Nature: The Global Security Implications of the Illegal Wildlife Trade repeated calls for collaboration and coordination among sectors over the short and long-term.

2.2 The Limits of Criminology for Conservation Practice

Conservation criminology, as an interdisciplinary tactic for thinking about framing the questions and solutions to the problem of natural resource exploitation (Gore, 2011), is an academic cousin of green criminology (e.g., Lynch & Stretskey, 2014).

The approach has much to offer in terms of research, teaching, and practice. However, from the perspective of proactively preventing wildlife crimes, criminology may be limited. These limits have been enumerated and explored in depth by prominent criminologists within the context of non-conservation crimes (e.g., Clarke, 2004). In reviewing critiques of criminology we were intrigued by claims about limits in the face contemporary challenges of crime in general (e.g., mass shootings, cyber crime, organized crime). A number of critiques in particular appeared relevant to conservation, provoking thoughts about the implications for resolving the negative effects of overexploitation of natural resources on species and the people that depend on them. Below, we review these critiques and apply them to conservation. For example, under the standard for criminological research theory testing and methodological diligence takes precedence over the timeliness and pragmatic relevance of the findings. In instances where wildlife species are being rapidly decimated by non-subsistence-based poaching, such as Central Africa's okapi, continuing with research objectives, methods, and timelines that answer distant questions of *why* wildlife crimes occur rather than answering the immediate questions of *how* is functionally irrelevant in conservation. Or, since criminology has largely been invested in understanding why someone has committed a crime, criminologists have typically focused on offenders (Clarke, 2004). They then might interpret results to determine the socialization mechanism generating deviance so that programs can work to reform deviance (Forsyth & Marckese, 1993). For example, in conducting interviews with poachers to elucidate their motivations to poach, scholars often measure participant's thrill of outsmarting game wardens and demonstration of their hunting skills in an effort to inform interventions designed to reduce the thrill.

One important limit of criminology in conservation involves the focus on the distant causal roots of crime and associated calls for long-term social change. In following this approach, criminologists often engage in research with little realistic or measurable policy relevance (Clarke, 2004) and offer little in terms of ways to reduce or prevent crimes in the near term (Clarke, 1995). Policy relevance is often not the objective of criminology, however, some criminologists feel that "striving for policy relevance uniquely distorts the quest for a 'pure' understanding of crime" (Clarke, 2004, p. 57). Conservation is an inherently applied field relying on a variety of context-based interventions, including policy; there is also a temporal urgency to many conservation problems.

A second potential limit of criminology in conservation is the detachment of theory and practice. For example, some social disadvantage-based theories of crime, such as social disorganization theory (Shaw & McKay, 1942) are criticized because evidence indicates that even after many of the conditions hypothesized to increase criminal dispositions, such as poverty and lack of education, are improved, crime rates continue or even may increase (Cohen & Felson, 1979). These theories are particularly inadequate for explaining cyber-crimes committed by individuals that are not socially or educationally disadvantaged (Clarke, 2004). Again, given the practical and ground level interventions deployed in diverse conservation contexts, strong linkages between the knowledge and implementation bases are desirable.

Within mainstream criminology, critical commentary also discusses how criminology can be interpreted as being sympathetic to criminals when such approaches and descriptions of offenders present them as disadvantaged or as failures of society (Clarke, 2004). Within the context of conservation, empathy with people that poach for subsistence under impoverished circumstances with few livelihood alternatives is arguably warranted and rarely debated. There is little question, however, that poaching for extreme profit is occurring and that many publics support action against offenders feeding the extreme luxury markets for wildlife. For example, CNN profiled the plight of Asian pangolins, arguing for intervention. Asian pangolins are currently being exploited at extremely high rates to satiate demand for meat (e.g., pangolin fetus soup is considered a delicacy and regularly served in some Vietnamese restaurants) or wine (e.g., pangolins are steeped in rice wine sold by the glass or bottle) (Sutter, 2014). Pangolin meat has been known to retail in some restaurants for $U.S. 350 per kilo; whole animals regularly weigh 5 kilos and thus can retail for $U.S. 1750 (Sutter, 2014).

To prevent becoming obsolete in a global society where environmental, and other, crime control and prevention techniques are in high demand, some criminologists (e.g., Clarke, 2004; Gradon, 2013; Junger *et al.*, 2012) have argued a sea change is warranted.

Specifically, criminology can (a) abandon notions of theoretical purity for an applied science approach; (b) reduce the over-reliance on dispositional and disadvantage-based theories to explain why crime occurs; (c) use methods that examine how crimes are committed and are consistent with an applied-science approach; (d) engage a broader array of cross sectoral practitioners in policing, business, and industry in interventions designed to reduce crime and its negative effects.

2.3 Overcoming the Limits of Criminology with Crime Science

Crime science is a crime-centric approach with a primary mission of crime control and prevention (Clarke, 2004) and policy-relevant analysis (Wellsmith, 2010); it emerged as a complement to criminology yet sought to overcome key shortcomings, many of which are discussed above. If the criminological mission is concerned with explaining *why*, the mission of crime science is concerned with discovering *how*. The theoretical foundation of crime science draws on diverse disciplines, such as biology, economics, computer science, and geography (Clarke, 2004). It embraces the tenets of environmental criminology, often rejected by conventional criminology, that approaches should focus on proximate, situational factors that create opportunities for crime (Clarke, 1999). Crime science is applied, problem-led, and embraces policy and other interventions. Theories that dominate crime science focus how criminal opportunities are generated, such as how our daily routines may affect our chances of becoming a victim of crime, and how they are perceived by the offender (Clarke, 2004).

Crime science methods focus on how a crime was committed and can include victim surveys, how to predict crime and crime patterns, and how to alter criminal opportunities to reduce or prevent crime (Clarke, 2004). Under a crime science paradigm the importance of providing timely and relevant results, which can include using rapid appraisal methods and technical reports, is prioritized over concerns about theoretical loyalty and single method techniques (Clarke, 2004). Prevention-driven objectives necessitate that crime science broadly engage the enforcement community, many of whom bear the primary responsibility for detecting crime and apprehending offenders (Clarke, 2004). Significant emphasis is placed on designing social and technological crime-reduction systems according to the needs of a variety of stakeholders from government, businesses, security and general public (Bouhana, 2013).

Importantly, crime science research generates results that are context-specific, resulting in proactive crime prevention strategies that are based on understanding the situational factors that are more likely to lead to certain crime events (Gradon, 2013). Although informed by theory, crime science-related outcomes are not intended to test or build theory. Generalizability (i.e., external validity) is often diminished at the expense of developing case-by-case problem solving (i.e., reliability). Additionally, crime science moves beyond legal definitions of crime adhered to in criminology and criminal justice pursuits, and may include broader contexts such as socially deviant and antisocial behavior, disorder, and social misconduct (Gradon, 2013).

Crime science is relatively recent addition, joining criminal justice and criminology, approaches for studying crime (Clarke, 2010). Some criminologists argue crime science is an extension of environmental criminology while others argue that crime science is a separate discipline with theories and methods devoted exclusively to understanding crime—not criminals (Clarke, 2010). Environmental criminology focuses on explaining how opportunities for crime arise from the built environment, such as tangible factors like the availability of weapons and illicit markets that immediately precipitate a crime event. The differences between crime science and environmental criminology may have consequences downstream in terms of the recommended courses of action and the consumers of information generated through scientific inquiry.

Considering the differences between criminology and crime science in dealing with conventional crimes encouraged us to reflect on the implications for conservation. Conservation criminology represents advancement in the interdisciplinary research of environmental crimes, yet given this state of the real world problems associated with natural resource exploitation, the question becomes: Do we need conservation crime science?

2.4 State of Knowledge: Conservation Criminology and Conservation Crime Science

As a first step to answering our question we reviewed the contemporary literature associated regarding wildlife poaching. We used the Web of Science to search the peer-reviewed literature from the years 1990 to 2014 using the keyword search function and the terms "poach* wildlife." We chose not to elaborate on variations of this concept so as not to bias the sample toward specific types of poaching, such as literature on bushmeat, or confound the activity with poaching of domesticated animals (e.g., cattle rustling). We used the Web of Science's Results Analysis function to determine the article theme, publication year, and the top ten research areas and journals in which articles appeared. We expected our search would exclude fish, fresh water organisms, and marine species largely due to a difference in language in the literature stemming from the nature of violations and the historical disciplinary separation of aquatic (e.g., fisheries) and terrestrial (e.g., wildlife) systems. For example, many marine and freshwater species are harvested legally but have restrictions on equipment used, quotas, and equipment used to harvest. Studying violations in these systems often refer to "illegal harvest, illegal fishing, and over-harvest" to name a few. After our initial query of the database, we read each article's abstract to confirm the primary research topic was wildlife poaching. We recorded the conservation context of the research (e.g., country/region, species/genera). Within the 15-year sample, we examined the most recent third (2010–2014) to record the primary research objective(s) of each study and match it with the mission of crime science, criminal justice, criminology, and forensic science. Articles were not exclusively matched with a discipline, as many articles had multiple objectives, which often bridged these distinctions. For example, Kahler, Roloff, and Gore (2013) used participatory risk ranking and mapping combined with incident reports of poaching to quantify the extent of poaching and detection (i.e., criminal justice), examine spatial patterns of poaching (i.e., crime science), and corroborate stated motivations to poach (Kahler & Gore, 2012) in Namibian conservancies. We defined the disciplinary missions as follows:

- Crime science as how poaching takes place, situational predictors of crime (e.g., poacher process, crime patterns), or policy-related research on crime prevention (e.g., trade bans, wildlife farming).
- Criminal justice as crime detection, quantifying the poaching problem (e.g., number of poachers), or prosecution, punishment or the criminal justice system (e.g., conviction rates).
- Criminology as biological or ecological consequences of poaching (e.g., population effects), causes of or why poaching takes place (e.g., motivations of poachers), or consequences of poaching on human systems (e.g., food security, instability).
- Forensic science as evidence collection (e.g., crime scene procedures), evidence preservation, and scientific interpretation (e.g., DNA analysis)

Our conceptualization of these missions was based on assumptions about the organizational relationship of these disciplines and how they work differently to address a primary research question (Figure 2.1).

2.4.1 Describing the Literature

Our initial search uncovered 319 articles; of these 148 directly related to wildlife poaching. Over time, there has been a dramatic increase in the number of publications on the topic (Figure 2.2).

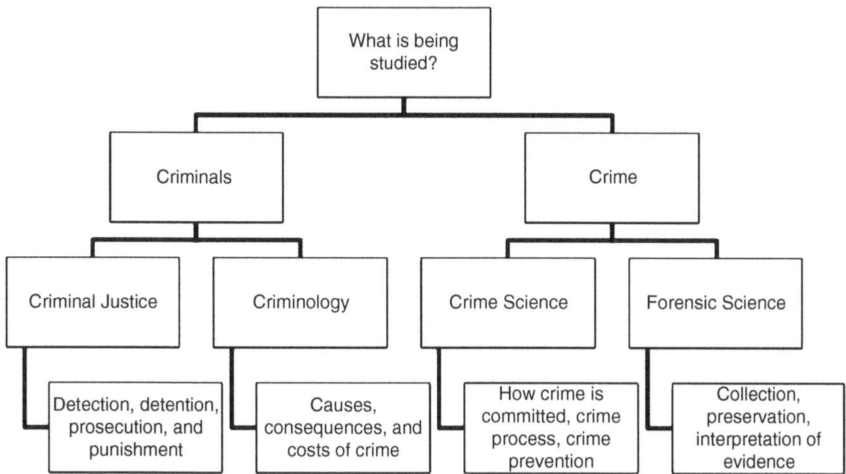

Figure 2.1 A conservationist's opinion on the sub-disciplines that study crime, criminal behavior and the criminal justice system.

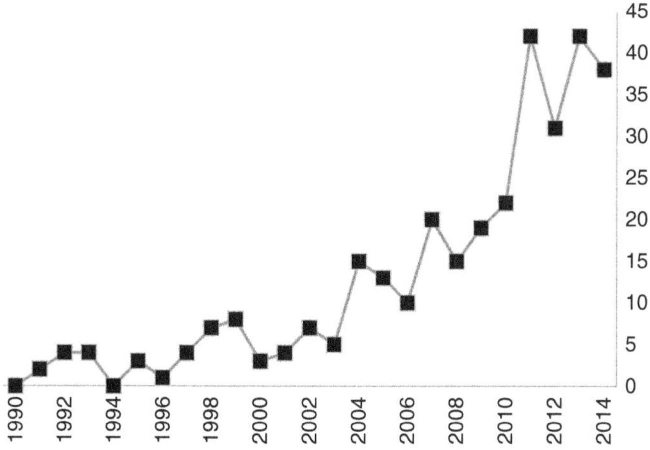

Figure 2.2 The total number of peer-reviewed journal articles published between 1990 and 2014 detected by the Web of Science in January 2015 using the terms "poach*wildlife."

Paralleling the increase in number of publications on wildlife poaching, the interdisciplinary aspects of research amplified to over 40 research areas and 125 journals publishing on the topic; the 10 most common research areas and journals were varied (Table 2.1).

Less than one-third of our sample (n = 93) was published between 2010 and 2014. This literature was mostly based on conservation issues situated in Africa. The majority of research was not species or taxa specific; unsurprisingly mammals were the most common subject of recent poaching research with elephants being the most commonly researched species. Fishes were

Table 2.1 Top 10 research areas and journals based on a search of Web of Science on articles (n = 319) related to wildlife poaching from the years 1990 to 2014.

Research Areas	Number	Percent
Environmental sciences, ecology	177	55
Biodiversity conservation	102	32
Zoology	63	20
Legal, medicine	20	6.3
Science technology, other topics	19	6.0
Business, economics	15	4.7
Life sciences, biomedicine, other topics	11	3.4
Criminology, penology, genetics, heredity, veterinary sciences	10	3.1
Agriculture, sociology	9	2.8
Forestry	6	1.9
Journals	**Number**	**Percent**
Biological Conservation	23	7.2
Oryx	19	6.0
Conservation Biology, Pachyderm	14	4.4
Biodiversity and Conservation	12	3.8
J. Wildlife Management, PLoS One	11	3.4
African J. Ecology	10	3.1
Ecological Economics, Environmental Conservation, Forensic Science International	6	1.9
Animal Conservation, Forensic Science International Genetics, PNAS, Tropical Conservation Science	5	1.6
Deviant Behavior, Environmental Management, J. Nature Conservation, J. Forensic Sciences, Ursus, Wildlife Research	4	1.3
British Journal of Criminology, Conservation Society, International J. Sustainable Development and World Ecology, J. Environmental Management, J. Medical Entomology, Revista de Biologia Tropical, Science Justice, South African J. Wildlife Research, Wildlife Society Bulletin, Zoology of the Middle East	3	1.0

dramatically under-represented in this sample with only 2% of the articles focusing on fisheries resources (Table 2.2).

The majority of our sample (n = 59, 63%), much like conventional criminology, was dominated by answering the why questions or examining root causes of crime and establishing the consequences and costs of poaching to human and natural systems (e.g., Lindsey, Romanach, & Matema, 2011; Lui, McShea, & Garshelis, 2011). For example, Lindsey *et al.* (2011) researched the underlying

Table 2.2 A description of peer-reviewed literature on wildlife poaching published between 1990-2014 (n = 93).

		Number	Percent	Example
Criminal focus	**Criminal Justice**	**25**	**27**	Evaluated long-term enforcement records to determine the effect of patrol size & length on snare detection (Becker *et al.*, 2013)
	Crime detection	21	23	
	Prosecution, punishment	4	4	
	Criminology	**59**	**63**	Quantitative analysis fish & wildlife offenses in Florida to develop a typology & examine racial & ethnic differences of offenders (Crow, Shelley, & Stretesky, 2013)
	Biological consequences	19	20	
	Causes of crime	26	28	
	Human consequences	14	15	
Crime focus	**Crime Science**	**33**	**35**	Examined the situational factors, such as distant to cities, that affect which species of parrots in Bolivia are most commonly poached (Pires & Clarke, 2011)
	Crime pattern, how	15	16	
	Policy prevention	18	19	
	Forensic Science	**15**	**16**	Developed baseline health assessments of wild & confiscated tortoises to use as forensic evidence (Henen, Hofmeyer, & Ernst, 2013)
	DNA, forensics	15	16	
Geographical context	Africa (N = 40, 43%)	Sub-Saharan, Tanzania (8), South Africa (5) Kenya, Zimbabwe (4)		
		Democratic Republic of Congo, Zambia (2), Botswana, Cameroon		
		Cote d' Ivoire, Ethiopia, Ghana, Namibia, Uganda (1)		
	Asia - Pacific (N = 13, 14%)	China, India (3), Nepal, Thailand (2), Australia, Malaysia		
		Myanmar (1)		
	Europe (N = 8, 9%)	Europe, Spain (2), Cyprus, Italy, Portugal, Scandinavia (1)		
	North America (N = 11, 12%)	United States (5), Mexico (3), North (2), Belize (1)		
	South America (N = 5, 5%)	South (2), Bolivia, Brazil, Galapagos (1)		
	Other (N = 16,17%)	Computer modeling, non-specified, laboratories, web-based		

(Continued)

Table 2.2 (Continued)

Species or group	General (N = 52, 56%)	Wildlife (39), Bushmeat (11), Vertebrates (2)
	Birds (N = 7, 8%)	Parrots (5), Cockatoos, Thrushes (1)
	Fishes (N = 2, 2%)	Freshwater, Sharks (1)
	Mammals (N = 33, 35%)	
	Carnivores (N = 8, 9%)	Bears, carnivores (general), tiger (2), Snow leopard, Wolf (1)
	Herbivores (N = 25, 27%)	Elephant (10), Rhino (3), Deer (2), African buffalo, Elk, Herbivores
		Migratory ungulates, Mountain nyala antelope, Oribi antelope, Ovis spp., Reedbuck, Sardinian mouflon, Tapir (1)
	Reptiles (N = 4, 4%)	Tortoise (2), American alligator, Sea turtles (1)

causes of the illegal bushmeat trade in Zimbabwe, identifying poverty, unemployment, food shortages, and the failure of programs to establish stakes for communities in wildlife resources, to name a few, as key drivers of wildlife crime. However, the sample did include articles detailing the application of crime science theories (e.g., routine activity theory) to wildlife poaching (e.g., Eliason, 2012b; Pires & Clarke, 2011). Pires and Clarke (2012) found CRAVED to be useful in analyzing what species of parrots were targeted for the pet trade in Mexico.

Many of the methods utilized by crime science practitioners are applicable to wildlife crime and are being employed in research; our sample of recent literature indicated 35% of articles included a crime science methodology. For example, examinations of poaching crime patterns, hot spot identification, and species-specific case studies are established in research on wildlife related crime. For example, Mackenzie, Chapman, and Sengupta (2012) examined the spatial patterns of illegal poaching and wood extraction, conducted observational studies in villages looking for signs of illegal activity, and compared villages based on whether they had negotiated resource access agreements.

2.5 Limitations

We recognize the sampling frame favored disciplinary journals more traditionally associated with conservation and natural resources management. Although there was a wide array of journals and disciplines represented in our sample, we are aware of the limitations that the Web of Science poses in terms of the fields of crime science, criminal justice, and criminology in particular. For example, in May of 2012 the International Journal of Comparative and

Applied Criminal Justice published a special issue on "Wildlife Crime and Enforcement." The articles in this journal were not captured in our sample because the search engine does not include this journal. However, this could represent a legitimate concern in terms of conservation managers and researchers incorporating the best practices from criminology and crime science. Additionally, although crime science approaches comprised 35% of the sample of recent literature, over half of these were examinations, policy choice simulations, and critique of policy used to prevent wildlife crime. Other methods in crime science, in addition to the aforementioned crime pattern and spatially explicit methods, which would be advantageous to understanding crime prevention at a site-specific level come from the situational crime prevention approach. There is a dearth of research in this are and not one paper in our sample used this approach, however, Lemieux (2014) published a book on the topic.

2.6 Utility of Using Conservation Crime Science

Conservation crime science would likely expand the suite of tools available to diagnose problems and scaffold solutions by expanding understanding of conservation-related criminals and crime: the why and the how. Further, conservation crime science might promote innovation and discovery of long and short-term approaches that sustainably reduce negative effects of wildlife crimes. What might conservation crime science look like in terms of mission, theory, research methods, application, and audience? Fundamentally, fully embracing the mission of crime science would require crime-centered research objectives such as understanding rhino poaching rather than rhino poachers; results would produce recommendations for policy-relevant interventions that are tested and evaluated in the near term (Clarke, 2004). Much of the tenets of crime science are complementary to contemporary approaches to address wildlife crime, indeed some are already being employed, and other areas need further exploration. Conservation-based organizations, such as World Wildlife Fund, Wildlife Conservation Society, TRAFFIC the wildlife trade-monitoring network, International Fund for Animal Welfare, and government agencies (e.g., U.S. Department of State) regularly use policy to address wildlife crimes. There is strong support within the field of conservation to engage in research that both increases understanding of the causes and consequences of wildlife crimes in order to inform preventative programs that immediately reduce risk (e.g., Wellsmith, 2010); these goals are consistent with the mission of crime science.

Conservation crime science could have diverse applications and audiences, including but not limited to state and federal agencies, police, wildlife rangers and wardens, protected area managers, communal and private conservancy managers, conservation organizations, business (e.g., ecotourism, hunting operations) and industry (e.g., fishing, forestry). This approach would be consistent with the crime science tradition of accommodating diverse applications and audiences with a stake in reducing crime. Crime science often works with businesses, management, police, planners and the security sectors to address crime prevention and control needs, through application of detection, deterrence and situational prevention techniques, applied to specific crime problems (Clarke, 2004). Many of these stakeholders are already poised to receive, assess and react to information that could be provided via a crime science approach, particularly centered around poaching associated with organized crime syndicates.

Conservation criminology offers a progressive lens for thinking about the problem and solution sets for environmental crime and harm; conservation crime science is the logical next arena in which we can advance the diversity and effectiveness of environmental crime interventions. This is because despite substantial efforts by diverse stakeholders, wildlife crime is still a proximate threat to species conservation in numerous contexts worldwide. Many gaps persist in understanding of conservation-based crimes and it there is a growing sentiment that new innovations are needed to provide answers. There is widespread agreement that to increase understanding and discover these innovations, interdisciplinary approaches are uniquely qualified for informing the complexity of the interactions between diverse offenders, natural resource stakeholders, the targeted species, and the environment in which these interactions occur.

2.7 Setting Expectations for Conservation Crime Science

Crime science has positioned itself well to address the practical, theoretical and methodological demands of a risk-based, post-modern, technologically driven world in a state of constant crime crisis (e.g., terrorism, human body part trafficking) (Clarke, 2004). But is crime science the prevention cure it seems? Some approaches embraced by a crime science, such as situational crime prevention (Bouhana, 2013) have been criticized for advocating top-down controls, promoting the militarization of natural resources, restricting civil liberties, and blaming the victim (Clarke, 2008). Like these general critiques of crime science, ethical issues with natural resource-based crime controls abound as well. For example, the use of "shoot-to-kill" anti-poaching policies in countries such as Zimbabwe and Kenya (Messer, 2010) and "fortress conservation" or "fences and fines" approaches in conservation have long been criticized due to the potential for human rights violations (Duffy, 2014). Additionally, crime science has been criticized for paying little attention to the offender part of the crime equation and relying on overly simplistic models of decision-making (e.g., rational choice perspective, see Bouhana, 2013). Therefore, within the context of wildlife crimes, conservation crime science can mirror conservation criminology and integrate theories from disciplines with a more robust and theoretically sound understanding of natural resource stakeholder decision-making, namely the disciplines of natural resources management and risk and decision sciences.

Importantly, the most obvious and direct victims of poaching are non-human and given that many of them are considered natural resources managed legally for the sustenance, enjoyment, and economic benefit of people, questions of why violations occur and how hegemony produces resource disadvantaged groups and environmental injustice will never be completely irrelevant. Although many of the high profile, visually shocking and violent wildlife crimes such as rhino and elephant poaching are likely crimes of greed, the more ubiquitous, chronic wildlife crimes like illegal harvest of firewood or wild meat for household consumption are activities of need. Social inequity and disadvantage must be dealt with when it is a proximate factor to wildlife crime and pursuing an intervention agenda that contains short-term and long-term crime reducing solutions is good conservation practice.

Finally, there are diverse legal, historical, and geographic contexts that define the concept of poaching. Yet from the perspective of conserving biodiversity, reducing overharvest, legal or illegal, of threatened and endangered species are priorities regardless of legal definitions. These contexts are arguably essential to consider in any solution and regardless of the diversity of stakeholders that would be the consumers or end-users of information and strategies to reduce wildlife crimes. In order to effectively reduce wildlife crimes any forthcoming strategies would ideally be put in the hands of a diverse group of natural resource stakeholders on the ground. This could include stakeholders with both legal jurisdiction (e.g., police, park rangers, private citizens, communities and businesses with ownership rights over natural resources), and those with a stake in biodiversity conservation (e.g., non-governmental organizations).

2.8 Conclusion

There is a dire need is to achieve measurable wildlife crime reduction in the short-term across a variety of environmental and social contexts (Nellemann *et al.*, 2014). Conservation criminology offers a needed advancement in interdisciplinary scholarship, infusing theoretical and methodological vigor into research on wildlife crimes, to increase understanding of the motivations, dispositions and the why of environmental crimes. This will be important to generate approaches to affect long-term social changes, such as market demand reductions, that reduce wildlife crimes. However, if it follows suit as a sub-discipline of criminology it could run the risk of the limitations discussed above, in particular failure to produce and provide more immediate, contextually appropriate crime reduction strategies for the appropriate stakeholders on the ground. The most progressive way forward may be to develop a conservation crime science alongside development of conservation criminology as an interdisciplinary, applied, and necessary endeavor to increase the efficacy of research on environmental crimes and harms, from poaching to pollution. The two would be complementary (Table 2.3). The advantage of the late stage of interaction between conservation-based sciences with criminology and crime sciences is that the former can adopt and adapt the most rigorous, relevant and tried and tested theories, methods and approaches from the later. Continued research into the applicability

Table 2.3 Characterizing the differences between research on wildlife poaching under conservation criminology versus conservation crime science (adapted from Clarke, 2004).

Conservation Criminology	Conservation Crime science
Mission	
Understand poachers	Understand poaching
Poverty elimination	Immediate poaching reduction
Human development	Protect species populations
Theory-led	Problem-led
Policy critiques	Policy changes
Theory	
Cause is distant (poverty)	Triggers based on proximate situations
Opportunity secondary	Opportunity central
Poaching deviant	Poaching routine
The WHY of poaching	The HOW of poaching
Poacher criminally inclined	Poacher calculated decision-maker
Poachers motivations	Cost and benefits of poaching
Conflict theory, political ecology, risk theories	Routine activities, rational choice
Development studies, law, sociology, psychology	Economics, geography, biology, ecology, computer sciences (GIS)
Applicable Research Methods	
Hunting ethnographies	Seasonal, spatial poaching patterns
Historical analysis	Hot spot, spatial congruence
Regression analysis	Participatory mapping
Random response techniques	Species CRAVED analysis
Long-term studies in depth	Rapid appraisal techniques
Application and Audience	
Environmental non-compliance	Specific poaching problems (regions, species)
Sentencing/treatment/social prevention	Detection/deterrence/situational prevention
Development workers, conservationist	Rangers, conservationists, traditional authorities
Social policy-makers	Conservation, wildlife management
Peer-reviewed publications	Policy briefs
Career in academia	Careers in enforcement, management

of the crime science approach to wildlife crimes, theoretically and otherwise, is needed given the breadth of species and contexts where wildlife crimes are a serious concern, our dearth of knowledge of factors that influence poaching opportunities and how wildlife crimes are committed.

References

Becker, M., McRobb, R., Watson, F., Droge, E., Kanyembo, B., Murdoch, J., & Kakumbi, C. (2013). Evaluating wire-snare poaching trends and the impacts of by-catch on elephants and large carnivores. *Biological Conservation*, 158, 26–36.

Bouhana, N. (2013). The reasoning criminal vs. Homer Simpson: Conceptual challenges for crime science. *Frontiers in Human Neuroscience*, 7, 1–6.

Brashares, J. S., Abrahms, B., Fiorella, K. J., Golden, C. D., Hojnowski, C. E., Marsh, R. A.,...& Withey, L. (2014). Wildlife decline and social conflict. *Science*, 345, 376–378.

Challendar, D. W. S., & Cooney, R. (2016). Informing decisions on trophy hunting: A briefing paper for European Union decision-makers regarding potential plans for restriction of imports of hunting trophies. International Union for the Conservation of Nature. Retrieved from www.iucn.org/about/union/commissions/ceesp_ssc_sustainable_use_and_livelihoods_specialist_group/news_from_suli/

Clarke, R. V. (1995). Situational crime prevention. *Crime and Justice*, 19, 91–150.

Clarke, R. V. (1999). *Hot products: Understanding, anticipating and reducing demand for stolen goods*. Police Research Series, Paper 112. Policing and Reducing Crime Unit, Research Development and Statistics Directorate. London: Home Office.

Clarke, R. V. (2004). Technology, criminology and crime science. *European Journal on Criminal Policy and Research*, 10, 55–63.

Clarke, R. V. (2008). Situational crime prevention. In Wortley, R. & L. Mazerolle (Eds.). *Environmental criminology and crime analysis*. London and New York: Rutledge.

Clarke, R. V. (2010). Crime science. In E. Mclaughlin & T. Newburn (Eds.). *Handbook of Criminological Theory*. United Kingdom: Sage Publications.

Clinton, H. (2012). Remarks at the partnership meeting on wildlife trafficking. Retrieved from http://www.state.gov/secretary/20092013clinton/rm/2012/11/200294.htm

Cohen, L. E., & Felson, M. (1979). Social change and crime rate trends: A routine activity approach. *American Sociological Review*, 44, 588–608.

Crow, M. S., Shelley, T. O., & Stretesky, P. B. (2013). Camouflage-collar crime: An examination of wildlife crime and characteristics of offenders in Florida. *Deviant Behavior*, 34, 635–652

Duffy, R. (2010). *Nature crime: How we're getting conservation wrong*. New Haven, Connecticut: Yale University Press.

Duffy, R. (2014). Waging a war to save biodiversity: The rise of militarized conservation. *International Affairs*, 90, 819–834.

Eliason, S. (2012a). From the King's deer to capitalist commodity: A social historical analysis of poaching law. *International Journal of Comparative and Applied Criminal Justice*, 36, 133–148

Eliason, S. L. (2012b). Trophy poaching: A routine activities perspective. *Deviant Behavior*, 33, 72–87.

Forsyth, C.J., & Marckese, T.A. (1993). Thrills and skills: A sociological analysis of poaching. *Deviant Behavior*, 14, 157–172.
Gore, M. L. (2011). The science of conservation crime. *Conservation Biology*, 25, 659–661.
Gradon, K. (2013). Crime science and the internet battlefield: Securing the analog world from digital crime. *Security & Privacy, IEEE*, 11, 93–95.
Henen, B., Hofmeyr, M., & Ernst, B. (2013). Body of evidence: Forensic use of baseline health assessments to convict wildlife poachers. *Wildlife Research*, 40, 261–268.
Junger, M., Laycock, G., Hartel, P., & Ratcliffe, J. (2012). Crime science: Editorial statement. *Crime Science* 1: 1–3.
Kahler, J. S., & Gore, M. L. (2012). Beyond the cooking pot and pocket book: Factors influencing noncompliance with wildlife poaching rules. *International Journal of Comparative and Applied Criminal Justice*, 36, 103–120.
Kahler, J. S., Roloff, G., & Gore, M. L. (2013). Poaching risks in a community-based natural resource system. *Conservation Biology*, 27, 177–186.
Lindsey, P., Romanach, S., & Matema, S. (2011) Dynamics and underlying causes of illegal bushmeat trade in Zimbabwe. *Oryx*, 45, 84–95.
Lemieux, A. M. (2014). *Situational prevention of poaching*. United Kingdom: Routledge.
Lui, F., McShea, W., Garshelis, D., & Shao, L. (2011). Human-wildlife conflicts influence attitudes but not necessarily behaviors: Factors driving the poaching of bears in China. *Biological Conservation*, 144, 538–547.
Lynch, M.J., & Stretesky, P.B. (2011). Similarities between green criminology and green science: Toward a typology of green criminology. *International Journal of Comparative and Applied Criminal Justice*, 35(4), 293–306.
Mackenzie, C. A., Chapman, C. A., & Sengupta, R. (2012). Spatial patterns of illegal resource extraction in Kibale National Park, Uganda. *Environmental Conservation*, 39, 38–50.
McLellan, R. (2014). World Wildlife Fund 2014 Living Planet Report. World Wildlife Fund International, Gland, Switzerland.
Messer, K. D. (2010). Protecting endangered species: When are shoot-on-sight policies the only viable option to stop poaching? *Ecological Economics*, 69, 2334–2340.
Morse, W. B. (1973). Law enforcement-one third of the triangle. *Wildlife Society Bulletin*, 1, 39–44.
Pires, S. F., & Clarke, R. V. (2011). Sequential foraging, itinerant fences and parrot poaching in Bolivia. *British Journal of Criminology*, 51, 314–335.
Pires, S., & Clarke, R. V. (2012). Are parrots CRAVED? An analysis of parrot poaching in Mexico. *Journal of Research in Crime and Delinquency*, 49(, 122–146.
Nellemann, C., Henreiksen, R., Raxter, P., Ash, N., & Mrema, E. (2014). *The environmental crisis-threats to sustainable development from illegal exploitation and trade in wildlife and forest resources*. United Nations Environment Programme: Gland, Switzerland.
Shaw, C. R., & McKay, H. D. (1942). *Juvenile delinquency and urban areas: A study of rates of delinquents in relation to differential characteristics of local communities in American cities*. Chicago: University of Chicago Press.

Sutter, J. (2014). The most trafficked mammal you've never heard of. CNN. Retrieved from http://www.cnn.com/interactive/2014/04/opinion/sutter-change-the-list-pangolin-trafficking/

Wellsmith, M. (2010). The applicability of crime prevention to problems of environmental harm: A consideration of illicit trade in endangered species. In White, R. (Ed.), *Global Environmental harm: Ecological perspectives*. Portland: Willan Publishing.

3

Deterrence, Legitimacy, and Wildlife Crime in Protected Areas

William D. Moreto and Jacinta M. Gau

More and more, criminologists are exploring wildlife crimes, including poaching (Moreto & Lemieux, 2015a; Pires & Clarke, 2012), illegal fishing (Petrossian & Clarke, 2014), and illegal wildlife markets (Moreto & Lemieux, 2015b; Warchol, Zupan, & Clack, 2003). Other scholars are enhancing the knowledge base on various aspects of the criminal justice system, particularly wildlife law enforcement in a variety of contexts and settings (e.g., Eliason, 2014; Moreto, 2015b; Moreto, Brunson & Braga, 2015; 2016; Warchol & Kapla, 2012). Although the development of sub-criminological genres, including conservation (Gibbs, Gore, McGarrell, & Rivers, 2010) and green (White & Heckenberg, 2014) criminology, are important to the interdisciplinary scholarship of wildlife crime, examining the application and relevance of traditional criminological and criminal justice perspectives are also worthwhile (e.g., Eliason, 2012; Pires & Moreto, 2011). Deterrence theory is a central framework within criminology and criminal justice. Deterrence also features prominently in efforts to reduce wildlife crime in protected areas (PAs).

A diverse set of stakeholders, including policymakers, continuously endorse policing, prosecution, and punishment as the most effective and efficient prevention methods. There is widespread belief that more stringent arrest, charging, and sentencing policies will successfully turn offenders away from wildlife crime (Becker, 1968). At the same time, however, there are many reasons to question how well deterrence works, or could ever work, to accomplish this goal. Recognizing these potential limitations, alternative solutions warrant consideration. In particular, a legitimacy-enhancing approach may prove superior at promoting widespread compliance with wildlife-protection rules.

Our objective in this chapter is to provide an overview of deterrence theory as it applies to wildlife crime within PAs. We first review the relevant literature, the theoretical underpinnings of deterrence theory as it relates to the criminology, and the benefits and limitations of deterrence-based approaches in the management and monitoring of PAs. We also discuss the relevance and role of the government-legitimacy literature as it relates to natural resource management. We end by providing a road map for future scholarship.

Conservation Criminology, First Edition. Edited by Meredith L. Gore.

3.1 Wildlife Crime in Protected Areas

Protected areas clearly defined geographical spaces, recognized, dedicated, and managed, through legal or other effective means, to achieve the long-term conservation of nature with associated ecosystem services and cultural values (Dudley & Stolton, 2008). According to the World Database on Protected Areas (WDPA) there are over 200,000 terrestrial and marine PAs spanning more than 30 million km^2 in the world today (IUCN and UNEP-WCMC, 2016). In this chapter we focus solely on terrestrial PAs. Broadly speaking two main strategies are employed in the protection of PAs: traditional protectionist and community participation models (see Hayes, 2006). The traditional protectionist model focuses on restricting human residents and limiting their access to resources within PAs. Conversely, community participation models recognize the central role that local people living adjacent to or within PA boundaries have in the effective management and monitoring of PAs. Protectionist and participation models are not mutually exclusive and many PAs utilize both approaches in varying degrees (Braga, 2012).

Due to the abundance of natural resources within PAs, they are often subject to a variety of forms of resource extraction. The taking of these natural resources, including poaching, encroachment, logging, charcoal burning, and plant harvesting, among others, is often considered a criminal act and against the rule of law. In other instances, resource extraction is normatively prohibited. Beyond the ecological and environmental risks associated with resource extraction, wildlife crimes in PAs can also adversely impact local communities by unsustainably removing resources that they may depend upon for economic and subsistence purposes. Although other forms of criminal activity can occur within PAs as well, such as marijuana cultivation (Milestone *et al.*, 2012), we focus our discussion primarily on wildlife crimes or the illegal exploitation of the world's fauna that occur within PAs.

3.2 Criminological and Criminal Justice Perspectives on Deterrence

3.2.1 Theoretical Foundations

Deterrence theory has garnered sustained attention within criminology and criminal justice due to its link with the classical school of criminology (Beccaria, 2009) as well as the simplicity in its explanation of and solution to crime (Pratt, Cullen, Blevins, Daigle, & Madensen, 2006). Simply put, deterrence tells us individuals choose to commit a criminal act when the apparent benefits outweigh the perceived costs. The theory assumes that offenders are rational individuals that are mindful of the potential costs and benefits of particular criminal activities and based on these assessments choose to commit criminal acts (Pratt & Cullen, 2005). Consequently, in order to reduce or prevent crime, the costs or risks of illegal activity, often associated with laws and related sanctions, must dwarf the possible returns from the act. This contention is based on the three main elements of deterrence: severity, certainty, and celerity. In essence, punishment needs to be justly severe, likely to occur, and swiftly applied. Deterrence theory serves as a bridge between criminology and criminal justice since the criminal justice system is primarily responsible for establishing and enforcing criminal laws and penalties. Importantly, the extant literature on deterrence heavily derives from research conducted in the global north; it is therefore difficult to state whether the theory is culturally bounded. Further complicating matters is the varying capability of criminal justice responses in different settings and for different types of crime. Ultimately more research is needed to determine the extent to which the principles discussed herein hold true across settings (e.g., urban versus rural, criminal justice contexts, culture).

Traditionally, criminologists have investigated and distinguished between the general and specific deterrent effects of punishment. General deterrence refers to the "imposition of sanctions on one person" as a means to "demonstrate to the rest of the public the expected costs of a criminal act, and thereby discourage criminal behavior in the general population" (Nagin, 1978, p. 96). Specific or special deterrence occurs when an individual is "deterred by the actual experience of punishment" (Andenaes, 1968, p. 78). Both general and specific deterrence carry with them several assumptions that often do not hold true in practice. Regarding general deterrence, the cost-benefit calculus of individuals who are able to effectively avoid punishment should differ from those who are subject to punishment, thereby altering their perceived certainty and severity of legal sanctions. Additionally, specific deterrence is limited in recognizing the indirect effects of punishment on specific individuals. For example, the effectiveness of deterrent measures will be influenced by an offender's familiarity or knowledge of other individuals' experiences in similar circumstances, whether they are punished or not (Stafford & Warr, 1993). As a result of the limitations associated with how general and specific deterrence were initially conceptualized, revisionists proposed general and specific deterrence focus on personal experiences rather than unique populations (Stafford & Warr, 1993). As a result, general deterrence may be also be conceptualized as the "deterrent effect of indirect experience with punishment and punishment avoidance" while specific deterrence refers to the deterrent effect of "direct experience with punishment and punishment avoidance" (Stafford & Warr, 1993, p. 127).

A critical yet often overlooked element of deterrence is that it is fundamentally psychological in nature (Decker, Wright, & Logie, 1993). Deterrence depends entirely upon would-be offenders' perceptions of the certainty and severity of punishment. Irrespective of the objective probability of arrest or harshness of sanctions, offenders will not be deterred if they perceive they are likely to evade capture or penalty. Importantly, the general public is notoriously poor at accurately predicting arrest certainty or sanction severity (Sever, Li, & Gertz, 2005). People who have been arrested in the past do no better at estimating the probability of arrest than those with no history of criminal justice contact (Kleck, Sever, Li, & Gertz, 2005) and in fact may have even more distorted beliefs about their chances of being caught again in the future (Pogarsky & Piquero, 2003).

3.3 Empirical Findings

Given the potential implications of deterrence theory on state-based responses to crime, it is not surprising that it has generated much empirical attention. Beginning in the 1960s, scholars empirically examined deterrence from primarily macro- and micro-level perspectives. The former often comparing official crime data to various levels of punishment (e.g., arrests to offenses ratio) and the latter focused on exploring self-reported criminal behavior and perceptions of punishment (Kleck *et al.*, 2005). These studies derived from three main distinct methodological perspectives: interrupted-time series, ecological, and perceptual (Nagin, 1998).

In general, the effectiveness of deterrence-based strategies are mixed at best. For instance, the most comprehensive macro-level study of deterrence examined over 200 aggregate-level studies (Pratt & Cullen, 2005). Investigating the impact of specific variables, including increased police size, arrest ratios and clearance rates, and "get tough" policies, the authors found weak support for deterrence preventing overall crime rates. Micro-level studies delve deeper into perceptual manifestation of deterrence, particularly as it relates to perceived certainty and severity of punishment. These studies provided limited support for deterrence theory. The very fact that certain acts are criminalized and penalized probably instills sufficient dread into large portions of the public that they refrain from these behaviors (Walker, 2001). Most crimes, however, also carry moral stigmas and informal sanctions (e.g., job loss), and non-offenders' abstention may have little to do with criminal justice system considerations. Nonparticipation might be grounded in a desire not to invite disapproval from family and friends or imposition of social and economic penalties (Paternoster, 1989). Additionally, offenders may engage in neutralization techniques that permit them to distort their beliefs about the harm they are causing (e.g., denial of injury; see Sykes & Matza, 1957), their likelihood of being caught, and the types of punishments they could face (Copes & Vieraitis, 2006). This calls into question the presumption that offenders are rational and suggests instead that they are highly selective in the information they use when judging the cost–benefit ratio of committing a crime (Challender, 2014).

3.4 Limitations with Deterrence-based Approaches in Protected Areas

Enforcement strategies are an integral element of PAs and other natural resource management (Ostrom, 1990). Ranger foot patrols are the primary method utilized in the monitoring, detection, and prevention of illegal activities (Gray & Kalpers, 2005; Hilborn *et al.*, 2006; Stokes, 2010). Similar to the policing literature (e.g., Nagin, Solow, & Lum, 2015) studies examining wildlife law enforcement have largely been evaluative with findings alluding law enforcement reduces illegal activities within PAs. For example, ranger manpower variables (e.g., (km^2/scout, km^2/carrier, effective patrol days/km^2, effective investigation days) were associated with the number of elephants killed in Luangwa Valley, Zambia (Jachmann, 2003). Also, a decline in poaching activities (e.g., ratio of arrests per patrol) in Serengeti National Park, Tanzania was attributed to anti-poaching efforts by the enforcement community (Hilborn *et al.*, 2006). In a comprehensive study examining 16 PAs in 11 African nations, effective law enforcement was found to be one of the most important aspects in overall PA success (Struhsaker, Struhsaker, & Siex, 2005). The most effective law enforcement in PAs has been associated with adequate internal support (e.g., bonus system, sufficient equipment), coupled with positive public attitudes, and low human population densities. Based on these studies, it appears that law enforcement can have an impact, including a deterrent effect, on illegal activities within PAs.

Although law enforcement initiatives are undoubtedly an important element within a broader conservation agenda (e.g., U.S. National Strategy for Combating Wildlife Trafficking), several limitations need to be considered. One of the main limitations in many PAs is the vast and often dangerous setting that rangers are required to transverse on foot making it extremely difficult to detect illegal activities (Nolte, 2015). Technological advancements, including GPS-linked video cameras and unmanned aerial vehicles (Koh & Wich, 2012) have improved detection probabilities, however, effectively monitoring an entire PA still poses considerable logistical challenges. Moreover, these technologies also assume that the resources available to most ranger agencies are sufficient to produce a swift response. Unfortunately, that is not always the case. For instance, as of 2013, Uganda's Queen Elizabeth National Park rangers have had ten vehicles on hand to cover 1,978km^2 and with only one allocated specifically for law enforcement operations (Moreto, 2013).

Another limitation is that swift capture of an offender requires an appropriate response from other elements of the criminal justice system. The criminal justice system must have a vested interest in appropriately and consistently punishing offenders and having laws that outline sanctions that are severe enough to deter recidivism (i.e., repeat offenses) and other would-be offenders. This is not always the case in many countries in the global South, where much of the world's biodiversity exists. Beyond the potential for corruption and the lack of knowledge of international and national conservation agreements, treaties and laws, sanctions are often lax and insufficient to deter offenders from recidivating, especially in situations where no livelihood alternatives to rule breaking are present.

Third, from a community perspective, "fences and fines" approaches to deterrence are widely criticized for the socially exclusive nature of such strategies (Inamdar, de Jode, Lindsay, & Cobb, 1999) and the role they play in removing needed resources from local communities, the imposition of Northern biases to conservation, and the explicit criminalization of traditional, customary behaviors (Agrawal & Gibson, 1999). Indeed even community-based conservation initiatives, which theoretically have "shorter fences," have been critiqued on their inability to wholly facilitate local involvement and incorporate public opinion (see Brockington, 2004; Duffy, 2010).

Another limitation of deterrence-based approaches rests within the scope of PA management and anti-poaching patrols. Crime data management and technological issues related to the collection of information on illegal activities

(Moreto, Lemieux, Rwetsiba, Guma, Driciru, & Kirya, 2014), as well as challenges in determining the "dark figure" or unknown number of actual offenses that occur of wildlife crime make it difficult to assess the effectiveness of deterrence-based strategies (Wellsmith, 2011). This is further complicated by the reality that law enforcement patrols are at times retrospectively deployed based on data from previous patrols. Although data-driven patrols are probably better than randomly patrolling a vast landscape, the rarity in conducting a complete and comprehensive survey of an entire PA raises the possibility of illegal activity hot spots simply being a function of patrol activities (Moreto *et al.*, 2014). In other words, unlike urban or even other forms of rural law enforcement where citizens can call and provide an exact location to police (e.g., street address), the "silent victim" problem almost ensures that the identification of illegal activities with PAs are limited to the activities and practices of law enforcement personnel (Lemieux, Bernasco, Rwetsiba, Guma, Driciru, & Kirya, 2014).

Corruption can undermine the efficacy of deterrence-based law enforcement strategies (Wellsmith, 2011). Incidents of bribery, willful neglect of duties, and active participation in illegal activities can undermine and reduce the credibility and legitimacy of authorities (Kahler & Gore, 2012). Non-compliance with conservation regulations can be influenced by the corrupt behaviors of authorities (Gore, Ratsimbazafy, & Lute, 2013). Jenks, Howard, and Leimgruber (2012) examined the role that ranger stations may have in deterring poaching activity in a National Park in Thailand. The authors surmised that if ranger stations had a deterrent effect, they would find an abundance of ungulates and little to no poaching near ranger stations. Although the authors did find increased presence of ungulates, they also found a high probability of poachers nearby park headquarters and stations. The surprising presence of poachers may have been due to the location of targets, accessibility due to road infrastructure, or the complicity of park staff.

Law enforcement rangers' perceptions of ranger wrongdoing further highlight the complexity of low-level forms of corruption and misconduct (Moreto *et al.*, 2015b). Surprisingly little attention has been given to understanding the perspectives of law enforcement personnel, considering deterrence-based strategies tend to be based on "boots-on-the-ground" approaches, or ranger patrols. Failing to acknowledge the variety of occupational stressors on rangers (e.g., lack of proper field equipment; Moreto, 2015b) might not only hinder patrol effectiveness and efficiency, but may foster an environment where ranger corruption or misconduct is viewed acceptably. Importantly, despite having minimal resources, recent emphasis on the use of specific forms of technology such as unmanned areal vehicles in conservation law enforcement has broadened discourse to include dimensions of privacy and the ethics of militarization. The militarization of conservation or the increased use of military technologies and responses to conservation issues (Duffy, 2014; Lunstrum, 2014) may stem from a deterrence-based perspective, which can result in further developing and entrenching division between local communities and PA management (Duffy, St. John, Buscher, & Brockington, 2016). Such divisions may hamper community engagement, involvement, and trust, as well as foster resentment toward PAs.

3.5 Legitimacy and Its Role in Establishing Normative and Instrumental Forms of Compliance in Conservation

Deterrence is ultimately a fear-based approach. It uses the threat of psychological or physical pain to coerce people into compliance with the law and authority figures. Deterrence, moreover, presumes that all law breaking is done for personal gain; the theory leaves no room for disobedience arising from desperation or mass protest against patently unjust laws or governments. Many scholars have found wildlife rule violation can be categorized as a collective form of resistance and a direct violation of culturally valued norms (Bell, 2007). Deterrence, therefore, can be thought of as a form of instrumental compliance, whereby people obey laws out of concern for what will happen to them if they rebel.

Normative compliance stands in stark contrast to instrumental compliance. Normative compliance occurs when a populace internalizes a moral belief that laws should be obeyed, and thus abide not out of fear but, rather, out of the sense that it is the right thing to do. This type of compliance springs from Weber's (1978) conception of rational-legal authority, which holds that governments and their various agencies and representatives garner compliance most effectively when they operate according to policies of openness and accountability. The public is more supportive of, and therefore more likely to obey, laws they feel are just and authority figures they believe are morally upstanding (Jackson, Bradford, Hough, Myhill, Quinton, & Tyler, 2012). A large body of research confirms the proposition that people are more likely to cooperate with rules and obey government authorities they deem trustworthy (e.g., Jackson & Gau, forthcoming).

The key to normative compliance is governmental legitimacy. Legitimacy is governance by consent; it is a form of authority derived from the will of the people whereby all persons voluntarily relinquish some freedom in exchange for a government that regulates social behavior in a manner promoting widespread peace and order. A legitimate government abides by the rule of law and eschews corruption and brutality. Although deterrence undoubtedly has a part to play in legitimate governments, greater levels of compliance with rules is ultimately achieved through the fair, equitable distribution of goods and services.

Procedural justice plays a central role in establishing a government as a legitimate authority figure. Procedural justice entails high-quality treatment of individuals during face-to-face contacts with governmental representatives, and is theorized to enhance citizens' beliefs in the legitimacy of the authority figure. This concept has met with empirical support in the context of civil court proceedings (Thibaut & Walker, 1978), regulatory authorities (Braithwaite & Makkai, 1994), and police in Northern, developed nations (Gau, 2011; 2014; 2015). When an authority figure treats an individual fairly and respectfully, the authority conveys an important message about that person's social worth (Tyler, 1997). High-quality treatment makes the individual feel valued and accepted by society, while disrespect demeans the person and creates a sense of anger and alienation. Widespread unjust treatment of certain groups in society can foster a culture of rebellion wherein established social norms are rejected (Anderson, 1999). Violence and lawlessness flourish where the government has lost its claim on legitimacy (Kubrin & Weitzer, 2003).

3.6 Alternatives to Deterrence-Based Approaches

3.6.1 Enhancing Legitimacy

Legitimacy and normative compliance have clear theoretical relevance to the prevention of wildlife crime, although the literature on compliance within natural resource management and enforcement of conservation regulations is limited compared to other fields (Keane, Jones, Edwards-Jones, & Milner-Gulland, 2008; Solomon, Gavin, & Gore, 2015). Nonetheless, recent compliance research within the conservation literature highlights its relevance. For example, we know that villager perceptions of trust and legitimacy can have a stronger impact on voluntary compliance than deterrence-based strategies and that trust and legitimacy can be vital in fostering compliance in situations where support for PA laws and regulations is low (Stern, 2008). Despite the lack of empirical attention thus far, there are several logical applications of the theory of normative compliance to wildlife protection in PAs. For example, procedural justice and police legitimacy in Africa and the Caribbean is based on people in these regions placing a premium on police effectiveness (see Bradford, Huq, Jackson, & Roberts, 2014; Johnson, Maguire & Kuhns, 2014). Citizens of countries that are economically underdeveloped and commonly susceptible to geopolitical conflict often assign police the responsibility for establishing and enforcing order and civility (Neumann, 2004). As noted previously, corruption and severe underfunding often plagues policing in the nations that are most in need of strong, high-quality public servants. Consistent, fair, even-handed enforcement of laws may greatly contribute to public trust in police and willingness to comply with conservation rules. This has relevance to PAs because if the public views wildlife rangers as unknowledgeable, corrupt, or arbitrary, they may not recognize these law enforcement officials as legitimate authority figures. The end result is that these publics may distrust authorities and not comply with conservation rules.

Normative compliance may be achieved through government taking a more active role in promoting the health and wellbeing of local people living around and near PAs. A critical element of legitimacy is moral alignment, or the public's belief that authority figures share their viewpoints and orientations (Jackson *et al.*, 2012). Indeed, it has been argued that "managing PAs to reflect local values may help build support for and reduce resistance to them and allow governments to justify and explain conservation in terms that has real meaning to local communities" (Infield, 2001, p. 801). If individuals poach because they are hungry, yet the government treats this activity as no more valid than poaching for simple pecuniary gain, people may view the government as uncaring, arbitrary, and untrustworthy. Efforts to sanction poachers may further delegitimize the government because the public will see sanctions being levied upon people trying to sustain their livelihoods. In this regard, normative compliance is particularly relevant to the future of effective PA management particularly if funding for PAs and wildlife-law enforcement increases. These areas are comprised of vast areas, many of which are inaccessible due to rugged terrain or dense vegetation cover and it will likely remain impossible for law enforcement to fully patrol these areas, even with technology. The probability that any given poacher will be caught, at least in the act of hunting, before the damage has been done, will remain low. This will make it very hard for governments and other authorities to establish credible deterrent messages, even if the local criminal justice system is functioning. An alternative if for these authorities to focus efforts on enhancing legitimacy so that local people internalize and cultivate a sense of obligation to comply with conservation rules. Ultimately, poaching violations may be decreased when people believe the activity is wrong, rather than fearing arrest and sanctioning.

3.7 Future Considerations

In this chapter, we outlined the strengths and limitations of using deterrence-based strategies to realize compliance with conservation rules in PAs. We also profiled the legitimacy literature to highlight the potential role that legitimacy-based approaches may have in attaining compliance. Drawing on the criminological and criminal justice literature, our review demonstrates the importance of normative compliance, as well as the role of procedural justice and trust on police legitimacy. We do not consider deterrence-based or legitimacy-enhancing strategies to be mutually exclusive; each has a contribution to make in achieving a broader conservation agenda. The dynamic and complex nature of conservation problems makes them "wicked" (Rittel & Webber, 1973). As such, interdisciplinary and multi-pronged approaches are warranted. Also justified are strategies and tactics that recognize and address the short-, medium-, and long-term aspects of exploitation in PAs. For example, short-term strategies might aim to improve law enforcement effectiveness through technical and financial support, medium-term strategies may include securing sustainable funding, improving morale and quality of PA staff, and limiting and regulating access to PAs. Long-term strategies could address the attitudes of the neighboring communities towards the PAs alongside human population growth need consideration (Struhsaker, Struksaker, & Siex, 2005). Short-term objectives understandably remain a huge focus of the conservation enforcement community. Given the transnational nature of some wildlife crimes, including wildlife trafficking, increasing the capabilities for local law enforcement is essential in advancing information sharing and collaboration with other vested agencies (e.g., INTERPOL, World Customs Organization), possibly within an intelligence-led conservation policing framework (Moreto, 2015a). Moreover, since it is unlikely that legitimacy-enhancing strategies will occur overnight and will undoubtedly require a significant amount of time, resources, and investment from all parties involved, a multi-stage approach is necessary to reduce or at least minimize losses. This may be especially the case in settings where negative associations with the legitimacy of authority figures are exacerbated by a nation's history with colonial and neocolonial regimes.

The quickening pace and scale of natural resources exploitation should not dissuade governments, vested agencies, and citizens from engaging in multi-pronged strategies and tactics. Simply put, deterrence-based strategies are not sufficient to stop all illegal activities within PAs. Not all offenders will be arrested or prosecuted and those who are punished are often punished lightly. Although deterrence-based strategies may be needed for those involved in transnational wildlife trafficking operations or organized crime groups, such approaches may be ineffective at a local level where poaching behavior may be linked to livelihood preservation. On-the-ground tactics can rely heavily on identifying ways to engender local cooperation and buy-in; even more important is a willingness to begin this conversation on a level playing field where local concerns and traditional and cultural beliefs are equalized alongside other conservation stakes. Only by doing so will governments and agencies have the legitimacy to effectively and efficiently manage PAs with nearby communities.

References

Agrawal, A., & Gibson, C. C. (1999). Enchantment and disenchantment: The role of community in natural resource conservation. *World Development*, 27, 629–649.

Andenaes, J. (1968). Does punishment deter crime? *Criminal Law Quarterly*, 11, 76–93.

Anderson, E. (1999). *Code of the street: Decency, violence, and the moral life of the inner city*. New York: W. W. Norton & Company.

Beccaria, C. (2009). *On Crimes and punishments*. Philadelphia: Seven Treasures Publications.

Bell, S., Hampshire, K., & Topalidou, S. (2007). The political culture of poaching: A case study from Northern Greece. *Biodiversity and Conservation*, 16: 399–418.

Bradford, B., Huq, A., Jackson, J., & Roberts, B. (2014). What price fairness [sic] when security is at stake? Police legitimacy in South Africa. *Regulation & Governance*, 8, 246–268.

Braithwaite, J., & Makkai, T. (1994). Trust and compliance. *Policing & Society*, 4, 1–12.

Brockington, D. (2004). Community conservation, inequality and injustice: Myths of power in protected area management. *Conservation & Society*, 2, 411–432.

Challender, D. W. S., & MacMillan, D. C. (2014). Poaching is more than an enforcement problem. *Conservation Letters*, 7, 484–494.

Copes, H., & Vieraitis, L. M. (2006). Bounded rationality of identity thieves: Using offender-based research to inform policy. *Criminology & Public Policy*, 8, 237–262.

Decker, S., Wright, R., & Logie, R. (1993). Perceptual deterrence among active residential burglars: A research note. *Criminology*, 31, 135–147.

Dudley, N., & Stolton, S. (2008). *Defining protected areas: an international conference in Almeria, Spain*. International Union for the Conservation of Nature: Switzerland.

Duffy, R. (2010). *Nature crime: How we're getting conservation wrong*. New Haven: Yale University Press.

Duffy, R. (2014). Waging a war to save biodiversity: The rise of militarized conservation. *International Affairs*, 90, 819–834.

Duffy R., St. John, F. A. V., Buscher, B., & Brockington, D. (2016). The militarization of anti-poaching: Undermining long-term goals? *Environmental Conservation*, 42, 345–348.

Eliason, S. L. (2012). Trophy poaching: A routine activities perspective. *Deviant Behavior*, 33, 72–87.

Eliason, S. L. (2014). Life as a game warden: The good, the bad and the ugly. *International Journal of Police Science and Management*, 16: 196–204.

Gau, J. M. (2011). The convergent and discriminant validity of procedural justice and police legitimacy: An empirical test of core theoretical propositions. *Journal of Criminal Justice*, 39, 489–498.

Gau, J. M. (2014). Procedural justice and police legitimacy: A test of measurement and structure. *American Journal of Criminal Justice*, 39, 187–205.

Gau, J. M. (2015). Procedural justice, police legitimacy, and legal cynicism: A test for mediation effects. *Police Practice and Research*, 16, 402–415.

Gibbs, C., Gore, M. L., McGarrell, E. F., & Rivers, III., L. (2010). Introducing conservation criminology: Towards interdisciplinary scholarship on environmental crimes and risk. *The British Journal of Criminology*, 50, 124–144.

Gore, M. L., Ratsimbazafy, J., & Lute, M. L. (2013). Rethinking corruption in conservation crime: Insights from Madagascar. *Conservation Letters*, 6, 430–438.

Gray, M., & Kalpers, J. (2005). Ranger based monitoring in the Virunga-Bwindi region of East-Central Africa: A simple data collection tool for park management. *Biodiversity and Conservation*, 14, 2723–2741.

Hayes, T. M. (2006). Parks, people, and forest protection: An institutional assessment of the effectiveness of protected areas. *World Development*, 34, 2064–2075.

Hilborn, R., Acrese, P., Borner, M., Hando, J., Hopcraft, G., Loibooki, M.,... & Sinclair, A. R. E. (2006). Effective enforcement in a conservation area. *Science*, 314, 1266.

Infield, M. (2001). Cultural values: A forgotten strategy for building community support for protected areas in Africa. *Conservation Biology*, 15, 800–802.

Inamdar, A., de Jode, H., Lindsay, K., & Cobb, S. (1999). Capitalizing on nature: Protected area management. *Science*, 283, 1856–1857.

IUCN and UNEP-WCMC. (2016). The World Database on Protected Areas (WDPA). Retrieved from www.protectedplanet.net

Jachmann, H. (2003). Elephant poaching and resource allocation for law enforcement. In Oldfield, S. (Ed.). The trade in wildlife: Regulations for conservation. London, U.K.: Earthscan Publications, Inc.

Jackson, J., Bradford, B., Hough, M., Myhill, A., Quinton, P., & Tyler, T. R. (2012). Why do people comply with the law? Legitimacy and the influence of legal institutions. *British Journal of Criminology*, 52, 1051–1071.

Jackson, J., & Gau, J. M. (forthcoming). Carving up concepts? Differentiating between legitimacy and trust in public attitudes towards legal authority. In Shockley, E., Neal, T. M. S., Pytlik Zillig, L., & Bornstein, B. (Eds.) *Interdisciplinary perspectives on trust: Towards theoretical and methodological integration*. New York: Springer.

Jenks, K. E., Howard, J., & Leimgruber, P. (2012). Do ranger stations deter poaching activity in National Parks in Thailand? *Biotropica*, 44, 826–833.

Johnson, D., Maguire, E. R., & Kuhns, J. B. (2014). Public perceptions of the legitimacy of law and legal authorities: Evidence from the Caribbean. *Law & Society Review*, 48: 947–978.

Kahler, J. S., & Gore, M. L. (2012). Beyond the cooking pot and pocket book: Factors influencing noncompliance with wildlife poaching rules. *International Journal of Comparative and Applied Criminal Justice*, 36, 103–120.

Keane, A., Jones, J. P. G., Edwards-Jones, G., & Milner-Gulland, E. J. (2008). The sleeping policeman: Understanding issues of enforcement and compliance in conservation. *Animal Conservation*, 11, 75–82.

Kleck, G., Sever, B., Li, S., & Gertz, M. (2005). The missing link in general deterrence research. *Criminology*, 43, 623–660.

Koh, L. P., & Wich, S. A. (2012). Dawn of drone ecology: Low-cost autonomous aerial vehicles for conservation. *Tropical Conservation Science*, 5: 121–132.

Kubrin, C. E., & Weitzer, R. (2003). Retaliatory homicide: Concentrated disadvantage and neighborhood culture. *Social Problems*, 50, 157–180.

Lemieux, A. M., Bernasco, W., Rwetsiba, N., Guma, N., Driciru, M. & Kirya, H. K. (2014). Tracking poachers in Uganda: Spatial models of patrol intensity and patrol efficiency. In Lemieux, A. M. (Ed). *Situational Prevention of Poaching*. New York: Routledge.

Lunstrum, E. (2014). Green militarization: Anti-poaching efforts and the spatial contours of Kruger National Park. *Annals of the Association of American Geographers*, 104, 816–832.

Milestone, J. F., Hendricks, K., Foster, A., Richardson, J., Denniston, S., Demetry, A.,...& Fireman, D. (2012). Continued cultivation of illegal marijuana in U.S. Western National Parks. In Weber, S. (Ed.). *Rethinking protected areas in a changing world: Proceedings of the 2011 George Wright Society Biennial Conference on Parks, Protected Areas, and Cultural Sites*. The George Wright Society.

Moreto, W. D. (2013). To conserve and protect: Examining law enforcement ranger culture and operations in Queen Elizabeth National Park, Uganda. Doctoral dissertation, Rutgers University Graduate School: Newark.

Moreto, W. D. (2015a). Introducing intelligence-led conservation: Bridging crime and conservation science. *Crime Science*, 4, 15.

Moreto, W. D. (2015b). Occupational stress among law enforcement rangers: Insights from Uganda. Oryx, available on CJO2015. doi:10.1017/S0030605315000356.

Moreto, W. D., Brunson, R. K., & Braga, A. A. (2015). Such misconducts don't make a good ranger: Examining law enforcement ranger wrongdoing in Uganda. *British Journal of Criminology*, 55, 359–380.

Moreto, W. D., Brunson, R. K., & Braga, A. A. (2016). Anything we do, we have to include the communities: Law enforcement rangers' attitudes towards and experiences of community-ranger relations in wildlife protected areas in Uganda. *British Journal of Criminology*. Advanced access: DOI: doi: 10.1093/bjc/azw032

Moreto, W. D., & Lemieux, A. M. (2015a). From CRAVED to CAPTURED: Introducing a product-based framework to examine illegal wildlife markets. *European Journal on Criminal Policy and Research*, 21, 303–320.

Moreto, W. D., & Lemieux, A. M. (2015b). Poaching in Uganda: Perspectives of law enforcement rangers. *Deviant Behavior*, 36, 853–873.

Moreto, W. D., Lemieux, A. M., Rwetsiba, N., Guma, N., Driciru, M. & Kirya, H. K. (2014). Law enforcement monitoring in Uganda: The utility of official data and time/distance-based ranger efficiency measures. In Lemieux, A. M. (Ed). *Situational prevention of poaching*. New York: Routledge.

Nagin, D.S. (1978). General deterrence: a review of the empirical evidence. In A. Blumstein, J. Cohen, & D. Nagin (Eds). *Deterrence and incapacitation: Estimating the effects of criminal sanctions on crime rates*. Washington, D.C.: National Academy of Sciences.

Nagin, D.S. (1998). Deterrence research at the outset of the twenty-first century. *Crime and Justice*, 23, 1–42.

Nagin, D.S., Solow, R.M., & Lum, C. (2015). Deterrence, criminal opportunities, and police. *Criminology*, 53, 74–100.

Neumann, R. P. (2004). Moral and discursive geographies in the war for biodiversity in Africa. *Political Geography*, 23, 813–837.

Nolte, C. (2016). Identifying challenges to enforcement in protected areas: Empirical insights from 15 Colombian Parks. Oryx, 50, 317–322.

Ostrom, E. (1990). *Governing the commons: The evolution of institutions for collective action*. New York: Cambridge University Press.

Paternoster, R., & Piquero, A. (1995). Reconceptualizing deterrence: An empirical test of personal and vicarious experiences. *Journal of Research in Crime and Delinquency*, 32, 251–286.

Petrossian, G. A., & Clarke, R. V. (2014). Explaining and controlling illegal commercial fishing: An application of the CRAVED theft model. *British Journal of Criminology*, 54, 73–90.

Pires, S. F., & Clarke, R. V. (2012). Are Parrots CRAVED? An analysis of parrot poaching in Mexico. *Journal of Research in Crime & Delinquency*, 49, 122–146.

Pires, S. F., & Moreto, W. D. (2011). Preventing wildlife crimes: Solutions that can overcome the Tragedy of the Commons. *European Journal on Criminal Policy and Research*, 17, 101–123.

Pogarsky, G., & Piquero, A. R. (2003). Can punishment encourage offending? Investigating the "resetting" effect. *Journal of Research in Crime and Delinquency*, 40, 95–120.

Pratt, T. C., & Cullen, F.T. (2005). Assessing macro-level predictors and theories of crime: A meta-analysis. In Tonry, M. (Ed.), *Crime and Justice: A Review of Research*. Chicago: University of Chicago Press.

Pratt, T. C., Cullen, F. T., Blevins, K. R., Daigle, L. E., & Madensen, T. D. (2006). The empirical status of deterrence theory: A meta-analysis. In Cullen, F. T., Wright, J. P., & Blevins, K. R. (Eds.). *Taking stock: The status of criminological theory*. New Brunswick: Transaction Publishers.

Rittel, H. W. J., & Webber, M.M. (1973). Dilemmas in a general theory of planning. *Policy Sciences*, 4, 155–169.

Solomon, J. N., Gavin, M. C., & Gore, M. L. (2015). Detecting and understanding non-compliance with conservation rules. *Biological Conservation*, 189, 1–4.

Stafford, M. C., & Warr, M. (1993). A reconceptualization of general and specific deterrence. *Journal of Research in Crime and Delinquency*, 30, 123–135.

Stern, M. J. (2008). Coercion, voluntary compliance and protest: The role of trust and legitimacy in combating local opposition to protected areas. *Environmental Conservation*, 35, 200–210.

Stokes, E. J. (2010). Improving effectiveness of protection efforts in tiger source sites: Developing a framework for law enforcement using MIST. *Integrative Zoology*, 5, 363- 377.

Struhsaker, T. T., Struksaker, P. J., & Siex, K. S. (2005). Conserving Africa's rainforests: Problems in protected areas and possible solutions. *Biological Conservation*, 123, 45–54.

Sykes, G. M., & Matza, D. (1957). Techniques of neutralization: A theory of delinquency. *American Sociological Review*, 22, 664–670.

Thibaut, J., & Walker, L. (1978). A theory of procedure. *California Law Review*, May, 541–566.

Tyler, T. R. (1997). The psychology of legitimacy: A relational perspective on voluntary deference to authorities. *Personality and Social Psychology Review* 1, 323–345.

Walker, S. (2001). *Sense and nonsense about crime and drugs: a policy guide* (5th ed). Belmont, California: Wadsworth.

Warchol, G., & Kapla, D. (2012), Policing the wilderness: A descriptive study of wildlife conservation officers in South Africa. *International Journal of Comparative and Applied Criminal Justice*, 36, 83–101.

Warchol, G. L., Zupan, L. L., & Clack, W. (2003). Transnational criminality: An analysis of the illegal wildlife market in Southern Africa. *International Criminal Justice Review*, 13, 1–27.

Weber, M. (1978). *Economy and society*. Berkeley, California: University of California Press.

Wellsmith, M. (2011). Wildlife crime: The problems of enforcement. *European Journal on Criminal Policy and Research*, 17, 125–148.

White, R, & Heckenberg, D. (2014). *Green criminology: An introduction to the study of environmental harm*. United Kingdom: Routledge.

Part II

Case Studies and Examples

4

Governance for Conservation Risks and Crime

Mark A. Axelrod, Austin Flowers, Katherine Groff, and Julia Novak Colwell

4.1 Defining Governance

Governments and other decision-makers have developed various measures intended to reduce risks associated with the causes and consequences of natural resource declines. Governance is the process by which these measures are selected, enacted, and implemented. The 1995 United Nations (UN)-appointed Commission on Global Governance defined governance as the sum of the many ways individuals and institutions, public and private, manage their common affairs. Law may formally require such arrangements or they may develop through social norms. No matter their origin, governance provisions identify who gets to participate in decision-making, risk management, and each participant's role in doing so (Lockwood, Davidson, Curtis, Stratford, & Griffith, 2010). Governance is important because these provisions allocate decision-making authority, thereby determining which interests are prioritized in natural resource management decisions. Natural resource policy and management, coupled with traditional criminological efforts, provide important routes to reduce negative effects of conservation risks, but the resulting interventions are incomplete without understanding how decision-making authority is allocated among stakeholders. This chapter, therefore, examines how governance can interact with different management options when addressing conservation risks and crimes.

Governance rarely provides equal footing to all participants. Rather, some stakeholders gain more power than others, benefiting those with the most influence (Raik, Wilson, & Decker, 2008) and placing some in a position to benefit from governing in unlawful or harmful ways. Included among these concerns are management decisions that lack participation (Lockwood *et al.*, 2010) or override scientific evidence (Lute & Gore, 2014), as well as corrupt demands for financial benefit in the decision-making process. Indeed, weaker conservation policies are often correlated with increased corruption (Pellegrini & Gerlagh, 2006). As a result, both people and natural resources may suffer from poorly designed governance arrangements because harmful effects of risk are not sufficiently reduced.

Conservation Criminology, First Edition. Edited by Meredith L. Gore.

4.2 General Concepts of Governance for Conservation Risks

Although the complementarity of conservation and sustainable development policies is often debated (Adams *et al.*, 2004; Kaimowitz & Sheil, 2007; Roe & Walpole, 2010), we focus on management efforts that intend to limit exploitation of natural resources because of the associated harms. Two broad governance frameworks, strict enforcement and people-centered approaches, each of which will be discussed in further detail below, have been employed to reduce conservation risks. Biodiversity conservation is a primary goal of both approaches, but they suggest different means to best achieve that outcome, likely with different results for resource users and their livelihoods as well.

Strict enforcement proponents promote deterrence of conservation and other harms by increasing punishments for undesirable behavior, thereby increasing the cost of such behaviors. This approach requires severe punishments, as well as the capacity to identify violations and enforce these penalties when a rule violation is identified (Beccaria, 1963). In contrast, people-centered approaches suggest people willingly bear the risk of heavy punishments unless they have some other means of gaining and maintaining economic security. For instance, we discuss below how strict enforcement did not deter Guatemalan villagers from harvesting resources in a Belizian protected area because they perceived no other alternatives for maintaining livelihoods. Proponents of people-centered approaches suggest that heavy-handed enforcement alienates stakeholders (Ancrenaz, Dabek, & O'Neil, 2007), raises concerns about rule legitimacy (Suškevičs, 2012), fails to account for livelihood necessities (Lewis *et al.*, 2011), and in some circumstances may even encourage the undesirable behavior (Kaimowitz, 2003). In response, conservation strategies, within this framework, must provide alternative livelihood opportunities so that resource users can change their behavior without risking financial ruin or food insecurity (Groff & Axelrod, 2013). In this sense, people-centered approaches may enhance both human livelihoods and natural resource conservation.

These governance strategies provide opportunities for limiting conservation crime by reducing human impacts on natural resources. However, it is also important to consider possible, unintended, harms that such programs may create. In particular, policies designed to address a specific type of resource use (e.g., logging, mining) may have disproportionate impacts on groups whose livelihoods depend most directly on a particular resource or harvest method, or who are excluded from the decision-making process. For example, as we discuss below, fisheries rules often target and consider fishers without considering the impact on allied sectors such as those who work in fish processing or vending. As a result, conservation governance may have unintended consequences that should be constantly assessed and addressed. We proceed by comparing case studies of governance to limit resource poaching across the Guatemala-Belize border and global electronic waste (i.e., e-waste) shipments. These cases demonstrate strengths and limitations of the strict enforcement and people-centered approaches at reducing harm. We then present a third case study demonstrating unintended consequences of coastal fisheries governance in India. All case studies demonstrate the significance of understanding local natural resource and community characteristics, while identifying broader lessons for effective natural resource governance at reducing conservation risks and crime.

4.3 Strict Enforcement by Official Authorities and Governments

Globally, governments have used strict enforcement techniques to limit e-waste shipments and dumping. In this case study, we show how governance has been used, to varying degrees of success, to limit such dumping and reduce associated risks. Deterrence models provide for centralized punishment of behavior deemed to be criminal. After rules are enacted, formal authorities such as governments govern behavior. Rules provide an opportunity to raise the opportunity costs of conservation crime by punishing socially undesirable behavior. At this stage, resource users play a limited role in enforcement, ideally limiting incentives to evade responsibility.

E-waste is composed of consumer and business electronic equipment that is near or at the end of its useful life (CalRecycle, 2013). Improper disposal, in local dumping and incineration, is known to result in primary and secondary exposure to toxic metals, such as lead, which is linked to multiple diseases and other negative human health impacts. Exposure to other materials in e-waste can result in digestive, neurological, respiratory, and bone problems (McAllister, 2013). In addition to human health effects, e-waste chemicals enter the air, water, or soil-crop-food pathway, harming natural and agricultural ecosystems. Such harms include groundwater contamination (Grossman, 2006) and streams that can no longer support fish populations (Silicon Valley Toxics Coalition, 2010). These concerns are exacerbated in developing countries because of the limited infrastructure accompanying disposal and the resulting disproportionate exposure of poor communities and their natural resources to e-waste pollution; for this reason e-waste attracts the attention of criminologists working on environmental injustice. Due to the transnational flows of the waste stream and the global market structure for its disposal, the complexities of enforcing and punishing criminal behavior within the marketplace have allowed for a highly profitable and often illegal trade in e-waste. As a result, managing risks from transnational trade in e-waste has been elevated to a high policy priority (e.g., Basel Convention on the Control of Transboundary Movements of Hazardous Waste and their Disposal, Rotterdam, and Stockholm Conventions) and resulted in new international collaborations (e.g., International E-Waste Management Network).

4.4 International Movement of Electronic Waste

An estimated 40 million tons of e-waste are generated globally each year (Rucevska *et al.*, 2015; Gibbs, McGarrell, Axelrod, & Rivers, 2011), with anticipated increases due to expanded technology. E-waste disposal costs grew nearly 10% from 2009 to 2011 ($U.S. 6.2 billion to 6.8 billion); there is reasonable cause for concern about ecological risks associated with e-waste disposal. Risks are compounded by the fact that e-waste streams are projected to grow three times the rate of any other waste and the global market. Up to 90% of the world's e-waste, nearly $U.S. 19 billion is illegally traded. INTERPOL estimated the price per ton of e-waste at approximately $U.S. 500 (Rucevska *et al.*, 2015).

Examining the infrastructure of developed versus developing countries' disposal methods exposes trends of exploitation and the punishments (or lack thereof) for improper disposal of e-waste. Waste has an inverse incentive structure due to its negative value; owning e-waste entails transaction costs associated with disposal (Bisschop, 2014). Because e-waste holds a negative value in cost, there is an economic incentive to find a lower cost structure to deal with it. Exporting becomes advantageous and waste trade occurs. Transboundary shipments are illegal in some circumstances, and are often unregulated (Gibbs *et al.*, 2011). This combination of illegal and unregulated trade results in a volatile legal status, as the transfer of legality can happen at any stage of trade and or disposal (Bisschop, 2014). Even when e-waste shipments themselves do not violate law, conservation and human health harms often accompany their movement and particularly disposal (e.g., exposure to lead and mercury, involvement of organized crime in tax fraud and money laundering associated with large volumes of e-waste trade).

The cost structure surrounding e-waste promotes exploitation on a global scale. E-waste was originally generated in countries such as the U.S. and United Kingdom (U.K.) so quickly that streams were not easily handled; recyclers were not prepared for the volume or costs associated with the market. Proper recycling programs within countries like the U.S. were forced to export to developing countries because of these volume-related issues. Underdeveloped and unenforced environmental laws in the global South promoted more permanent export (Greenpeace, 2009). Today, developed nations easily exploit developing nations, weak regulations and minimal enforcement capacity. By circumventing the environmental regulations and processes that developed country e-waste recyclers would have to follow for proper recycling at home, they eliminate part of the costs associated with disposal even when shipped legally. Economic growth and globalization promotes a positive feedback loop of the phenomena; it is less expensive to ship e-waste between nations legally or illegally than it is to recycle (Thomas, 2011). Because of different cost margins in regulated versus unregulated disposal, such as the ten-fold increase of cost from China to the U.S. of glass-to-glass computer monitor recycling (Thomas, 2011), exploitation for profit is a highly motivating factor. The globalized illegal trade results in externalization of e-waste's human and environmental costs to countries with limited enforcement capacity (Gibbs *et al.*, 2011). This transfer of costs abroad also allows for more actors to become involved, limiting individual countries' ability to effectively police e-waste shipments.

Illegal e-waste streams fuel demand as well. Improper recycling through various forms of dumping provide jobs and income for people in developing nations receiving the waste. E-waste contains valuable metallic, but sometimes highly toxic, components that can be removed and sold for a profit following dumping or incineration storage. Children are often involved in removing metal such as copper from electronics, exposing a vulnerable population to toxic fumes and chemicals (Rucevska *et al.*, 2015). This is a cause for concern due to the issue of recycling towns appearing adjacent to dump sites. For example, in 2003, California followed the E.U. example, requiring lower hazardous content in electronic products and implementing a recycling fee at the point of sale (2003). Exporters make profits by cutting costs and illegally dumping and importers provide demand for the waste in the form of dangerous jobs and income for its citizens.

E-waste from computer hard drives or cellular devices often contain private information that e-waste recyclers exploit for profit. For instance, Ghanaian organized criminals scan materials for private health and financial information to use in scams, helping Ghana achieve unenviable leadership status in cybercrime (Frontline, 2009). Cybercrime is enabled by the e-waste exporters who provide Ghanaians with reliable sources of private information for use in illegal markets. High-profile examples include a $U.S. 22 million Northrop Grumman military contract that was found on an illegally discarded computer hard drive, causing major security concerns. Corporate banking and financial information has also been found (Frontline, 2009).

4.5 Regulatory Efforts to Limit E-waste Trade

Multiple factors contribute to the transnational criminality associated with e-waste, including absent or ineffective regulation, understaffed regulatory agencies, lack of administrative follow-up, or a combination thereof (Bisschop, 2014). Agencies put in place to regulate the market of e-waste recycling and disposal are unable to keep up with the high volume of waste and activity within the market. To compound the issue, rules are not centrally coordinated. The E.U., for example, has implemented the Waste Electrical and Electronic Equipment (WEEE) Directive. However, each state has its own legislation under the WEEE Directive, making individual exporting states the responsible actor for tracing illegal activity (Bisschop, 2014). In response, legislation has been put into place to combat exploitations. The U.S., for example, has established a large number of different state and federal policy instruments (e.g., 92), including three at the federal level and 87 (81 in force) spread over 38 states (Solving the E-Waste Problem [2014b]). The U.K. has five federal level policy instruments (Solving the E-Waste Problem (2014a)) in force, proposed, or approved. Despite the wide range of legislative efforts, their effectiveness remains limited as we discuss below.

The E.U. WEEE Directive requires producers who place EEE on the market to provide for the costs of collection, treatment, recovery and environmentally sound disposal of WEEE (European Union, 2012). This rule makes producers of EEE legally responsible for environmentally sound disposal. Because producers incur disposal costs the law may actually discourage proper recycling due to high costs, though it may also incentivize producers to develop less wasteful products in the long term. This requirement creates a demand for illegal exporters and importers because producers look to cut costs in recycling and disposal.

In response, the U.K. has passed legislation banning the export of hazardous waste and developed the most substantial intervention to address illegal exports of e-waste. The Environment Agency of England (and previously Wales) uses intelligence-based enforcement to prevent illegal hazardous waste exports. Intelligence-led policing is a policing strategy that draws on prior evidence to identify likely locations and sources of subsequent criminal behavior (McGarrell, Freilich, & Chermak, 2007). In this case, information gathered using traditional investigative methods is cross-referenced with public and secure databases to establish targets (e.g., individuals, companies shipments) for further investigation. Interventions are matched to the actor and the nature of the activity to maximize crime prevention and deterrence. Theoretically, this approach increases both the level and the likelihood of punishment for illegal export (Environmental Investigation Agency, 2011).

In contrast, the U.S. has not banned the export of e-waste. Three federal instruments exist, but none are mandatory regulations of e-waste. The U.S. encourages Sustainable Materials Management (U.S. Environmental Protection Agency, 2013) and Responsible Recycling Practices (Lingelbach, 2008), providing guidelines to producers on how to properly recycle e-waste. However, these guidelines are not legally enforceable so no producer is federally required to recycle e-waste in an environmentally and socially just manner. In addition, most electronic devices (or parts of electronic devices) are either exempt or excluded from the Resource Conservation and Recovery Act (RCRA) legislation on hazardous waste, classified as products or commodities rather than waste (Tonetti, 2007). Regulations covering the export of cathode ray tubes (CRTs) (i.e., glass video display component in computers and televisions) represent the only explicit regulation of e-waste at the federal level. U.S. firms exporting CRTs only incur liability under very specific and limited conditions related to reporting requirements (e.g., failure to maintain paperwork, failure to notify Environmental Protection Agency, failure to wait 60 days before export of CRTs, exporting broken yet intact equipment). In addition to the relative leniency of the legislation, an enforcement program has not followed. In fact, the U.S. Environmental Protection Agency has been criticized for failing to enforce these minimal regulations (United States Government Accountability Office, 2008a; 2008b). Instead, the U.S. has decentralized e-waste legislation. For example, in 2003, California followed the E.U. example, requiring lower hazardous content in electronic products and implementing a recycling fee at the point of sale. Thirty-five other states followed with new laws between 2004 and 2012 (Solving the E-Waste Problem (StEP)). Nonetheless, e-waste legislation in the U.S. has been deemed insufficient. The American Chemical Society concluded existing e-recycling laws on the books in 13 U.S. states are largely ineffective (Anderson, 2013). As such, the lack of federal requirements results in a lack of deterrence for e-waste export.

Policies in both the U.S. and U.K. are considered to be somewhat ineffective by criminologists, as measured by the number and size of ongoing e-waste shipments that governments intended to reduce with the aforementioned policies (Gibbs *et al.*, 2011). Nonetheless, the U.K. has experienced a steady rise in recycling, along with a shallow decline in the amount of e-waste that had to be treated, for an overall increase in treatment efficiency (Eurostat, 2014). One caveat is that it remains difficult to obtain accurate measures of illegal exports. This modest improvement suggests enforcement efforts—by limiting the role of resource users themselves—may deter unsustainable actions. This result fits with findings that regulations lacking strictness or enforcement lead people to commit illegal acts due to low perceived risk (Erickson, Gibbs, & Jensen, 1977). Despite the suite of U.K. actions, scholars have noted limits to regulatory methods for reducing illegal e-waste trade at all stages of the supply chain. First, such interventions require substantial resources that governments may not have available (Weidner, Jänicke, & Jörgens 2002). Second, policies of this nature are often politically unpalatable because they raise the costs of doing business without substantially raising each individual resident's quality of life (Lizzeri & Persico, 2001). Third, even if such punishments are put in place, they are often open to influence of corrupt officials due to the high volume of money involved (Pellegrini & Gerlagh, 2006). Finally, lack of stakeholder involvement may limit the positive incentives provided for avoidance of harmful behavior. The e-waste case demonstrates the need for greater understanding of supply chain and trade linkages, stricter rules, and more sophisticated enforcement when criminal networks can exploit regulatory loopholes. Indeed, the risk management strategy proposed by the United Nations Environment Programme includes strengthened awareness, monitoring, and information sharing; strengthened international treaties and compliance measures; promoting prevention measures and synergies; and strengthening legislation and enforcement (Rucevska *et al.*, 2015). In contrast to this risk management strategy to combat a conservation crime, the next case study demonstrates the limits to strict enforcement strategies when people depend on natural resource use for food security and livelihoods and highlights an alternative governance approach.

4.6 People-Centered Approaches Focused Local Livelihoods

Since 2007 the Government of Belize has employed strict enforcement to limit Guatemalan residents from encroaching across the border and harvesting protected species in Belize's Chiquibul National Park (CNP) (Salas & Meerman, 2008). In this case, despite potential severe punishments (e.g., arrest, beating, seizure of guns and animals) this strict enforcement approach to governance has been constrained by resource users' perceived need for poaching as the only available livelihood strategy. Despite their value in contexts such as global e-waste trade, strict enforcement strategies are limited by their confrontational nature, resistance to conservation rules (Ancrenaz, Dabek, & O'Neil, 2007; Dahlberg & Burlando, 2009), and lack of resources to devote to enforcement (Kaimowitz, 2003; Lee *et al.*, 2005), as well as people's need to maintain livelihoods (Hutton & Leader-Williams, 2003; McElwee, 2010). As a result, a number of innovative strategies have emerged to prevent conservation crime by incentivizing positive behavior rather than only punishing infractions. The case of CNP illustrates the breadth and depth of this well known approach.

4.7 Limits to Enforcement Actions in Chiquibul National Park, Belize

CNP provides a useful setting for understanding how human behavior can be influenced by regulatory interventions. As Belize's largest national park encompassing one-seventh of the country's territory, CNP has a high level of floral and faunal biodiversity and straddles the international border with Guatemala. Species including kinkajous, jaguars, ocelots, tapirs, and scarlet macaws have been found within the park. Communities bordering the park, particularly in Guatemala, have developed livelihoods that depend on access to natural resources conserved within the park such as timber extraction, hunting for food, and harvesting of xaté leaves for the global floral industry. Additional activities include scarlet macaw poaching to fuel the illegal pet trade market, panning for gold, and clearing land for milpa farming. While hunting and xaté harvesting have been the focus of Guatemalan sustainable development projects, both activities are illegal on the Belizean side of the border in CNP (Bridgewater *et al.*, 2006; Salas & Meerman, 2008).

Authorities regularly patrol for poachers. Rangers have enforced sanctions, including incarceration and confiscation of harvested resources, for people caught removing xaté or poaching wildlife in CNP. However, illegal resource extraction has continued despite these enforcement efforts (Salas & Meerman, 2008). Guatemalan communities demonstrated a correlation between lower levels of hunting and awareness of strict regulations. However, regulatory awareness was a weaker predictor of behavior change than livelihood needs. Residents consider the risks and benefits of enforcement, and they are often willing to risk punishment due to a lack of economic alternatives (Groff & Axelrod, 2013). This finding is reinforced by diverse literature (Bassett, 2005; Brashares *et al.*, 2011; Grey-Ross, Downs, & Kirkman, 2010) confirming people use more natural resources when they lack alternative employment or income opportunities (Angelsen & Kaimowitz, 1999). CNP resource users indicated there would be great value in conservation crime interventions that focused on livelihood preservation in addition to the narrow natural resource protection-based approach. Positive incentives that preserve local livelihoods would theoretically reduce conservation risks while benefiting natural resources and their human users. In the Guatemalan communities bordering CNP, as in other subsistence-based contexts worldwide, providing alternative and supplemental incomes may change the economic calculus of engaging in illegal activities (Bassett, 2005; Roe & Walpole, 2010). In some areas, resource managers have successfully implemented programs that identify motivated natural resource users and collaborated with them to develop and pursue other, and legal, sources of income that are not otherwise related to the resource to be conserved (Lewis *et al.*, 2011).

4.8 Limits of Alternative Livelihood Strategies

Alternative livelihood interventions are not a cure-all in subsistence-based contexts. First, livelihoods are culturally driven, leading some people to resist change even when options are available (Coulthard, 2008). For instance, one Guatemalan resident confirmed it would be difficult to accept an alternative because people are accustomed to hunting (Groff & Axelrod, 2013). Second, as in the Chiquibul region, promised livelihood alternative projects may fall short when community leaders are given the primary responsibility for implementation by international donors or external stakeholders. In some situations, local people do not have the necessary resources to carry out such projects or they do not adequately consider factors such as business planning, ecological management, infrastructure, appropriateness for the area, time-frame, or benefit structure (Blom, Sunderland, & Murdiyarso, 2010; Pires & Moreto, 2011; Tallis, Kareiva, Marvier, & Chang, 2008). Third, livelihood alternative projects may not produce sufficient compensation to provide adequate disincentives to carry out the illegal activity, or the compensation may be distributed unevenly among stakeholders (McElwee, 2010). In additional contexts, leaders may not have sufficient incentive to implement projects because consequences of conservation risks (e.g., water pollution from gold panning) are not locally concentrated (Blom *et al.*, 2010; Brown, 2002). There are also instances where leaders or powerful community members may want personal benefits or payoffs in order to implement changes and engage in corrupt behavior (Brown, 2002). This type of personal demand may be sufficiently engrained in certain areas, so as to limit community members' interest in responding. Ideally then, alternative livelihood programs also develop appropriate governance regimes that incentivize and enable leaders to accept new governance arrangements without blocking their implementation. For instance, by honoring innovative community leaders, or identifying regional or national employment opportunities for leaders who successfully implement such programs, local actors may have greater incentive to accept changes in leadership structure that facilitate alternative livelihood programs beneficial to the community.

4.9 Unintended Effects and Collateral Impacts of Conservation Governance

Despite the best intentions and implementation of science-based practice, conservation governance may sometimes result in unintended consequences that disadvantage groups of stakeholders and unintentionally harm natural resources. The most obvious examples involve management policies that restrict resource use for extended periods of time, ultimately limiting livelihood options. As noted earlier, if local people have limited livelihood alternative options they are likely to increase pressure on other less restricted resources (Angelsen & Kaimowitz, 1999; Brasheres *et al.*, 2011). Perverse outcomes are not always the case; there are some instances where fewer alternative livelihood options couple with greater dependence on the natural resources, resulting in increased natural resource stewardship.

Indian coastal fisheries management illustrates how collateral impacts and unintended effects of well-intended conservation governance can unfold. Tamil Nadu is one of the leading states in Indian marine fisheries; the tropical climate and diverse ecosystems produce diverse aquatic resources. There is a huge diversity of fish found in these different aquatic environments and the fisheries are a vital source of food security for the region. Fisheries governance in this context is focused on regulating fishing behavior. For example, a seasonal ban is enforced to restrict mechanized (e.g., trawler, gill netter), and sometimes other fishing for 45 days each year. The seasonal ban does not address criminal behavior per se (e.g., noncompliance with regulations), but the policy has deviant impacts insofar as it may unintentionally disadvantage a particular social group. The governance regime aims to incorporate many of the lessons noted above, particularly the need for careful monitoring and consistent sanctions, as well as local implementation and attention to resource users' livelihoods when restricting their resource use. In addition to strict enforcement of the seasonal ban the government provides subsidies to fishermen who abstain from fishing during this period (Tamil Nadu Fisheries Department, 2014). These subsidies are intended to minimize the negative impacts of the policy on local livelihoods (e.g., revenue loss for those near the poverty line) for those engaged directly in fishing. Many other groups other than fishers themselves depend on the fishing industry in Tamil Nadu. Indeed, for every one fisher there are approximately three allied workers who rely on those fish resources for their livelihoods (International Collective in Support of Fishworkers, 2005). Pre- and post-harvest (i.e., allied) sectors such as fish drying and marketing have limited business during the seasonal ban period. Because these groups do not physically engage in the act of fishing themselves, they are not granted government subsidies to cover expenses during the 45-day ban. These sectors are particularly important in terms of livelihood opportunities for women, who do not participate in fishing due to cultural norms (Subramanian, 2009). As a result, women's livelihoods, and households headed by women, are disproportionately harmed by the seasonal fishing ban due to the lack of funds replacing their usual income. These harms may manifest on an annual basis during the fishing ban in particular, but also accumulate over time and decrease the overall resiliency of women's livelihoods.

Disproportionate burdens from this type of conservation governance are partially a function of not treating allied fishworkers as stakeholders. Such a lack of attention to certain community members may result from poorly designed governing frameworks or from traditional village leadership that purposefully excludes certain groups from decision-making. This exclusion is exemplified in many cases by fishing-caste panchayats, who are the local governing authority in all matters of fishing behavior. Although composed of elected membership, only males may serve in many communities' panchayats (Kruks-Wisner, 2011). After the devastation caused by the 2004 Indian Ocean tsunami in particular, a lack of representation on behalf of women and lower caste members of the community was identified as a major factor in the uneven distribution of aid resources and a barrier to the rehabilitation of allied sector livelihoods overall (Gautham, 2007). In other situations, corrupt decision-makers, who have an incentive to only consider the most powerful participants in a particular community, may cause the disproportionate burdens. The collateral impacts of governance that reproduces existing and exclusionary power dynamics are significant given the region's importance in supporting local food security. The inability for conservation governance to wholly achieve objectives is problematic.

4.10 Conclusion

These case studies demonstrate multiple types of governance are available for reducing negative effects of illegal and other damaging behavior on biodiversity conservation and the people that depend on it. Lessons learned across cases indicate governance processes ideally account for and promote participation of relevant stakeholders. This principle is foundational to risk governance; the limits of failing to account for it can be seen repeatedly. E-waste policies have been constrained by their unintended market effects, including the propensity to ship waste abroad due to the increased cost from local disposal requirements. Transboundary poaching restrictions have fallen short in CNP due to the lack of alternative livelihood opportunities provided to communities living adjacent to the park. Although Tamil Nadu's fishing ban does account for changes to fisher livelihoods, it is limited by ignoring key participants in allied fishworker sectors. Beyond building the knowledge base to better accommodate the linkages between conservation risk and crime, determining how decision-makers can best involve local people or groups previously excluded from decision-making would be valuable. Efforts can be made to confront justice implications of existing and proposed changes to governance regimes.

Clearly, different conservation contexts require different governance and management techniques in order to best limit harms to natural resources and the people that depend on them. Management practices also must vary according to available resources for both enforcement and livelihood activities. Available infrastructure, state of ecological health, community structure, and related factors also may affect conservation management policies. For instance, including allied fishworkers (e.g., fish marketers) in the Tamil Nadu compensation program would have a greater impact on the government budget, meaning that other policy alternatives may need to be considered if sufficient resources are not available. Conservation policy interventions should ideally consider likely reactions in order to produce the best possible conservation and livelihood results.

In the end, despite some examples of success (e.g., Chhatre & Agrawal, 2009), studies suggest that there often is no determined formula for achieving win-win results (Agrawal & Redford, 2006; Campbell, Sayer, & Walker, 2010; Tumusiime & Vedeld, 2012) and a conservation or development goal must be prioritized over the other. In these situations, which is generally more the rule rather than the exception, decision-makers can consider how governance influences and is influenced by conservation risk and crime.

References

Adams, W. M., Aveling, R., Brockington, D., Dickson, B., Elliott, J., Hutton, J.,... Wolmer, W. (2004). Biodiversity conservation and the eradication of poverty. *Science*, 306, 1146–1149.

Agrawal, A., & Redford, K. (2006). Programmatic interventions to alleviate poverty and conserve biodiversity and discussion. In A. Agrawal & Redford, K. (Eds.). *Poverty, development, and biodiversity conservation: Shooting in the dark?* Wildlife Conservation Society Working Paper.

Ancrenaz, M., Dabek, L., & O'Neil, S. (2007). The costs of exclusion: Recognizing a role for local communities in biodiversity conservation. *PLoS Biol*, 5, e289.
Anderson, M. (2013). Electronics waste programs ineffective in most U.S. states. *IEEE Spectrum*. Retrieved from http://spectrum.ieee.org/energy/environment/electronics-waste-programs-ineffective-in-most-us-states
Angelsen, A., & Kaimowitz, D. (1999). Rethinking the causes of deforestation: Lessons from economic models. *The World Bank Research Observer*, 14, 73–98.
Baland, J. M. & Platteau, J-P. (1999) The ambiguous impact of inequality on local resource management. *World Development*, 27, 773–788.
Bassett, T. J. (2005). Card-carrying hunters, rural poverty, and wildlife decline in northern Côte d'Ivoire. *Geographical Journal*, 171, 24–35.
Beccaria, C. (1963). *On crimes and punishments*. Indianapolis: Bobbs-Merrill.
Bisschop, L. (2014). How e-waste challenges environmental governance. *International Journal for Crime, Justice and Social Democracy*, 3, 81–95.
Blom, B., Sunderland, T., & Murdiyarso, D. (2010). Getting REDD to work locally: Lessons learned from integrated conservation and development projects. *Environmental Science & Policy*, 13, 164–172.
Brashares, J. S., Golden, C. D., Weinbaum, K. Z., Barrett, C. B., & Okello, G. V. (2011). Economic and geographic drivers of wildlife consumption in rural Africa. *Proceedings of the National Academy of Sciences*, 108, 13931–13936.
Bridgewater, S. M., Pickles, P., Garwood, N., Penn, M., Bateman, R., Morgan, H.,...Bol, N. (2006). Chamaedorea (xaté) in the Greater Maya Mountains and the Chiquibul forest reserve, Belize: An economic assessment of a non-timber forest product. *Economic Botany*, 60, 265–283.
Brown, K. (2002). Innovations for conservation and development. *Geographical Journal*, 168, 6–17.
CalRecycle. (2013). What is e-waste? Retrieved from http://www.calrecycle.ca.gov/electronics/whatisewaste/
Campbell, B. M., Sayer, J. A., & Walker, B. (2010). Navigating trade-offs: Working for conservation and development outcomes. *Ecology and Society*, 15, 16.
Chhatre, A., & Agrawal, A. (2009). Trade-offs and synergies between carbon storage and livelihood benefits from forest commons. *Proceedings of the National Academy of Sciences*, 106, 17667–17670.
Commission on Global Governance. (1995). *Our global neighborhood: The report of the Commission on Global Governance*. Oxford: Oxford University Press.
Coulthard, S. (2008). Adapting to environmental change in artisanal fisheries—Insights from a South Indian Lagoon. *Global Environmental Change*, 18, 479–489.
Dahlberg, A. C., & Burlando, C. (2009). Addressing trade-offs: Experiences from conservation and development initiatives in the Mkuze Wetlands, South Africa. *Ecology and Society*, 14, 37.
Environmental Investigation Agency. (2011). *System Failure: The U.K.'s harmful trade in electronic waste*. Retrieved from London: http://www.greencustoms.org/docs/EIA_E-waste_report_0511_WEB.pdf
Erickson, M. L., Gibbs, J. P., & Jensen, G. F. (1977). The deterrence doctrine and the perceived certainty of legal punishments. *American Sociological Review*, 42, 305–317.

European Union. (2012). *Directive 2012/19/EU of the European Parliament and of the Council of 4 July 2012 on waste electrical and electronic equipment (WEEE).*

Eurostat. (2014). Environmental data centre on waste. Retrieved from http://epp.eurostat.ec.europa.eu/portal/page/portal/waste/key_waste_streams/waste_electrical_electronic_equipment_weee

Frontline. (2009). Ghana: Digital dumping ground. Retrieved from http://www.pbs.org/frontlineworld/stories/ghana804/video/video_index.html

Gautham, S. (2007). Katta panchayats denying relief to women. *India Together.* Retrieved from http://indiatogether.org/kattarule-society

Gibbs, C., McGarrell, E. F., Axelrod, M., & Rivers III., L. (2011). Conservation criminology and the global trade in electronic waste: Applying a multi-disciplinary research framework. *International Journal of Comparative and Applied Criminal Justice,* 35(4), 269–291.

Greenpeace. (2009). Where does e-waste end up? Retrieved from http://www.greenpeace.org/international/en/campaigns/toxics/electronics/the-e-waste-problem/where-does-e-waste-end-up/

Grey-Ross, R., Downs, C. T., & Kirkman, K. (2010). An assessment of illegal hunting on farmland in KwaZulu-Natal, South Africa: Implications for oribi (Ourebia ourebi) conservation. *South African Journal of Wildlife Research,* 40, 43–52.

Groff, K., & Axelrod, M. (2013). A baseline analysis of transboundary poaching incentives in Chiquibul National Park, Belize. *Conservation and Society,* 11, 277–290.

Grossman, E. (2006). *High tech trash: Digital devices, hidden toxics & human health.* Washington: Island Press/Shearwater Books.

Hutton, J. M., & Leader-Williams, N. (2003). Sustainable use and incentive-driven conservation: Realigning human and conservation interests. *Oryx,* 37, 215–226.

Iles, A. (2004). Mapping environmental justice in technology flows: Computer waste impacts in Asia. *Global Environmental Politics,* 4(4), 76–107.

International Collective in Support of Fishworkers (ICSF). (2005). *Post-tsunami rehabilitation of fisheries livelihoods.* Retrieved from http://bhoomikatrust.org/downloads/icsfdossier.pdf

Kaimowitz, D. (2003). Forest law enforcement and rural livelihoods. *International Forestry Review,* 5, 199–210.

Kaimowitz, D., & Sheil, D. (2007). Conserving what and for whom? Why conservation should help meet basic human needs in the tropics. *Biotropica,* 39, 567–574.

Kruks-Wisner, G. (2011). Seeking the local state: Gender, caste, and the pursuit of public services in post-tsunami India. *World Development,* 39, 1143–1154.

Lee, R. J., Gorog, A. J., Dwiyahreni, A., Siwu, S., Riley, J., Alexander, H.,...Ramono, W. (2005). Wildlife trade and implications for law enforcement in Indonesia: A case study from North Sulawesi. *Biological Conservation,* 123, 477–488.

Lewis, D., Bell, S. D., Fay, J., Bothi, K. L., Gatere, L., Kabila, M.,...Travis, A. J. (2011). Community markets for conservation (COMACO) links biodiversity conservation with sustainable improvements in livelihoods and food production. *Proceedings of the National Academy of Sciences,* 108, 13957–13962.

Lingelbach, J. (2008). *Responsible recycling practices for use in accredited certification programs for electronics recyclers.* Retrieved from http://www.decideagree.com/R2%20Document.pdf

Lizzeri, A., & Persico, N. (2001). The provision of public goods under alternative electoral incentives. *American Economic Review*, 91, 225–239.
Lockwood, M., Davidson, J., Curtis, A., Stratford, E., & Griffith, R. (2010). Governance principles for natural resource management. *Society & Natural Resources*, 23, 986–1001.
Lute, M. L., & Gore, M. L. (2014). Knowledge and power in wildlife management. *The Journal of Wildlife Management*, 78, 1060–1068.
McAllister, L. (2013). The human and environmental effects of e-waste. *Population Reference Bureau*. Retrieved from http://www.prb.org/Publications/Articles/2013/e-waste.aspx
McElwee, P. D. (2010). Resource use among rural agricultural households near protected areas in Vietnam: The social costs of conservation and implications for enforcement. *Environmental Management*, 45, 113–131.
McGarrell, E. F., Freilich, J. D., & Chermak, S. (2007). Intelligence-led policing as a framework for responding to terrorism. *Journal of Contemporary Criminal Justice*, 23, 142–158.
Pellegrini, L., & Gerlagh, R. (2006). Corruption, democracy, and environmental policy: An empirical contribution to the debate. *The Journal of Environment Development*, 15, 332–354.
Pires, S., & Moreto, W. (2011). Preventing wildlife crimes: Solutions that can overcome the 'Tragedy of the Commons'. *European Journal on Criminal Policy and Research*, 17, 101–123.
Raik, D. B., Wilson, A. L., & Decker, D. J. (2008). Power in natural resources management: An application of theory. *Society & Natural Resources*, 21, 729–739.
Roe, D., & Walpole, M. J. (2010). Whose value counts? Trade-offs between biodiversity conservation and poverty reduction. In N. Leader-Williams, W. M. Adams, & R. J. Smith (Eds.). *Trade-offs in conservation: Deciding what to save.* London, United Kingdom: Wiley-Blackwell.
Rucevska, I., Nellemann, C., Isarin, N., Yang, W., Liu, N., Yu, K.,...Nilsen, R. (2015). *Waste crime - waste risks: Gaps in meeting the global waste challenge.* Retrieved from Nairobi and Arendal: http://www.unep.org/delc/Portals/119/publications/rra-wastecrime.pdf
Salas, O., & Meerman, J. (2008). *Chiquibul National Park Management Plan 2008-2013.* Retrieved from http://www.biodiversity.bz/downloads/Chiquibul_National_Park_Management_Plan_finalv_090330.pdf
Silicon Valley Toxics Coalition. (2010). *Living in fear: A story of e-waste pollution on the Erren River in Taiwan.* Retrieved from cherrypal.blogspot.com/2008/08/story-of-e-waste-pollution-on-erren.html (accepted 14 November 2016).
Solving the E-Waste Problem (2014). United Kingdom of Great Britain and Northern Ireland. Retrieved from http://step-initiative.org/index.php/Overview_United_Kingdom.html#Regulatory
Solving the E-Waste Problem (2014). United States of America. Retrieved from http://step-initiative.org/index.php/Overview_USA.html#Regulatory
Subramanian, A. (2009). *Shorelines: space and rights in South India.* Stanford: Stanford University Press.
Suškevičs, M. (2012). Legitimacy analysis of multi-level governance of biodiversity: Evidence from 11 case studies across the E.U. *Environmental Policy and Governance*, 22, 217–237.

Tallis, H., Kareiva, P., Marvier, M., & Chang, A. (2008). An ecosystem services framework to support both practical conservation and economic development. *Proceedings of the National Academy of Sciences*, 105, 9457–9464.

Tamil Nadu Fisheries Department. Marine Fisheries Development. Retrieved from http://www.fisheries.tn.gov.in/marine-main.html

Thomas, J. (2011). E.U. criminals corner e-scrap market. *E-Scrap News*. Retrieved from http://resource-recycling.com/esn_mag

Tonetti, R. (2007). *EPA's regulatory program for 'e-waste'.* Retrieved from http://www.epa.gov/epaoswer/hazwaste/recycle/ecycling/rules.htm

Tumusiime, D. M., & Vedeld, P. (2012). False promise or false premise? Using tourism revenue sharing to promote conservation and poverty reduction in Uganda. *Conservation and Society*, 10, 15–28.

United States Government Accountability Office. (2008). *Electronic waste: EPA needs to better control harmful U.S. exports through stronger enforcement and more comprehensive regulation*. Retrieved from http://www.gao.gov/new.items/d081044.pdf

United States Government Accountability Office. (2008). *Electronic waste: Harmful U.S. exports flow virtually unrestricted because of minimal EPA enforcement and narrow regulation*. Retrieved from http://www.gao.gov/assets/130/121163.pdf

US Environmental Protection Agency. (2013). EPA's sustainable materials management. Retrieved from http://www.epa.gov/smm/

Weidner, H., Jänicke, M., & Jörgens, H. (2002). *Capacity building in national environmental policy: a comparative study of 17 countries*. Berlin London: Springer-Verlag.

5

Gaining Compliance and Cooperation with Regulated Wildlife Harvest

Brent A. Rudolph and Shawn J. Riley

Consumptive uses of wildlife provide food, cultural and recreational values, and economic benefits. Conserving the opportunity to derive these benefits requires that consumption not exceed sustainable levels. In some cases, conservation may benefit from ensuring citizens have a vested utilitarian interest in long-term maintenance of wildlife populations by managing for high levels of sustainable consumptive use. In yet other instances, human impacts on habitat and simplification of ecosystems (e.g., through removal of predators) may produce conservation dilemmas that require increasing harvest above typical levels demanded. Our intent in this chapter is to provide readers with a holistic yet practical overview of concepts and supporting research for understanding citizen compliance and cooperation with regulated harvest as a component of wildlife conservation efforts. We review this spectrum of needs from restricting to promoting to maximizing harvest through regulations and management regimes at scales from local levels to sovereign states. We focus on factors that are most likely to influence collective behaviors of individual actors, and not efforts for pursuing nation-state commitment to multinational agreements and treaties.

Numerous factors influence the ability of governments to protect the public good by reducing frequency of harmful behaviors and increasing frequency of beneficial behaviors. Consumption of wildlife and other natural resources typically is difficult to restrict (Weimer & Vining, 2005). Given modern trends toward increased democratization and egalitarianism, political regimes have been pressured and overthrown over efforts to entirely prohibit consumption of natural resources by all or subsets of citizens, such as in and around protected areas (Hauck & Kroese, 2006; Rudolph, Schechter, & Riley, 2012). Governments, therefore, commonly allow but regulate wildlife consumption. Assessing harvest compliance behavior provides decision-makers opportunities to account for noncompliance directly through efforts to increase compliance or indirectly by restricting legally allowable take to sustainable levels even in combination with expected illegal take.

Conservation capacity is constrained by narrowly focusing on a simple dichotomy of compliance: citizens either behaving or not behaving exactly as dictated by regulations. More proactive decisions can be informed through efforts to understand conservation behaviors that are more nuanced than this

Conservation Criminology, First Edition. Edited by Meredith L. Gore.

simple dichotomy. Conservation depends on a variety of behaviors potentially influenced by an array of public policy instruments through evolving processes by which governments exercise power (Bemelmans-Videc, Rist, & Vedung, 2003; Rudolph *et al.*, 2012). We review these overarching considerations of conservation behavior, public policy instruments, and government power, and then present a conceptual approach to understanding compliance and cooperation with harvest management and practical considerations for influencing these behaviors.

5.1 Importance of Compliance and Cooperation

Human harvest of wildlife has a variety of direct and indirect effects on wildlife populations, habitats, and ecosystem functions. Some such effects help and some hinder conservation efforts. Wildlife managers and conservationists seek to restrict or regulate harvest to achieve a variety of outcomes. Though objectives vary widely, three distinct categories of harvest management include strong restrictions or outright bans on harvest, allowing sustainable levels of harvest for sustenance or recreation, and maximizing harvest to reduce populations deemed overabundant. The relevance of a spectrum of behaviors to conservation under these differing categories of harvest management objectives should be considered. These behaviors range from non-participation, which will avoid all risk of illegal acts but will not constitute cooperation where harvest is desired, through basic regulatory compliance, to expenditure of extra effort in pursuit of effective cooperation.

The strongest restrictions involve near or complete bans on harvest. In the context of conservation, attention on addressing compliance often brings to mind concerns over limiting the effect of poaching, or taking of wildlife in violation of laws or regulations, in locations where these substantial restrictions are in place (Kahler & Gore, 2012). In impoverished regions food insecurity, human-wildlife conflict, or commercial value of wildlife may create strong motivations for poaching, yet sustainable hunting can provide critical food resources or sources of income. Illegal harvest in these cases can be particularly difficult to quantify and control, and may jeopardize future existence of critically imperiled wildlife populations as well as the people that depend on them for their livelihood.

Under a second category of restriction, where management objectives involve regulating sustainable harvest to allow sustenance or recreation, violations may be an overlooked issue. Well-developed governance structures are typically in place where harvest is regulated but commonly allowed, providing funding and coordination of research, monitoring, and management. Yet, even sophisticated efforts to identify optimal resource allocations often directly explore implications of producing specific harvest levels. Decision-makers, however, are not able to directly manipulate harvest. Rather, compliance and cooperation and a host of other factors influence the effectiveness with which regulations affect harvest levels and conservation outcomes (Anderson & Lee, 1986; Hunter & Runge, 2004). The imperfect control by regulations of both legal and illegal harvesting activities contributes to partial controllability, one of four sources of

Table 5.1 Components of resource management uncertainty. See Nichols *et al.* (1995) and Hunter and Runge (2004).

Source of Uncertainty	Definition
Partial controllability	Imprecise control of resource impacts by management efforts
Environmental variation	Unpredictable influence of weather and habitat conditions on population vital rates and distribution
Structural uncertainty	Imperfect knowledge of biological systems and responses to management
Partial observability	Imperfect monitoring of population status

uncertainty in wildlife management (Nichols, Johnson, & Williams, 1995). Partial controllability is the only source of uncertainty that relates directly to intentional management actions (Table 5.1). Decision-makers, therefore, have an opportunity to mitigate the interference of partial controllability with meeting conservation objectives by evaluating and adapting their own management actions (Hunter & Runge, 2004). Management even of abundant populations that are consistently harvested (e.g., deer in North America) may therefore be improved by efforts to assess factors driving noncompliance as a contributor to partial controllability that confounds reaching harvest objectives.

Partial controllability is also an obstacle to addressing cases that fall under the third category of harvest management, where conservation objectives create needs for maximizing harvest to reduce populations deemed overabundant. Some situations involve abundant game populations that theoretically may be reduced through liberalized recreational harvest regulations. Pressures of herbivory by abundant red deer in Scotland, for example, threaten the integrity of ecosystems upon which they and other wildlife depend (MacMillan & Leitch, 2008). Agencies cannot coerce recreational hunting participants to kill game in adequate quantity to bring about population reductions. Voluntary hunter cooperation through effort extending beyond simple compliance is necessary to effectively reduce populations in such instances (Rudolph & Riley, 2014).

Conservation can critically depend upon effectively implementing and enforcing government regulations that restrict harvest to sustainable levels, but efforts should not be limited to these activities. Management effectiveness may be maximized by comprehensively assessing factors that influence behaviors. Benefits include opportunities to prevent crime or promote cooperation (rather than simply reacting to crime and unsuccessful conservation efforts after resources are exploited or degraded) and expanding the tools and suite of actors that support conservation behavior.

Up to this point, we have only addressed restricting harvest through the adoption of government regulations. Regulations, however, are just one of three distinct public policy instruments that may influence behavior (Bemelmans-Videc *et al.*, 2003). Other options include economic instruments (e.g., providing payments, levying or exempting taxes) and communication (e.g., awareness, persuasion, transfer of knowledge). Regulations are the exclusive province of governments, but governments increasingly are moving toward collaborative governance approaches (Sandström, Pellilekka, & Ratamäki, 2009; Rudolph *et al.*, 2012). Collaborative governance includes coordination among multiple governments, agencies, or organizations (e.g., formation of treaties, partnerships with non-governmental organizations). Benefits of collaborative governance include coordinated use of a greater pool of financial and personnel resources, applying diverse expertise possessed across multiple actors, and exerting a broader nature of influence through an expanded set of actors (Kretser, Glennon, & Smith, 2014; Prideaux, 2014). Collaborative governance may facilitate broader engagement in the course of establishing regulations, and may especially facilitate coordinated application of economic instruments and communication efforts.

In light of the broad range of behaviors relevant to conservation efforts and the variety of policy instruments that may be applied, effectiveness of conservation practices can be improved by evaluating broader approaches than simply government action to adopt regulations and apply enforcement. Such broader consideration supports promotion of a diversity of behaviors that contribute to conservation, informs implementation of all available policy instruments, and supports roles for an expanded set of actors pursuing collaborative governance of wildlife resources. We review important factors that may contribute to this spectrum of behaviors, drawing upon general compliance literature and theory and providing brief examples and research findings to illustrate their significance to wildlife harvest management. We then provide key considerations to guide approaches to increasing compliance and cooperation.

5.2 What Drives Violations of Natural Resource Regulations?

Most individuals comply with laws and regulations out of deference to authority or belief that behavior prohibited by law is morally wrong (Tyler, 1990; 2003). In other words, most people comply because they believe it is the right thing to do. For some others, violations result from unintentional acts due to lack of awareness or inability to comply with regulations. In other cases still, individuals are motivated to intentionally violate laws and regulations. The framework we present is intended to aid conservationists in recognizing the likelihood of either intentional or unintentional violations and considering what factors may motivate violations along with practical means for gaining compliance. Social and political context strongly shape violation motivations (von Essen *et al.*, 2014). Our framework may not be useful for addressing instances of noncompliance that are acts specifically intended to protest or rebel against authority or specific political regimes (e.g., Malagasy farmers setting fire to Ankarafantsika National Park forests in frustration with national election results). In the most extreme of such cases, resolution may require governance changes much broader than adjusting conservation policies and practices.

5.3 Unintentional Violations

Insufficient knowledge of regulations and inadequate skill to comply are fundamental factors that can influence unintentional illegal harvest. Basic awareness of harvest restrictions may not be a significant barrier to achieving adequate compliance in consistently regulated systems. Unintended violations may be more common in systems that are inconsistently regulated, or where regulations are complex, require specific knowledge or specialized skill, or change frequently. North American waterfowl hunting regulations bear such characteristics, and have been the subject of more compliance evaluations than most other hunting pursuits. Regulations vary in complexity, and in some instances rely on hunters' abilities to properly identify sex and species of birds in flight. Special knowledge and skills are needed to correctly identify and target waterfowl.

An assessment of waterfowl hunting outcomes in Michigan, U.S. demonstrated greater complexity of regulations did not result in considerably greater violation rates (Mikula, Martz, & Bennett, 1972). The experimental design, however, randomly assigned hunters at a public hunting area to be subject to regulations of varying levels of complexity. The approach provided detailed explanations of the regulations assigned to each hunting party. This likely limited the influence of lack of knowledge relative to the typical situation in which hunters must determine applicable regulations on their own. A broad assessment of waterfowl hunting, over multiple years and across 12 states within the Mississippi Flyway region of North America, indicated rates and justification of violations differed across states of the region even though regulations did not differ substantially (Gray & Kaminski, 1994). The authors could not determine if regulatory changes directly influenced violation rates. Respondents, however, indicated that among various violations, 53 – 84% were intentional. In some cases, a considerable majority of acknowledged infractions were due to some motivation to violate rather than occurring due to lack of knowledge or ability to comply. Thus, ensuring individuals are well informed of regulations, while important, should not be assumed to be sufficient for securing compliance.

5.4 Intentional Violations

Individuals may make intentional behavioral choices to violate rules and illegally harvest wildlife. That is, at times they knowingly and deliberately do not comply with regulations. Factors that may motivate violations include instrumental influence, which is a result of the perceived benefits of personal gains balanced against potential losses, and normative influence from factors that create an internal sense of duty to behave in particular ways regardless of personal gains and losses (Winter & May, 2001; Tyler, 2003). Most research has focused exclusively on either instrumental or normative drivers of violations, with little integration of these two perspectives (von Essen *et al.*, 2014). Development of strategies for enhancing compliance can benefit from assessing combined instrumental and normative influences on subsequent behaviors, and the integration of instrumental and normative insights is especially important when seeking to improve broader cooperation (Sutinen & Kuperan, 1999; Rudolph & Riley, 2014).

5.5 Violations Motivated by Direct Personal Gains

Financial gains can be a strong motivation to engage in illegal take of wildlife. Substantial restrictions on commercial trade even of legally harvested animals were established early in an era of wildlife recovery in North America (Geist, Mahoney, & Organ, 2001). In other settings, legal and sometimes unrestricted markets exist for wildlife and wildlife parts. Rather than the presence of a market for wildlife parts, however, impacts of trade on wildlife populations will be determined by specific local economic, political, and cultural factors that influence rates of compliance, dynamics of use and demand, and market activity (Garshelis, 2002).

For example, in North America a legal, regulated commercial market exists for pelts from species such as raccoon, gray fox, fisher, American marten, and bobcat. Enforcement of restrictive trapping regulations and the secretive nature of furbearers have combined to allow for sustainable management of these resources over time. Population dynamics or abundance trends of these elusive species are difficult to monitor, and are commonly assessed using information collected from harvested animals registered by and effort data reported by trappers (Skalski *et al.*, 2011). Changes in pelt prices appear to drive changes in furbearer harvest (Elsken-Lacy *et al.*, 1999; Gehrt, Hubert, & Ellis, 2002), but reported harvest of some highly regulated furbearers does not respond to prices (Hiller *et al.*, 2011; Kapfer & Potts, 2012). Wildlife managers have noted, however, that harvest or trapping effort associated with illegal activities will not be reported, which produces inaccurate data and confounds efforts to assess population dynamics or abundance of these species (Koen, Bowman, & Findlay, 2007; Skalski *et al.*, 2011). Increasing profit margins may increase motivation for users to engage in illegal harvest in order to enter additional furs into these regulated markets. Trappers may exceed restrictive bag limits by making use of licenses purchased by non-trappers, practicing high-grading (i.e., harvesting in excess of the quota, but keeping the most valuable pelts and discarding the excess), or taking furbearers within closed areas or during closed seasons and falsely register and report activities as legal. Lack of trapper compliance may place populations at risk from overexploitation, but also promote falsified data that results in ineffective harvest regulations or misinterpretation of effects on population dynamics created by regulated harvest.

Illicit trade in wildlife typically is thought of as problematic for endangered species whose rarity affects the supply relative to demand for them, in addition to making such populations sensitive to exploitation. Some observers conclude that the relationship between global wildlife trade and poaching even of still abundant, harvested species requires more attention due to indications that markets for game animal parts (e.g., American black bear gall bladder and antler velvet) are increasingly lucrative (Musgrave, Parker, & Wolok, 1993; Muth & Bowe, 1998). In particular, substantial concerns are raised by the increasing involvement of organized crime in illegal wildlife trade (Zimmerman, 2003).

Other personal gains that can motivate illegal harvest include use of wildlife for food resources and a variety of other factors associated with successfully harvesting game. Improving food security can be a substantial motivator for harvest in some situations, particularly those at the local level (Hauck, 2008). Wildlife may be illegally harvested to feed families directly, or this meat may be sold to others for consumption. Interventions in such cases often focus on implementing a variety of approaches to improving access to food and enhancing income, such as by subsidizing livestock ownership or enhancing wages or access to markets and credit (Moro *et al.*, 2013). The motivation for poaching wildlife to serve as a food resource is perceived to have decreased in the United States (and perhaps in other global North countries) due to changing modern views on the desirability and acceptability of game meat and increased availability of other food sources, including through social welfare programs for those in need (Eliason, 2004). Hunters that have already determined to go into the field in pursuit of game, however, indicate that perceived enhanced opportunity to harvest game is one reason they engage in illegal methods of take. Hunters report being more likely to engage in illegal baiting and hunting outside of allowed shooting hours due to perceived likelihood of increased harvest success in the course of hunting waterfowl and deer (Gray & Kaminski, 1994; Rudolph, 2012).

5.6 Violations Motivated by Indirect Personal Gains

Retaliation for or prevention of anticipated negative human-wildlife interactions such as crop damage, livestock depredation, competition between humans and predators for game species, or attacks or threats to human safety is often assumed to be a key motivation for illegal take of wildlife (Treves & Bruskotter, 2014). In such cases, noncompliance is motivated by indirect gains—by responding to losses or preventing future losses—rather than direct personal gains. Mixed evidence exists as to the motivation for retaliatory or preventative poaching. Residents of the Zambezi region of northeast Namibia perceived protection of property or human lives as motivations to poach, but these were considered substantially less important factors than poaching for financial gain and food (Kahler & Gore, 2012). Depredation of crops and livestock and attacks on humans by Asiatic black bears in the Sichuan Province of southwestern China affected attitudes toward bears, but illegal killing was more common in areas without human-bear conflicts, and was motivated by financial gains (Liu *et al.*, 2011). Conflicts with predators regarding livestock depredation and perceived competition with hunters for game were motivations for poaching in Scandinavia, and motivation to poach was not eliminated by opportunities for regulated legal harvest of predators (Andrén *et al.*, 2006). Though retaliatory or preventative poaching related to negative human-wildlife interactions may correspond to perceived risks of such encounters, these actions may also be an expression of general rebellion against government, or opposition to specific agencies or policies that restrict what are viewed as traditional practices or rights (Bell, Hampshire, & Topalidou, 2007; Muth & Bowe, 1998). Such considerations relate to instrumental judgments of government policies or regulators.

5.7 Violations and Instrumental Judgments of Government Policy and Regulators

Individuals engage in instrumental judgments regarding whether government policies or authorities are working to protect what they view as their personal interests (Levi & Stoker, 2000). Instrumental judgments pertaining to decision-makers as individuals in positions of authority include identification (i.e., perceived sharing of social bonds) and performance (i.e., judgment of authorities' abilities to produce valuable outcomes) (Braithwaite, 1995; Sunshine & Tyler, 2003). Instrumental judgments pertaining to regulations or overarching policies prompting their implementation consist of goal agreement (i.e., evaluations of whether agency goals are aligned with individuals' personal goals) and equity or distributive justice (i.e., judgments of equitability of treatment or fairness of allocation of resources relative to the needs of different individuals or groups) (Braithwaite, 1995; Tyler, 2000). Individuals may forego immediate personal gains that could be available through intentional violations if they are convinced through favorable instrumental judgments that authorities or regulations may effectively protect their personal interests over the long-term (Tyler, 2000; Rudolph & Riley, 2014).

Instrumental judgments of identification, performance, goal agreement, and equity may be closely linked, and several judgments may influence compliance behavior collectively. In Michigan, a ban on hunter use of bait was implemented in pursuit of bovine tuberculosis (bTB) eradication, which included dual goals to eliminate a self-sustained infection from a white-tailed deer population and to eliminate the disease from domestic cattle that were periodically affected by spillover infections from deer. Hunter compliance with the baiting ban differed based on goal agreement with those distinct but related goals of eradication from deer and livestock (Rudolph, 2012). The baiting ban was established after past evaluations indicated use of bait did not increase overall harvest of deer, but could potentially increase transmission of bTB from infected to uninfected deer, and thus continue to sustain the source for livestock infection (Rudolph *et al.*, 2006). Agreement with the agency goal to eradicate bTB from deer was negatively associated with past baiting violations, but hunters that agreed with the goal to eradicate bTB from livestock were more likely to have violated the ban. Individuals that believed reducing or eradicating bTB from livestock was important may have been more likely to violate if they negatively evaluated performance toward reaching that goal, such as if bait was believed to enhance the harvest of deer regardless of what past agency assessments indicated. Rudolph (2012) focused assessments of how individuals evaluated agency performance based on perceptions regarding deer hunting rather than agency performance at addressing livestock interests, but such comments in support of removing the baiting ban were regularly made at public meetings of hunters and livestock producers in the bTB infected area. As another example, among what they identified as contemplated violations, as opposed to unintentional and heat-of-the-moment violations, Gray and Kaminski (1994) found that 11 – 17% of waterfowl hunters that violated a variety of waterfowl hunting regulations justified their violations simply out of disagreement with the regulations, a likely reflection of one or more negative instrumental judgments of the regulations or regulators.

5.8 Violations and Normative Influence

Human behavior is influenced by normative factors arising from moral obligation to internalized values, social norms, and a sense of duty to obey or otherwise support authorities. Moral norms motivate individuals to do the right thing or avoid guilt or shame that may occur from behaving against internalized values (Grasmick & Bursik, 1990). Social norms originate from beliefs regarding behavior deemed acceptable by people whose views are considered important (Vaske & Manfredo, 2012). Moral or social norms may influence specific behaviors that are required or prohibited by regulations or may more generally apply to a tendency to comply with authorities or rule adherence. Procedural justice, or perceptions of fair processes and appropriate exercise of power, may produce an internalized sense of obligation to obey or otherwise support authorities, even if such behavior diminishes or does not promote individuals' personal benefits (Levi & Stoker, 2000; Tyler, 2003). Studies of diverse institutions including police agencies (Sunshine & Tyler, 2003), federal law making (Tyler, 1994), tax payment (Murphy, 2005), and environmental regulations (Winter & May, 2001) reveal that procedural justice is often more important than the outcome individuals experience or expect to experience (e.g., being arrested, seeing laws passed that are deemed unfavorable, bearing the expenses of taxes or fines) in determining compliance as well as broader cooperation.

Tyler (2000) identified four components of procedural justice, including treatment with dignity, participation, neutrality, and trustworthiness of authorities. Considerations of participation in a regulatory setting are based on opportunities to interact with decision-makers and provide input during development and enforcement of regulations. Neutrality is evaluated through perceptions that those in positions of authority are not overly guided by personal beliefs and desires. Individuals' judgments are based on whether impartial rules for making decisions exist and are followed, and assessments of whether decisions are made based on factual, objective considerations. Decisions are more likely to be viewed as factual if it can be demonstrated that scientific findings and technical expertise are considered when weighing alternative regulations (Stryker, 1994). Trustworthiness is determined to a large extent by the justification that is provided for decisions. To increase trustworthiness, a justification should involve explaining how alternative arguments or options were considered, and individuals are more likely to judge as trustworthy those authorities with whom they consistently share beliefs about what is likely to be accomplished by the laws and regulations they ultimately implement (Beetham, 1991; Tyler, 2000).

Most assessments of the influence procedural justice has on compliance have focused on core government functions such as police authority and tax collection rather than conservation laws and regulations. The earliest efforts to assess procedural justice in a conservation context involved research examining compliance with commercial fishing regulations. Assessments of commercial fishing compliance have increasingly expanded from applying economic models of purely instrumental factors to also incorporate normative factors. Instrumental factors are often identified of great importance in commercial fishing violations even when considered along with normative influence. Opportunities for financial gains through illegal harvest, however, are considerable in commercial fishing contexts. Nonetheless, commercial fishing compliance studies indicate normative factors can have a significant influence on compliance behavior (Hatcher *et al.*, 2000).

5.9 What Drives Cooperation?

Cooperative behavior, as with compliance, may be motivated by a combination of instrumental and normative influences. What differs, however, is that lack of cooperation does not produce potential personal losses through risk of sanctions. Cooperation by definition involves supportive behaviors extending beyond simple compliance with dictates of laws and regulations. Due to this voluntary nature, penalties cannot be applied for uncooperative behavior.

Agency objectives that depend upon voluntary cooperation as well as basic regulatory compliance cannot secure supportive behavior by applying deterrence effects. Thus, enforcement of restrictive regulations can restrain harvest, but implementation of liberalized recreational harvest opportunities with encouragement that hunters aid agencies with population reduction efforts have met with little success. Where they are not constrained by regulations, harvest rates can be constrained by inadequate hunter participation or success, adherence to hunting traditions, and opposition to policies that promote liberal regulations and reduction of game species populations (Hunter & Runge, 2004; Heberlein, 2012). Even instrumental personal gains of increased harvest are often less appealing than the perceived long-term benefits of foregoing this extra harvest in return for sustaining abundant game populations for future recreational opportunities (Holsman & Petchenik, 2006).

For example, eradicating bTB partially depends on hunters cooperating with deer population reduction efforts (Rudolph *et al.*, 2006). If hunters do not both comply and cooperate, with compliance in this case defined as following a ban on baiting deer and cooperation involving making an effort to kill additional antlerless deer, eradication is believed to be nearly impossible (Ramsey *et al.*, 2014). The effects of numerous instrumental personal gains and normative influences on hunter cooperation, measured through purchase of antlerless licenses that would allow harvest of female deer, were evaluated (Rudolph & Riley, 2014). The only statistically significant variable related to cooperation was an aspect of trustworthiness of authorities, a component of normative influence through procedural justice. Specifically, the trustworthiness variable assessed agreement by hunters that bTB eradication is possible, which was an important part of justification for the liberal harvest regulations that required hunter cooperation in order to be effective. The correlation between trustworthiness and cooperation was negative, such that hunters that believed it was possible to eradicate bTB were less likely to cooperate with efforts to reduce deer densities. This example demonstrates that even when authorities provide plausible justification for regulations, justification alone is unlikely to ensure cooperative behavior. More broadly, though procedural justice can be an important normative influence on behavior, moral, and social norms often are the strongest motivations for both compliance and cooperation (Tyler, 2000). Policies aligned with existing norms are those most likely to benefit from efforts extending beyond basic compliance into more proactive cooperation. Cooperation will be most difficult to secure with policies that are not aligned, or worse, opposed to, existing norms, for, agencies are constrained in their abilities to facilitate norm adoption or adaptation (Vaske & Manfredo, 2012).

5.10 Considerations for Increasing Compliance and Cooperation

Three public policy mechanisms are commonly implemented to influence behavior: government regulations, economic instruments, and communication (Bemelmans-Videc *et al.*, 2003). These policies apply different influences (Table 5.2). Regulations are the only mechanism that involves an authoritative relationship, mandating or prohibiting specific behaviors. Payments or taxes levied or exempted through economic instruments incentivize desirable behaviors, but create no obligation for particular actions to be taken; fines and penalties for violations are a feature of the regulations mechanism. Providing information may involve efforts of persuasion or to transfer knowledge. Communication may be implemented to attempt to persuade the public without application of the other policy mechanisms, but where regulations or economic instruments are in place, the intent may be to educate the public about the associated costs or benefits. Applying different types of policy mechanisms can offset the potential drivers of compliance and cooperation that we have reviewed herein.

Table 5.2 Policy mechanisms identified by Bemelmans-Videc *et al.* (2003), and the nature of their influence on compliance and cooperation.

Policy Mechanism	Influence on Compliance and Cooperation
Regulations	Create instrumental losses associated with non-compliance
Economic instruments	Create instrumental gains associated with compliance or cooperation
Communication	Explicate instrumental and normative gains and losses associated with compliance or cooperation

5.10.1 Applying Regulations to Influence Compliance

Regulations mandate or prohibit specific behaviors; they create instrumental losses in the form of sanctions that may be applied to those that commit noncompliant behaviors (Table 5.2). Theoretically, the instrumental influence of regulations involves a conceptual decision process in which individuals weigh deterrence costs with their perceived net personal gains associated with violations (Winter & May, 2001). For the instrumental influences to promote compliance the potential losses from sanctions must exceed the potential gains available through noncompliant behavior. Deterrence ideally operates by creating a credible threat of punishment through enforcement (Burby & Paterson, 1993).

Detection and apprehension comprise one element of enforcement, incorporating the likelihood that violators are discovered and caught by enforcement officers. Another element is sanctions and adjudication, which includes the severity of applicable penalties and the likelihood those penalties will be applied by enforcement officers and judicially upheld. Sanctions typically include fines, incarceration, loss of privileges (e.g., future hunting opportunities), or loss of equipment (e.g., hunting equipment or vehicles).

Improving detection and apprehension rates is more difficult than increasing severity of sanctions (Tyler, 2003). It is therefore problematic that the bulk of research indicates decisions to comply are more strongly influenced by perceived risk of punishment than expected costs of punishment (Burby & Paterson, 1993). Furthermore natural resources violations are notoriously challenging to detect and apprehend compared to other violations such as street crime. This difference stems from low ratios of conservation officers to resource users, the difficulties of detecting violations in often remote locations, and public resistance and legal challenges to the use of aggressive policing techniques for enforcing such violations (Falcone, 2004).

Despite a somewhat discouraging outlook regarding the effectiveness of deterrence efforts to reduce natural resource violations, several cases offer hope. Where hunting violations are concerned, perceptions of the severity and nature of penalties (in particular, the loss of hunting privileges) rather than the risk of punishment can be effective deterrents (Gray & Kaminski, 1994; Rudolph, 2012). Thus, identifying and applying sufficiently severe or particularly effective penalties may be a more effective strategy than devoting resources to increasing the certainty of punishment. Applying loss of hunting privileges as deterrence may be an optimal strategy, for there is also limited support within the legal system for increasing natural resource violation fines to levels equal or exceeding those of other criminal acts (Sutinen & Kuperan, 1999).

Understanding and influencing individuals' perceptions of the certainty and severity of punishment is the key to applying and evaluating deterrence. Whether or not individuals accurately assess those risks and costs, their estimates influence behavior (Tyler, 2003). Efforts to influence perceptions of certainty and severity of punishment may more effectively achieve deterrence, particularly considering the difficulties associated with detection and apprehension in natural resource contexts. These efforts may be implemented through policy mechanism of providing information, by highlighting successful prosecutions or increasing awareness of the ability to apply effective modes of deterrence such as loss of hunting privileges.

5.10.2 Applying Economic Instruments to Influence Compliance and Cooperation

Economic instruments differ from fines associated with regulations; they create instrumental gains for demonstrating desirable behavior rather than applying losses as punishment for violations (Bemelmans-Videc *et al.*, 2003). For example, financial rewards for hunters to increase take of deer in Wisconsin's chronic wasting disease eradication zone were offered, but were determined to be ineffective (Holsman & Petchenik, 2006). Programs that provide landowners payments for achieving conservation performance appear to hold promise, but many have been insufficiently monitored or not in practice long enough to empirically prove success (Dickman, Macdonald, & Macdonald, 2011). Although economic instruments primarily produce incentives for proactive engagement beyond compliance, such gains may also promote compliance with rules. For example, efforts to compensate livestock owners for losses or pay landowners for attracting carnivores to their property may promote active conservation, but may also offset motivation for retaliatory or preventative illegal killing of carnivores. Economic incentive and loss compensation programs have been linked to increased tolerance and reduced poaching of carnivores, though such programs have not been universally successful (Maclennan *et al.*, 2009). Effectiveness of economic instruments can be hampered by unsuccessful administration of payments, such as in settings with corrupt governments or where unstable or poorly defined property rights complicate verification of eligible landowners (Zabel & Holm-Müller, 2008). Programs may also exacerbate conflict and undermine conservation efforts if depredation becomes a significant opportunity for profit, incentivizing settlement near conservation areas that harbor carnivore populations and thereby degrading habitat through increased grazing and development (Bulte & Rondeau, 2005). Where suitable conditions exist for appropriately administering payments, paying landowners that maintain carnivores on their property may be preferable to depredation compensation to avoid incentivizing conflicts (Dickman *et al.*, 2011).

Other mechanisms have been implemented in addition to making payments to reduce economic expenses of restoring wildlife species and habitats, including cost-sharing, providing technical guidance, or alleviating land use restrictions (Wilcove & Lee, 2004). Apart from offering reprieve from regulatory restrictions, non-governmental organizations (NGOs) as well as government agencies may apply economic instruments through payments, cost- sharing, or providing technical expertise. NGOs have actively engaged in such programs to advance conservation, ranging from programs to benefit conservation of snow leopards in India to lions in Kenya to wolves in North America (Dickman *et al.*, 2011).

5.10.3 Applying Communication to Influence Compliance and Cooperation

Communication designed to affect behavior may enhance the influence of instrumental and normative gains and losses associated with compliance or cooperation. Communication efforts may seek to reduce unintentional violations through public information and education campaigns. These campaigns may address lack of awareness of restrictions, improve capacity to comply with complex regulations, or enhance skills required to successfully and legally participate in harvest. Alternatively, campaigns may seek to increase individuals' perceptions of the certainty and severity of punishment, as perceived rather than assessed risks and costs influence behavior (Tyler, 2003). In other cases, informative or persuasive communication may influence instrumental judgments or activate norms, as discussed below. As with economic instruments, communication efforts provide opportunities for collaborative governance (Rudolph *et al.*, 2012; Prideaux, 2014). Conservation or other community organizations may enhance agency communication efforts or conduct their own campaigns. Organizations may provide funding, personnel, or volunteers, and may have better access to or credibility with some population segments.

5.10.4 Communication to Influence Instrumental Judgments

Communication may strategically convey that authorities are working to protect public interests in order to enhance instrumental judgments of identification, performance, goal agreement, and equity. As wildlife management agency missions evolve, instrumental judgments by the public in the absence of persuasive communication may reduce compliance or cooperation. Many North American departments of game have been redefined as departments of natural resources. New mandates call for the conservation and protection of natural resources overall, beyond the initial narrow focus of establishing agencies solely to regulate hunting and trapping. This may produce an eroding sense of identification, which could be responsible for increased conflict between traditional constituencies such as hunters or trappers and wildlife managers or conservation officers (Falcone, 2004).

Conservation of some charismatic species creates tensions between demonstrating satisfactory performance and goal agreement, given the diverse personal interests of a global audience. Debates regarding conservation of elephants through limitations on the sale of ivory exemplify this challenge. Disagreement has persisted regarding the need for a total moratorium, based on the contested assumption that properly regulated limited trade in ivory can be sustainable and may provide an incentive to those states where elephants live. Some countries resent what they believe are unfair influences of NGOs in lobbying for increased protection, creating conflicting goals and assessments of conservation performance relative to their interests as individual states (Brown Weiss, 2000). Communication can emphasize points on which interests of diverse groups align, rather than marginalizing the views of those with different identities, goals, and expectations of performance. For example, regarding wildlife management in North America, communication has emphasized hunters and trappers provide important management capacity to address zoonotic diseases or conflicts arising from wildlife damage to crops or private property. Maintaining broad relevance to overall societal needs may gain public support to sustain opportunities to hunt and trap for the minority of the population that engages in these activities (Geist *et al.*, 2001).

5.10.5 Communication to Influence Behavior Through Norms

Moral and social norms vary in the strength by which they are held by individuals or groups but they commonly exert strong influence on behavior (Tyler, 2000). Unlike the application of deterrence through enforcement, norms have the potential to influence broader cooperation, but only if individuals have the necessary information to recognize connections between existing norms and behaviors required for resource protection (Vandenbergh, 2005). For example, a persuasive communication campaign designed to increase perceptions that individuals important to Michigan bTB area hunters (e.g., family, friends, fellow hunting camp members) supported bTB management goals. Exposure to the communication materials produced detectable increases in perceptions of the existence of social norms regarding bTB reduction, which created the potential to activate social norms (Triezenberg, Gore, Riley, & Lapinski, 2014). Communication can also enhance the influence of norms by creating a threat of informing the public when individuals violate social norms. Agencies or NGOs may publicly highlight occurrences of violations or unacceptable behavior, which may deter others from engaging in such activities in the future (May, 2005).

5.10.6 Communication to Influence Procedural Justice

Procedural justice is determined by judgment of processes, policies, and treatment of individuals. Intentionally addressing the four components that consistently contribute to procedural justice—treating individuals with dignity, providing opportunities for meaningful participation, and demonstrating that authorities are neutral and trustworthy—may improve compliance and cooperation. However, public involvement in wildlife agency decision-making processes is limited by lack of awareness of engagement opportunities (Lord & Cheng, 2006). Communication can increase public awareness of opportunities for input, which may create a need to increase capacity for taking input. For example, direct involvement in the regulatory process led fishermen to be more likely to comply with quota restrictions, but such beneficial outcomes were limited because a minority of fishermen felt that they were significantly involved (Hatcher *et al.*, 2000). Citizens, however, may only demand opportunities for personal input when they do not believe governments implement other aspects of fair and impartial processes for adopting regulations (Tyler, 2000; Rudolph & Riley, 2014). Communication can shape awareness of members of the public well beyond those individuals that directly experience procedurally just processes and policies, regardless of what components of procedural justice may be most critical to gaining compliance and cooperation in any specific context.

5.11 Conclusion

Conserving wildlife for future generations involves restricting consumption to sustainable levels. Regulations, a common method of restricting consumption, imperfectly control legal and illegal harvesting activities due to both unintentional and intentional violations. The imperfect relationship between setting regulations and achievement of intended outcomes can be termed partial controllability. As the only one of four sources of resource management uncertainty that relates directly to intentional management efforts, decision-makers may evaluate and adapt their own actions to realize opportunities to reduce the negative impact of partial controllability on meeting conservation objectives (Nichols, Johnson, & Williams, 1995; Hunter & Runge, 2004). Addressing the influence of partial controllability on regulatory compliance provides a constructive means of improving wildlife harvest management, whether of imperiled species, game animals that are consistently and sustainably harvested, or abundant species that must be reduced to achieve other conservation goals.

Most research exploring drivers of violations has focused exclusively on either instrumental or normative factors, with little integration of both perspectives (von Essen *et al.*, 2014). Considering both instrumental and normative influences can diversify opportunities to proactively prevent crime. Integrated assessment of instrumental and normative influences is especially important when seeking to improve broader cooperation not directly elicited through enforcement (Rudolph & Riley, 2014). Understanding these diverse influences can guide direction of all public policy tools, including government regulations, economic instruments, and communication efforts. When all public policy tools may be directed toward conservation efforts, the benefits of collaborative governance emerge. Collaborative governance approaches allow engagement of an expanded set of actors, and the pooled resources, expertise, and influence they possess can more effectively achieve compliance and cooperation to safeguard public benefits of sustainable use of wildlife (Rudolph *et al.*, 2012).

References

Anderson, L. G., & Lee, D. R. (1986). Optimal governing instrument, operation level, and enforcement in natural resource regulation: The case of the fishery. *American Journal of Agricultural Economics*, 68, 678–690.

Andrén, H., Linnell, J. D. C., Liberg, O., Andersen, R., Danell, A., Karlsson, J., ... & Segerström, P. (2006). Survival rates and causes of mortality in Eurasian lynx (Lynx lynx) in multi-use landscapes. *Biological Conservation*, 131, 23–32.

Beetham, D. (1991). *The legitimation of power*. Atlantic Highlands, NJ: Humanities Press International.

Bell, S., Hampshire, K., & Topalidou, S. (2007). The political culture of poaching: a case study from northern Greece. *Biodiversity and Conservation*, 16, 399–418.

Bemelmans-Videc, M., Rist, R. C., & Vedung, E. (2003). *Carrots, sticks, and sermons: Policy instruments and their evaluation*. Piscataway, NJ: Transaction Publishers.

Braithwaite, V. (1995). Games of engagement: Postures within the regulatory community. *Law and Policy*, 17, 225–255.

Brown Weiss, E. (2000). The five international treaties: A living history. In Brown Weiss, E., &. Jacobson, H. K. (Eds.). *Engaging countries: Strengthening compliance with international environmental accords*. Cambridge, MA: MIT Press.

Bulte, E. H., & Rondeau, D. (2005). Why compensating wildlife damages may be bad for conservation. *Journal of Wildlife Management*, 69, 14–19.

Burby, R. J., & Paterson, R. G. (1993). Improving compliance with state environmental regulations. *Journal of Policy Analysis and Management*, 12, 753–772.

Dickman, A. J., Macdonald, E. A., & Macdonald, D. W. (2011). A review of financial instruments to pay for predator conservation and encourage human–carnivore coexistence. *Proceedings of the National Academy of Sciences*, 108, 13937–13944.

Eliason, S. L. (2004). Accounts of wildlife law violators: Motivations and rationalizations. *Human Dimensions of Wildlife*, 9, 119–131.

Elsken-Lacy, P., Wilson, A. M., Heidt, G. A., & Peck, J. H. (1999) Arkansas gray fox fur price-harvest model revisited. *Journal of the Arkansas Academy of Science*, 53, 50–54.

Falcone, D. (2004). America's conservation police: Agencies in transition. *Policing: an International Journal of Police Strategies and Management*, 27, 56–66.

Garshelis, D. L. (2002). Misconceptions, ironies, and uncertainties regarding trends in bear populations. *Ursus*, 13, 321–334.

Gehrt, S. D., Hubert, G. F., Jr., & Ellis, J. A. (2002). Long-term population trends of raccoons in Illinois. *Wildlife Society Bulletin*, 30, 457–463.

Geist, V., Mahoney, S. P., & Organ, J. F. (2001). Why hunting has defined the North American model of wildlife conservation. *Transactions of the 66th North American Wildlife and Natural Resources Conference*, 66, 175–184.

Grasmick, H. G., & Bursik, R. J., Jr. (1990). Conscience, significant others, and rational choice: Extending the deterrence model. *Law and Society Review*, 24, 837–861.

Gray, B. T., & Kaminski, R. M. (1994). Illegal waterfowl hunting in the Mississippi flyway and recommendations for alleviation. *Wildlife Monographs*, 127, 1–60.

Hatcher, A., Jaffry, S., Thébaud, O., & Bennett, E. (2000). Normative and social influences affecting compliance with fishery regulations. *Land Economics*, 76, 448–461.

Hauck, M. (2008). Rethinking small-scale fisheries compliance. *Marine Policy*, 32, 635–642.

Hauck, M. & Kroese, M. (2006). Fisheries compliance in South Africa: A decade of challenges and reform 1994-2004. *Marine Policy*, 30, 74–83.

Heberlein, T. A. (2012). *Navigating environmental attitudes*. New York, NY: Oxford University Press.

Hiller, R. L., Etter, D. R., Belant, J. L., & Tyre, A. J. (2011). Factors affecting harvests of fishers and American martens in northern Michigan. *Journal of Wildlife Management*, 75, 1399–1405.

Holsman, R. H., & Petchenik, J. (2006). Predicting deer hunter harvest behavior in Wisconsin's chronic wasting disease eradication zone. *Human Dimensions of Wildlife*, 11, 177–189.

Hunter, C. M., & Runge, M. C. (2004). The importance of environmental variability and management control error to optimal harvest policies. *Journal of Wildlife Management*, 68, 585–594.

Kahler, J. S., & Gore, M. L. (2012). Beyond the cooking pot and pocket book: Factors influencing noncompliance with wildlife poaching rules. *International Journal of Comparative and Applied Criminal Justice*, 36, 103–120.

Kapfer, P. M., & Potts, K. B. (2012). Socioeconomic and ecological correlates of bobcat harvest in Minnesota. *Journal of Wildlife Management*, 76, 237–242.

Koen, E. L., Bowman, J., & Findlay, C. S. (2007). Fisher survival in eastern Ontario. *Journal of Wildlife Management*, 71, 1214–1219.

Kretser, H. E. Glennon, M. J. & Smith, Z. (2014). NGOs enhance state wildlife agencies' capacity to meet public trust doctrine obligations. *Human Dimensions of Wildlife*, 19, 437–447.

Levi, M., & Stoker, L. (2000). Political trust and trustworthiness. *Annual Review of Political Science*, 3, 475–507.

Liu, F., McShea, W. J., Garshelis, D. L., Zhu, X., Wanga, D., & Shao, L. (2011). Human-wildlife conflicts influence attitudes but not necessarily behaviors: Factors driving the poaching of bears in China. *Biological Conservation*, 144, 538–547.

Lord, J. K., & Cheng, A. S. (2006). Public involvement in state fish and wildlife agencies in the U.S.: A thumbnail sketch of techniques and barriers. *Human Dimensions of Wildlife*, 11, 55–69.

Maclennan S. D., Groom R. J., Macdonald D. W., & Frank L. G. (2009). Evaluating a compensation scheme to bring about pastoralist tolerance of lions. *Biological Conservation*, 142, 2419–2427.

MacMillan, D. C., & Leitch, K. (2008). Conservation with a gun: Understanding landowner attitudes to deer hunting in the Scottish Highlands. *Human Ecology*, 36, 473–484.

May, P. J. (2005). Regulation and compliance motivations: Examining different approaches. *Public Administration Review*, 65, 31–44.

Mikula, E. J., Martz, F. F., & Bennett, C. L. (1972). Field evaluation of three types of waterfowl hunting regulations. *Journal of Wildlife Management*, 36, 441–459.

Moro, M., Fischer, A., Czajkowski, M., Brennan, D., Lowassa, A., Naiman, L. C., & Hanley, N. (2013). An investigation using the choice experiment method into options for reducing illegal bushmeat hunting in western Serengeti. *Conservation Letters*, 6, 37–45.

Murphy, K. (2005). Regulating more effectively: The relationship between procedural justice, legitimacy, and tax non-compliance. *Journal of Law and Society*, 32, 562–589.

Musgrave, R. S., Parker, S., & Wolok, M. (1993). The status of poaching in the United States: Are we protecting our wildlife? *Natural Resources Journal*, 33, 977–1014.

Muth, R. M., & Bowe, J. F. (1998). Illegal harvest of renewable natural resources in North America: Towards a typology of the motivations for poaching. *Society and Natural Resources*, 11, 9–24.

Nichols, J. D., Johnson, F. A., & Williams, B. K. (1995). Managing North American waterfowl in the face of uncertainty. *Annual Review of Ecology and Systematics*, 26, 177–199.

Prideaux, M. (2014). Wildlife NGOs and the CMS family: Untapped potential for collaborative governance. *Journal of International Wildlife Law & Policy*, 17, 254–274.

Ramsey, D. S. L., O'Brien, D. J., Cosgrove, M. K., Rudolph, B. A., Locher, A. B., & Schmitt, S. M. (2014). Forecasting eradication of bovine tuberculosis in Michigan white-tailed deer. *Journal of Wildlife Management*, 78, 240–54.

Rudolph, B. A. (2012). *Enforcement, personal gains, and normative factors associated with hunter compliance and cooperation with Michigan white-tailed deer and bovine tuberculosis management interventions.* Unpublished doctoral dissertation, Michigan State University.

Rudolph, B. A., & Riley, S. J. (2014). Factors affecting hunters' trust and cooperation. *Human Dimensions of Wildlife*, 19, 469–479.

Rudolph, B. A., Riley, S. J., Hickling, G. J., Frawley, B. J., Garner, M. S., & Winterstein, S. R. (2006). Regulating hunter baiting for white-tailed deer in Michigan: Biological and social considerations. *Wildlife Society Bulletin*, 34, 314–321.

Rudolph, B. A., Schechter, M. G., & Riley, S. J. (2012). Governance of wildlife resources. In Decker, D. J., Riley, S. J., & Siemer, W. F. (Eds). *Human dimensions of wildlife management.* Baltimore, MD: Johns Hopkins University Press.

Sandström, C., Pellilekka, J., & Ratamäki, O. (2009). Management of large carnivores in Fennoscandia: New patterns of regional participation. *Human Dimensions of Wildlife*, 14, 37–50.

Skalski, J. R., Millspaugh, J. J., Clawson, M. V., Belant, J. L., Etter, D. R., Frawley, B. J., & Friedrich, P. D. (2011). Abundance trends of American martens in Michigan based on statistical population reconstruction. *Journal of Wildlife Management*, 75, 1767–1773.

Stryker, R. (1994). Rules, resources, and legitimacy processes: Some implications for social conflict, order, and change. *American Journal of Sociology*, 99, 847–910.

Sunshine, J., & Tyler, T. R. (2003). The role of procedural justice and legitimacy in shaping public support for policing. *Law and Society Review*, 37, 513–548.

Sutinen, J. G., & Kuperan, K. (1999). A socio-economic theory of regulatory compliance. *International Journal of Social Economics*, 26, 174–193.

Treves, A., & Bruskotter, J. (2014). Tolerance for predatory wildlife. *Science*, 344, 476–477.

Triezenberg, H. A., Gore, M. L., Riley, S. J., & Lapinski, M. K. (2014). Persuasive communication aimed at achieving wildlife-disease management goals. *Wildlife Society Bulletin*, 38, 734–740.

Tyler, T. R. (1990). *Why people obey the law.* New Haven: Yale University Press.

Tyler, T. R. (1994). Governing amid diversity: The effect of fair decision-making procedures on the legitimacy of government. *Law and Society Review*, 28, 809–831.

Tyler, T. R. (2000). Social justice: Outcome and procedure. *International Journal of Psychology*, 35, 117–125.

Tyler, T. R. (2003). Procedural justice, legitimacy, and the effective rule of law. *Crime and Justice*, 30, 283–357.

Vandenbergh, M. P. (2005). Order without social norms: How personal norm activation can protect the environment. *Northwestern University Law Review*, 99, 1101–1166.

Vaske, J. J., & Manfredo, M. J. (2012). Social psychological considerations in wildlife management. In Decker, D. J., Riley, S. J., & Siemer, W. F. (Eds.). *Human dimensions of wildlife management*. Baltimore, MD: Johns Hopkins University Press.

von Essen, E., Hansen, H. P., Källström, H. N., Peterson, M. N., & Peterson, T. R. (2014). Deconstructing the poaching phenomenon: A review of typologies for understanding illegal hunting. *British Journal of Criminology*, 54, 632–651.

Weimer, D. L., & Vining, A. R. (2005). *Policy analysis: Concepts and practice*. Upper Saddle River, NJ: Pearson Prentice Hall.

Wilcove, D. S., & Lee, J. (2004). Using economic and regulatory incentives to restore endangered species: Lessons learned from three new programs. *Conservation Biology*, 18, 639–645.

Winter, S. C., & May, P. J. (2001). Motivation for compliance with environmental regulations. *Journal of Policy Analysis and Management*, 20, 675–698.

Zabel, A., & Holm-Müller, K. (2008). Conservation performance payments for carnivore conservation in Sweden. *Conservation Biology*, 22, 247–251.

Zimmerman, M. E. (2003). The black market for wildlife: Combating transnational organized crime in the illegal wildlife trade. *Vanderbilt Journal of Transnational Law*, 36, 1657–1689.

6

Corruption and Organized Crime in Conservation

Aksel Sundström and Tanya Wyatt

Although corruption and organized crime affect most domains of societies where they are present, they are difficult to analyze since involved parties are keen to hide these practices. Both are illicit activities that function in the background of many formal processes. Regardless of their hidden nature there is still much research devoted to analysis of corruption and organized crime and a growing body of research addresses these issues in the conservation context. This chapter explores the impact of corruption and organized crime on conservation practices and the perpetration of conservation crime. The existing scholarly literature engages separately with corruption and organized crime as they relate to conservation. Few studies have analyzed how these concepts are interlinked and how they relate to conservation crime. The aim of this chapter is to synthesize these separate knowledge bases to give an increased understanding of the intertwined nature of corruption and organized crime as it relates to conservation. Drawing heavily from the fields of political science and criminology we seek to advance current thinking on the risks associated with corruption and organized crime in conservation.

The term conservation crime implies a violation of existing formal conservation regulations. This definition is nuanced, since legal actions related to the protection and extraction of resources are not always justifiable (e.g., certain large-scale logging concessions) and some illegal acts may in fact be normatively acceptable (e.g., subsistence gathering of wood in protected areas). A focus on crime in a conservation context potentially risks putting the blame on small individual actors instead of larger actors that are perhaps better equipped at hiding their practices continue their illicit behavior (Richards, Wells, Del Gatto, Contreras-Hermosilla, & Pommier, 2003). Therefore, scholars often use terms such as misuse or destruction of resources to define acts in conservation management that are morally unwanted (Hafner, 1998). Yet, these terms are imprecise and therefore not very useful in designing, implementing, and evaluating interventions designed to reduce risks from corruption and organized crime. This is partly the reason why some criminologists have suggested the term conservation crime instead of green or environmental crime, as it denotes a violation of formal conservation rules rather than an abuse of a vaguely defined environmental value (see Gibbs, Gore, McGarrell, & Rivers, 2010). Exactly what criminality is, and what actions are justifiable, in conservation are normative issues that are discussed elsewhere in the

Conservation Criminology, First Edition. Edited by Meredith L. Gore.

literature. Conservation crime for the purposes of this chapter involves people breaking codified laws created by governing bodies across the world.

The relationship between governance and conservation outcomes has a dynamic history. The literature within economics and political science on resource curses, or the insight that natural wealth may be harmful for the governance of a country, addresses how natural resource abundance (e.g., reserves of oils, diamonds, timber) may give rise to rent-seeking (i.e., a looting mentality among an elite that seek primarily to enrich itself and their kin). The literature also considers corruption within the state apparatus and how being embedded reduces incentives to improve governance (see Mehlum, Moene, & Torvik, [2006] for an overview). This chapter focuses on a different aspect of the connection between governance and natural resources. In particular, we explore the nexus of corruption and organized crime, specifically what enabling actions the presence of these two features has on conservation crime. Our exploration then considers possibilities are for overcoming risks associated with corruption and organized crime.

Corruption in conservation is not a new phenomenon. There is long-term evidence of corrupt practices surrounding extraction and exploitation of natural resources including timber, oil, minerals, and wildlife (Brack, 2003; Brack & Hayman, 2002). The theft of these natural resources not only benefits individuals, but also gives profits to corporations and states (Green & Ward, 2004). What arguably is a new evolution in terms of corruption in conservation is the link to organized crime and the resulting globally pervasive and resilient black environmental markets this connection has helped to fuel. Corruption and organized crime generally have negative implications for states, citizens, and natural resources, especially where they co-occur and in regions in which one group has a monopoly over resources.

At the extreme, corrupt access to natural resources such as water and arable land can be considered human rights violations. In Bolivia and other areas where water has been privatized, ownership over public goods can result in everyday people being unable to access and afford resources essential to survival (Kane, 2012). Corruption can divert finances and resources that support social services such as healthcare, education, and infrastructure. For instance, bribery of customs officers to avoid being charged import or export duties on timber or other natural resources means the government loses out on essential revenue designated to fund social services. Organized crime has been shown to have the power to destabilize regimes and operate with violence, thus threatening the ability of law enforcement officials to do their jobs effectively (Fijnaut, Bovenkerk, Bruinsma, & van de Bunk, 1998; Van Duyne, 1997). Moreover, organized crime, which is discussed in detail in the next section, is known to play an increased role in current natural resource trafficking (Brack & Hayman, 2002). This role has downstream implications for increased habitat degradation and biodiversity loss (Wyatt, 2013). Conservation and anti-corruption institutions can be aware of and address connections and synergies between the corruption and organized crime sectors because both impose environmentally damaging impacts as well as negative implications for human well being.

This chapter explores extant research in order to define and explain the role and extent to which organized crime and corruption factor into the conservation world; we draw heavily from political science and criminology. It then analyzes these connections through case studies of abalone poaching in South Africa and illegal trade of falcons in the Russian Far East. These two cases illustrate different aspects of how corruption and organized crime synergize in imposing risks to conservation initiatives as well as the biodiversity and humans the initiatives are designed to protect. Finally, there is a policy-oriented discussion of the possible solutions.

6.1 Connecting Corruption and Organized Crime to Conservation

6.1.1 Defining Corruption and Organized Crime

There are no universal definitions of corruption. Yet the concept of corruption can be defined as "the misuse of public power for private gain" (Treisman, 2007, p. 211). Generally, distinctions are made regarding where it occurs, who is involved, and on what scale. Whereas large-scale corruption focus on the decision-makers that shape policy, small-scale corruption often concerns petty bribes and involves public officers that implement such policy (Hellman, Jones, & Kaufmann, 2000). Corruption on a grand scale surely fuels the overexploitation of resources, since such actions can prevent policymakers from passing bills that, for instance, increase the area of land designated as a National Park. Yet, in terms of daily activities, corruption by local level officers is more relevant to conservation. Such small-scale transactions are more common and widespread, and therefore will be the focus of the chapter. Among the examples of small-scale bribery, there is an important distinction between collusive and non-collusive corruption. In collusive corruption, government officials overlook citizens' violations of laws in exchange for bribes, for example, to let loggers enter a protected area without sanctions. Non-collusive corruption, on the other hand, refers to the practice among bureaucrats to ask citizens for money to obtain services that they are legally entitled to, for example when giving out permits for exports of resources (Smith, Obidzinski, Wood, & Suramenggala, 2003).

Small-scale collusive and non-collusive corrupt acts are fairly common across cultures and societies and around the world. In many places, cultural norms and traditions seem to demonstrate widespread recognition of certain corrupt practices, thus making them more overt (see Gore, Ratsimbazafy, & Lute, 2013). Yet, although it may be more overt in some places than in others, there is little empirical support of the notion that corruption is actually more accepted in some countries than in others. In fact, although there are large differences in what has been seen to belong to the public and private sphere, there seems to be a norm across time and space that morally condemns behavior that enriches public servants and benefits a specific few individuals (see Rothstein & Torsello, 2014). There are actions that are viewed as corrupt in virtually all cultures and societies (Holmes, 2006). These acts are when a public official (be they elected or appointed) commits an act out of self-interest or for interest of an organization, instead of in the interest of the government or the public. Additionally, the act is often committed in secret to hide the inappropriateness or illegality. For example, even though it may be commonplace in some places for officials to ask for bribes to do work they are professionally tasked with doing, citizens still see engagement in such behavior as corruption.

Some types of corruption are not as universal. Specifically, many cultures have differing opinions on clientelism and nepotism. In many places, it is acceptable for a government employee to grant benefits to family members. Approval of these sorts of actions may depend heavily on culture and social conditions. Robbins (2000, p. 425) delineated this issue by recognizing, "corruption in natural resource management is defined as the use or overuse of community (state, village, city) natural resources with the consent of a state agent by those not legally entitled." Robbins (2000, p. 425) added, "it is the extension of existing non-economic relationships (family, 'friendship,' and other socially obligating relations) that determines access to these use rights through normative systems of expected exchange." Thus, corruption is not only the absence of strong state institutions but also the presence of differing institutions where deception, secrecy, and benefit are interlinked in social practices.

Similarly, there is no universal definition of organized crime. In general, organized crime groups are "structured groups committing serious crime for profit" (Buscaglia & van Dijk, 2003, p. 5). Key within this definition is that organized crime groups are non-ideological and motivated purely by profit (Abadinsky, 2007). This means, for example, that organized groups will smuggle any commodity that is economically favorable for them to smuggle. This is evident in the diversity of smuggling operations associated with organized crime such as counterfeit DVDs, weapons, drugs, and wildlife. In order to protect profits organized crime syndicate members are willing to resort to violence and to bribery (Fijnaut, Bovenkerk, Bruinsma, & van de Bunk, 1998; Van Duyne, 1997). Thus, corruption is an integral tool of organized criminal networks and the use of bribes is essential for such groups' survival. For instance, the anti-corruption resource center U4 (2008) found that criminal networks are reliant on both corrupt police forces and customs officials. These corrupt individuals enable smuggling by turning a blind eye, destroying evidence, providing intelligence, assisting in the registration of stolen vehicles, and misdeclaring or undervaluing shipments. There is also a temporal dimension within most definitions of organized crime. Organized criminal groups are not engaged in single criminal acts but rather have a history or the intention of continuing criminal acts over time (Abadinsky, 2007). The high level of profits acquired, the use of violence, and the longevity amount to the seriousness of crime committed by these groups in comparison to other crime. As we demonstrate in the case studies, many of the various elements of organized crime are present in conservation.

6.1.2 The Role and Extent of Corruption and Organized Crime in Conservation Crime

In regards to conservation, corruption features in the access, acquisition, and smuggling of natural resources. Corruption is in many cases an essential prerequisite for conservation crime to thrive. Large-scale corruption is important since it may be used to influence policymakers to relax conservation legislation and regulations. For example, a logging company may bribe politicians to downgrade the status of, or degazette, a protected forest to allow logging operations (see Smith, Obidzinski, Wood, & Suramenggala, 2003). The actual act of extracting such resources is then technically not illegal. The criminal act is the bribe before the extraction, which may be seen as an indirect conservation crime. More directly, small-scale types of collusive corruption are used to enable extracting agents to violate laws and regulations protecting natural resources. For instance, illegal logging within protected areas is often enabled when enforcement officers take bribes to overlook the extractive activity (see Robbins, 2000). In many contexts, such actions are violations of laws and are defined as criminal. Several studies provide evidence that corruption is one of the major culprits in failures of ineffective conservation interventions. Widespread corruption is correlated with increased deforestation, violations of regulations protecting marine resources and, more broadly, increased levels of pollution (e.g., Agnew *et al.*, 2009; Halkos, Sundström, & Tzeremes, 2015; Kyoucu & Yilmaz, 2009). Studies of corruption in natural resource management at the local level find that bribery tends to give rise to an increase of violations of regulations of fisheries and forest reserves (e.g., Miller, 2011; Sundström, 2012; 2013). For example, members of eastern Pakistan's timber mafia have bribed custom officers such that endangered timber is easily smuggled across borders. Members pull strings with certain politicians and pay bribes to control officers and enable the trafficking of timber. Other examples of collusion between corrupt forest officers and criminal networks that illegally harvest protected area resources exists in countries such as Indonesia (Palmer, 2001), Mexico (Klooster, 2000), Tanzania (Milledge, Gelvas, & Ahrends, 2007), Benin (Siebert & Elbert, 2004), Malaysia (Dauvergne, 1997), Brazil (Laurence, Albernaz, & Da Costa, 2001), and Honduras and Nicaragua (Richards *et al.*, 2003). These studies affirm corruption contributes to the failure of conservation efforts. Research from Uganda and Nepal suggests bribery diverted international aid funds from intended conservation schemes to the pockets of bureaucrats or politicians (Cavanagh, 2012; Iversen *et al.*, 2006).

Organized crime is centrally involved in smuggling natural resources around the world. Their involvement may be increasing because of the low risk and high profits that are often found in environmental black markets (Brack, 2003; Cook, Roberts, & Lowther, 2002). The greater the profits associated with the illegal activity, the greater the logistical complications, the greater the cost of avoiding law enforcement, and the greater the involvement of organized criminal groups in movement of natural resources (Wyatt, 2013). Seemingly, this is because of the lure of profits, the main motivation of organized crime groups, but also because the more complicated the smuggling operation, the more sophisticated the perpetration needs to be in order to achieve success. Prime examples of resources that are smuggled by organized crime syndicates include the widespread trade with wild parrots in Latin America and pangolins in East Asia. These smuggling operations are complicated in that they take place across long distances with numerous checks from regulatory and enforcement agencies (Wyatt, 2013). Organized criminal groups have the knowledge and experience as well as the connections to accept and overcome the potential risks of getting caught during multiple stages in the supply chain.

6.1.3 Why do Environmental Black Markets Exist?

It is important to understand which natural resource commodities are the primary targets of conservation crimes in order to help prevent these crimes from happening. We focus on the conditions that lead to the existence of environmental black markets because of their association with corruption and organized crime. Such insight can help analyze case studies of conservation crime. Corruption and organized crime protect environmental black markets both on the demand and supply side of the illicit trade. There are three factors that drive black markets (Brack, 2003). First, there needs to be demand for a product for which a suitable substitute does not exist. Second, there must be regulatory failures, in the form of lenient or absent structures to protect property and natural resources, that permit suppliers to source products and consumers to be able to access the products easily. Third, there must be a lack of effective enforcement against suppliers and consumers of illegal products. Regulatory and enforcement failures may have a diverse range of causes including lack of funding, resources and infrastructure, corruption, lack of political will or disruption of political processes, or because the methods of enforcement used are not what are needed (Brack, 2003).

The factors that predict the existence of environmental black markets are similar to the circumstances under which organized crime thrives. Although multiple factors are associated with thriving organized crime syndicates, none of them are individually necessary for organized crime to exist. There are five opportunity factors required for organized crime to persist (a) distinct economic conditions; (b) failure of government regulation; (c) lack of enforcement effectiveness; (d) demand for a product or service; (e) creation of new product or service market through technological or social change (Albanese, 2000). Synthesizing the suite of factors typically present where both black markets and organized crime thrive (Table 6.1), we present below two cases to give a brief illustration of how corruption and organized crime may be interlinked in their effects on conservation crime and how these links may play out in real world conservation situations.

6.2 Case Study on Abalone Poaching

6.2.1 The Context of Bureaucratic Corruption and Presence of Criminal Groups

Organized crime and corruption factor centrally in the illegal harvesting of abalone in South Africa (Sundström, 2016). Abalone is an edible marine mollusk also known as perlemoen that is harvested mainly through diving. It is a highly valuable export that is increasingly demanded as a gourmet food in East Asia. The abalone-harvesting sector was largely unregulated until 1998, when South Africa promulgated the Marine Living Resources Act (MLRA) to regulate marine fisheries. Following high levels of overexploitation, commercial fishing was closed in 2007 and 2008 and abalone was added as a protected species under the Convention on International Trade in Endangered Species of Wild Fauna and Flora (CITES), meaning it could not be exported without a permit (Platt, 2010). In 2010, the legal ban was lifted; however, the abalone fishery remains heavily regulated by the

Table 6.1 Characterizing the factors influencing the existence of black markets and the involvement of organized crime.

	Black Markets	Organized Crime
FACTORS		Economic Conditions • Poverty • Transitioning economies • Crises
	Regulatory Failure • Weak oversight • Lack of property rights • Little regard for protection	Government Regulation • Weak oversight • Lack of property rights
	Enforcement Failure • Law enforcement and regulators cannot (limited resources and staff) or choose not to try to prevent, investigate and prosecute offenders	Enforcement Effectiveness • Law enforcement and regulators cannot (limited resources and staff) or choose not to try to prevent, investigate and prosecute offenders
	Demand for Product • Consumers for the illicit good	Demands for Product/Service • Consumers for the illicit good
		Creation of New Product/Service Market • Influencing consumer demand by offering an innovative product

Adapted from Brack (2003) and Albanese (2000).

Compliance Directorate of the Department for Agriculture, Forestry and Fisheries (DAFF), whose enforcement officers have limited training in conservation and relatively low salary levels. DAFF officers are tasked with patrolling landing sites and harbors to ensure that fishers are compliant with the rules. The rate of noncompliance with fishing rules remains very high; some studies report that at times, almost the entire abalone catch has been caught illegally (Raemaekers & Britz 2009, p. 184). Apart from widespread noncompliance among fishers and perceptions of illegitimate management institutions, organized crime has complicated abalone fishery conservation and management. Organized criminal elements are thought to have entered into the fishery during the 1990s as extraction of this resource became increasingly profitable (Hauck & Fernández-Gallardo, 2013; Raemaekers *et al.*, 2011). Overtime, abalone poaching has become increasingly associated with violent groups protecting a steady source of income in distant localities along the coast where government enforcement is weak. At the same time regulatory changes were taking place, the South African fisheries sector was plagued by corruption in the compliance directorate (Hauck & Sweijd, 1999). Local enforcement officers within the directorate received monetary and non-monetary bribes (e.g., boxes of fish) from fishers in order to overlook rule violations (Sundström, 2013). In addition to turning a blind eye to conservation crimes, inspectors paid back those who bribed them by becoming informants for poachers, sharing secret details of enforcement operations, or an active part themselves in poaching activities (Sundström, 2015).

A cross-sectional analysis reveals several of the factors associated with organized crime and black markets are present in the case of South African abalone poaching. First, the fishers actively sought ways to supplement their fishing income, meaning that the socioeconomic conditions were favorable for organized crime to enter the sector. Additionally, national and international regulations made much of the abalone harvest illegal and enforcement effectiveness was perceived as being weak; ineffective regulations and poor enforcement are factors that are associated with organized crime prevalence in general. In terms of the factors contributing to the existence of black markets, abalone is a product without any substitute. Although unfortunate, it is somewhat unsurprising that organized criminal groups entered into this natural resource context, or that they emerged from established street gangs in the city of Cape Town. South African gangs traded abalone with criminal organizations connected to mainland China, Hong Kong, and Taiwan in exchange for crystal methamphetamine, known locally as "tik" (de Greef & Raemaekers, 2014, p. 6), complicating an already complex conservation problem.

6.2.2 The Investigation

The description of this case draws on insights from 34 confidential interviews that were performed with inspectors at the compliance directorate of DAFF in 2014 (Sundström, 2016). Former inspectors who no longer faced risks for speaking openly about bribe taking were also interviewed as well as a number of former senior managers of this directorate and key stakeholders.

6.2.3 Non-Corrupt Inspectors are Threatened

The presence and activities of violent groups in the abalone sector spotlight corruption. Both outright criminals that found an extra income from abalone poaching as well as fishers living off poaching abalone were able to bribe and coerce inspectors in order to conceal their activities. If the inspectors could not be bought off, a practice that evidently was widespread, they were instead threatened, as described below. Accounts from enforcement officers illustrated the presence of violent threats in their line of work. When approaching abalone poachers, they faced physical intimidation some feared might be lethal. For instance, one enforcement officer described:

> "Three years ago I did a bust [attempting to catch abalone poachers] and it went bad. They threw a firebomb, burning me. And we exchanged gunfire. So they put a price on my head, over 150 000 Rand. So I had to move to this station. And the sad thing is that it was my own people who had tipped them off, sharing information about this operation." *(Enforcement officer, Sundström, 2016).*

As the account suggests, the presence of corrupt officers who colluded with poachers and worked as informants caused honest inspectors to be targeted for violence. Honesty was, in this situation, a threat to both noncompliant abalone fishers and officers that benefited from corrupt practices. Accounts therefore showed how dangerous this situation could get:

> "Last week I almost got stabbed. I drove in my patrol car and saw how these guys were hiding their illegal catches. So I parked my car next to them. Then one broke a bottle, coming towards me and another one had a knife. ... So it is very risky. It is much easier to be blind. Some inspectors are more blind than others. And these officers will receive some fish. Not in the harbor, but to their homes, as a gratitude." *(Enforcement officer, Sundström, 2016).*

Therefore, if an enforcement officer was honest, they did so at high personal cost. It is noteworthy that being corrupt provided certain benefits to officers including both job security and personal protection against future violence. For example:

> "If you take bribes you are protected. You have a role in the community. You got organization protection and police protection. In the community this is a social thing. They will start helping you. Some inspectors even help the poachers drive their vehicles. So its protection, social protection." *(Enforcement officer, Sundström, 2016).*

In this corrupt context, some conservation officers chose to collude with criminal elements to protect themselves, at the expense of the abalone fishery. Corrupt inspectors, in turn, became informants that could tell when non-colluding officers would do random operations.

A lack of deterrence had severe consequences for conservation management as acts of conservation crime went unpunished. In this context, it became increasingly costly for conservation enforcement officers to remain honest. This case highlighted that, in a situation where organized crime had become present, taking bribes was one protection strategy for officers and it reduced the pressure of harassments. This seldom discussed conclusion is important as it implies that focusing on protecting the physical security of conservation officers may be a key measure to reduce incentives for bribe-taking.

6.3 Case Study on Illegal Trade in Russian Raptors

Falcons and other birds of prey such as some hawks and eagles have been used in the sport of falconry for centuries in the Near, Middle and Far East (Epstein, 1943). The practice became more widespread globally during the Middle Ages, but has recently retracted again mostly to the Middle and Far East. In these regions, people maintain the traditional of using these raptors to hunt small mammals, reptiles and other birds (Ash, 2007; Epstein, 1943). The supply of raptors for falconry either comes from captive bred birds or wild birds taken from their native habitats (Oswald, 1982). In both instances, if the trade is taking place internationally trade is regulated under CITES guidelines.

Several decades ago large populations of wild raptors were found in Central Asia (Lyapustin, 2006). Because these populations have collapsed due in large part to the illegal trade, smugglers have refocused their efforts to the Russian Far East to capture wild raptors to fill demand (Lyapustin, 2006). Eggs or live birds are taken from their nests by experts able to locate and identify the proper species. The raptors are then smuggled over thousands of miles to the Middle East by plane, ship, rail, and road (Wyatt, 2012). The final buyer pays an estimated $U.S. 50,000 to 100,000 for the bird when it arrives. Although Russia is a member of CITES and has implemented the required legislation to comply (in this case federal Article 188 prohibiting smuggling of contraband), there are few prosecutions, arrests, or seizures related to wildlife trafficking in general or raptor smuggling in particular in the nation (Wyatt, 2012). For instance, even though it is suspected that 500 to 600 raptors are captured every year, between 1992 and 2005 only six incidents were reported to CITES (Wyatt, 2012). This indicates that although regulation is present there is a lack of enforcement on multiple levels, which is one of the criteria for the creation of black markets. Additional enforcement failures including those linked to corruption will be detailed shortly. Compounding the probability of creation of a black market, there are no substitute "products" for raptors.

The eggs and raptors used for falconry are captured alive and highly valuable, thus smuggling is an extremely secretive practice that requires extensive coordination. The combination of high profits and complex perpetration in conjunction with little government enforcement appears to have attracted the services of organized crime (Albanese, 2000; Wyatt, 2012). These groups of organized criminals are based in the demand countries and then work within Russia. There are organized crime groups in Russia, however they thought to be involved only in other wildlife black markets, such as illegal caviar (Wyatt, 2012).

Integral to the success of trafficking falcons from the Russian Far East to the Middle East is bribery of border and custom agents as well as of transportation sector officials along the smuggling route. Those bribed are given money to look the other way as raptors are wrapped in cloth and tranquilized, stuffed into tubes and suitcases, and then carried on whichever form of transportation has been arranged. Alternatively, in some cases, transportation employees are paid to carry the falcons themselves or forge paperwork (Wyatt, 2012). The organized crime group generally coordinates the smuggling route, paying off the necessary agents as the raptors work their way from Russia through Central Asia to Saudi Arabia and the United Arab Emirates (Wyatt, 2012). There is little evidence of human violence being used in the perpetration of raptor smuggling, which may not correspond to most definitions of organized crime. Ultimately it is difficult to know the scope of crimes committed by the groups that are smuggling these birds, and there might be violence that goes unreported.

The case of illegal trade in live falcons from the Russian Far East through Central Asia and into the Middle East provides important insights. It highlights that the power of organized crime over corrupt individuals, be it customs personnel or transportation workers, enables these actors to avoid scrutiny of regulatory agencies and thus their conservation crime goes unnoticed. Attitudinal surveys indicate many Russians tolerate corrupt practices although they recognize it as corruption (Holmes, 2006). In other words, even though there is agreement that taking bribes in particular is morally wrong and denotes an abuse of power, there is recognition that corruption is required to do business. Thus, many people supposedly accept it as part of life (Holmes, 2006). In this sense, corruption is normalized. This acceptance could possibly mean that organized crime, which is so tightly intertwined with corruption, is also considered morally wrong yet accepted.

6.4 A Policy-Oriented Discussion of Solutions

The negative effects of corruption and organized crime on conservation may be reduced in part by reforming policies. Below, we identify key areas for policy reform that are based on our synthesis linking the two phenomena (Table 6.1). We critique how these reforms might effect corruption and organized crime in conservation.

6.4.1 Supporting Non-Corrupt Officials That Receive Threats

The experiences of law enforcement officers in the abalone sector in South Africa coupled with knowledge that many park guards in reserves that protect biodiversity face intimidations from organized poachers reminds us that control officers work under constant threat from criminals. As shown in the abalone case study, the presence of organized crime-related violence may push officers that would otherwise act honestly into situations where they collude with offenders and act against the law. In such situations, control officers may need support from institutions designed for this specific purpose. For example, enforcement officers working under threat of violent conditions can be supported by threat assessments that determine vulnerability and guide interventions (Fein & Vossekuil, 2000). Support would be ideally provided by external independent authorities not included in the sector and therefore not involved in local corrupt networks. Creating an independent agency could potentially offer effective protection for officers through threat assessments and security measures, but such agencies are not themselves completely immune to corruption. Future policies to counter organized crime and reducing incentives for corruption in conservation programs may benefit from designing similar protection schemes adapted to the local context. Although this policy reform does not offer a complete solution to the problem of threats to conservation officers, it does facilitate a systematized support structure and cultural norm of reform. Future research needs to unpack the details and impacts of such support and protections schemes.

6.4.2 Complement Merit-Based Reforms with External Monitoring Mechanisms

A second policy reform is that conservation officers can be better compensated in order to reduce their financial incentives for corrupt behavior (Pfaff, Amacher, & Sills, 2014). This reform is commonly suggested for officials in developing nations where salaries are notoriously low. Obviously, this reform can be difficult to implement with limited funds and stretched budgets. Empirically, there is mixed evidence about whether increased levels of the fixed salary for public officials reduce corruption rates (Dahlström, Lapuente, & Teorell, 2012; Treisman, 2007; Van Rijckeghem & Weder, 2001). Alternatively, performance-based pay to civil servants can incentivize officials to refuse bribery and other corrupt opportunities (Olken & Pande, 2012). Again, the case of South African abalone management provides insight into the challenges of such reforms, and shows anti-corruption polices may be easily taken over by existing corrupt networks. In South Africa, a reform of performance-related pay for enforcement officers in the DAFF intended to reduce corruption instead became an incentive for corrupt behavior (Sundström, 2014). In DAFF, senior managers charged with assessing the performance of junior enforcement officials were themselves corrupt. They therefore wound up rewarding the junior officers who they trusted to join in collusion, ultimately intending to keep the status quo of bribery from fishers. The salary bonuses allocated as part of this program wound up being used selectively as rewards to officers who were corrupt rather than officers who had a record of good enforcement. Officers that did not engage in bribery were professionally isolated and received no bonuses. The program ultimately created disincentives for honest behavior. These findings reaffirm claims that, "anticorruption efforts seem to ultimately have become entangled in the very corrupt networks that they were meant to fight" (Persson, Rothstein, & Teorell, 2013, p. 454). Such reforms may therefore need to be accompanied by external monitoring mechanisms, potentially by the third sector parties or NGOs to ensure that corrupt managers do not improperly redirect bonuses for honesty.

6.4.3 Public Awareness Campaigns May Help Decrease Demand for Illicit Goods

Both case studies profiled in this chapter demonstrate organized crime groups use corruption as a tool to perpetrate their crimes. In these instances, bribery was used as a means to secure access to natural resources and to clear pathways for smuggling those natural resources from source to markets. Corruption through bribery or force also allows trafficking of environmental commodities to go purposely unnoticed. Corruption and organized crime may be entangled with cultural norms. In Russia, research has shown that corruption, although viewed by the general public as morally wrong, is still widely practiced, and normalized. Such pervasiveness and acceptance may lead to both corruption and organized crime being culturally entrenched in some cultures. In these contexts, reform is particularly difficult to tackle because it is not solely a law enforcement problem. Different reform approaches can be applied in the contexts to reduce risks associated with conservation crimes. Public awareness campaigns or other communication techniques may be employed to help counter corruptions' culturally embedded nature and have proven successful in a number of conservation crime contexts. For instance, the World Wildlife Fund's "Hands Off My Parts" campaign and WildAid's use of celebrities such as Jackie Chan and Yao Ming as spokespersons employ persuasive communication techniques. The goal of these efforts is to change people's view of elephants, rhinos, and tigers not as products to be bought, but individuals who deserve to live; ultimately they aim to challenges social norms (Wyatt, 2013). Similar approaches may work to challenge acceptance of corruption and organized crime.

6.4.4 A Cooperative Network Approach to Combating Organized Crime

Organized crime cannot be combated by a single agency in isolation from larger support structures and organizations. Cooperative task forces can be stronger and more effective for conservation crimes in general (INTERPOL, 2013). In the conservation crime context, INTERPOL has advocated for having National Environmental Security Taskforces (NESTs), composed of police authorities, customs services, forensic scientists, prosecutors, and environmental regulators in a permanent collaboration administered at a national level. NESTs include the National Central Bureaus of INTERPOL as well as law enforcement that is tasked with fighting organized crime. Cooperation in fighting organized crime can also come from countries having signed the United Nations Convention Against Transnational Organized Crime, which ensures signatory states implement legislation to address organized crime including money laundering, obstruction and corruption (UNODC, 2014). Connections between organized crime and corruption persists in the conservation sector; more concerted efforts to disrupt the connections can be made.

6.5 Conclusion

Organized crime and corruption are often interlinked and together they function to facilitate conservation crimes. As is evident from the two examples detailed here, black markets involving the commercial trade of wildlife such as abalone and raptors arise when a number of factors are present. At a minimum, there must be demand for illegal goods for which there are no suitable substitutes in the eyes of the buyer. For example, although it is technically easy to produce ivory-like materials, there is still a demand for authentic ivory in East Asia. Moreover, there is a large amount of money to be made from such trafficking authentic natural resources, both in the short-term smuggling of high-value resources and the long-term income from smuggling resources with relatively smaller gains. The complexity of smuggling such items and the high profits attract the involvement of organized crime groups. These groups work to corrupt public and private officials to successfully sell their products without getting caught. Arresting the negative effects of corruption and organized crime may be achieved in part by more actively protecting non-corrupt officials, and supporting honest officials with incentive programs that are effectively monitored to prevent corruption from breeding more corruption. Additionally, governments can challenge the cultural ubiquity of corruption and organized crime in some areas and collaboratively combat organized crime, which will in turn also combat corruption. Because large-scale conservation crimes are so often associated with corruption and organized crime, policy solutions that minimize corruption and organized crime are an important step in the direction of reducing risks associated with conservation crime as a whole.

References

Abadinsky, H. (2007). *Organized Crime*, 8th edition. Belmont, CA: Wadsworth/ Thomson Learning.

Albanese, J. (2000). The causes of organized crime. *Journal of Contemporary Criminal Justice*, 16, 409–423.

Agnew J. D., Pearce, J., Pramod, G., Peatman, T., Watson, R., Beddington, J. R., & Pitcher, T. J. (2009). Estimating the worldwide extent of illegal fishing. PloSONE, 4, 1–8.

Ash, L. (2007). A Falconry Timeline. Retrieved from http://www.themodernapprentice.com/history.htm

Brack, D. (2003). Lessons from the control of the illegal trade in ozone-depleting substances, timber and fisheries. In Oldfield, S. (Ed.). *The trade in wildlife: Regulation for conservation*. London: Earthscan.

Brack, D., & Hayman, G. (2002). *International environmental crime: The nature and control of environmental black markets*. London: The Royal Institute of International Affairs.

Buscaglia, E., & van Dijk, J. (2003). Controlling organized crime and corruption in the public sector. *Forum on Crime and Society*, 2, 1–32.

Cavanagh, C. (2012). *Unready for REDD? Lessons from corruption in Ugandan conservation area*. U4 Brief 2012,3. Bergen: Christian Michelsen Institute.

Cook, D., Roberts, M., & Lowther, J. (2002). *The international wildlife trade and organized crime: A review of the evidence and role of the United Kingdom*. Retrieved from www.wwf.org.uk/filelibrary/pdf/organisedCrime.pdf

Dahlström, C., Lapuente, V., & Teorell, J. (2012). The merit of meritocratization: Politics, bureaucracy, and the institutional deterrents of corruption. *Political Research Quarterly*, 65, 656–668.

Dauvergne, P. (1997). *Shadows in the forest: Japan and the politics of timber in Southeast Asia*. Cambridge, MA: The MIT Press.

Epstein, H. (1943). The origins and earliest history of falconry. *Isis*, 34, 497–509.

Fein, R.A., & Vossekuil, B. (2000). *Protective intelligence and threat assessment investigations: A guide for state and local law enforcement officials*. Washington, D. C.: National Institute of Justice

Fijnaut, C., Bovenkerk, F., Bruinsma, G., & van de Bunk, H. (1998). *Organized crime in the Netherlands*. Leiden, The Netherlands: Brill Publishing.

Gibbs, C. E., Gore, M. L., McGarrell, E. F. & Rivers III, L. (2010). Introducing conservation criminology: Towards interdisciplinary scholarship on environmental crimes and risks. British Journal of Criminology, 50, 124–144.

Gore, M. L., Ratsimbazafy, J., & Lute, M. L. (2013). Rethinking corruption in conservation crime: Insights from Madagascar. Conservation Letters, 6, 430–438.

de Greef, K., & Raemaekers, S. (2014). *South Africa's illicit abalone trade: An updated overview and knowledge gap analysis*. Cambridge, United Kingdom: TRAFFIC International.

Green, P., & Ward, T. (2004). *State crime: Governments, violence and corruption*. London: Sterling.

Hafner, O. (1998). *The role of corruption in the misappropriation of tropical forest resources and in tropical forest destruction*. Transparency International Working Paper. Retrieved from http://resources.transparency.bg/download.html?id=235

Halkos, G., Sundström, A, & Tzeremes, N. (2015). Regional environmental performance and governance quality: A nonparametric analysis. *Environmental Economics and Policy Studies*, 17, 621–644.

Hauck, M., & Fernández-Gallardo, G. (2013). Crises in the South African abalone and Chilean loco fisheries: Shared challenges and prospects. *Maritime Studies*, 12, 1–20.

Hauck, M., & Sweijd, N.A. (1999). A case study of abalone poaching in South Africa and its impact on fisheries management. *ICES Journal of Marine Science*, 56, 1024–1032.

Hellman, J. S., Jones, G. & Kaufmann, D. (2000). *Seize the state, seize the day. State capture, corruption and influence in transition*. World Bank Policy Research Paper 2444. Retrieved from info.worldbank.org/etools/docs/library/17638/seize.pdf

Holmes, L. (2006). *Rotten states? Corruption, post-communism, and neo-liberalism*. Durham, NC: Duke University Press.

INTERPOL (2013). National Environmental Security Task Forces. Retrieved from https://www.interpol.int/Crime-areas/Environmental-crime/Task-forces (retrieved 14 November 2016).

Iversen, V., Chhetry, B., Francis, P., Gurung, M., Kafle, G., Pain, A., & Seeley, J. (2006). *High value forests, hidden economies and elite capture: Evidence from forest user groups in Nepal's Terai*. Ecological Economics, 58, 93–107.

Kane, S. (2012). *Where the rivers meet the sea: A political ecology of water*. Philadelphia, PA: Temple University Press.

Koyuncu, C., & Yilmaz, R. (2009). The impact of corruption on deforestation: Cross-country evidence. *The Journal of Developing Areas*, 42, 213–222.

Laurence, W. F., Albernaz, A. K. M., & Da Costa, C. (2001). Is deforestation accelerating in the Brazilian Amazon?' *Environmental Conservation*, 4, 305–311.

Lyapustin, S. (2006). The smuggling of falcons of the Far East – A threat to the existence of rare birds. *Preservation of Bioresources*, March, 89–100. In Russian.

Klooster, D. (2000). Institutional choice, community, and struggle: A case study of forest co- management in Mexico. *World Development*, 28, 1–20.

Mehlum, H., Moene, K., & Torvik, R. (2006) Institutions and the resource curse. *The Economic Journal*, 508,1–20.

Milledge, S. A. H., Gelvas, I. K., & Ahrends, A. (2007). Forestry, governance and national development: Lessons learned from a logging boom in Southern Tanzania. TRAFFIC East/Southern Africa, Tanzania Development Partners Group & Ministry of Natural Resources of Tourism: Dar es Salaam, Tanzania.

Miller, M. (2011). Persistent illegal logging in Costa Rica: The role of corruption among forestry regulators. *Journal of Environment & Development*, 20, 50–68.

Palmer, C. (2001). *The extent and causes of illegal logging: An analysis of a major cause of tropical deforestation in Indonesia*. CSERGE Working Papers. Centre for Social and Economic Research on the Global Environment: London, United Kingdom.

Persson, A., Rothstein, B., & Teorell, J. (2013). Why anticorruption reforms fail—Systemic corruption as a collective action problem. *Governance: An International Journal of Policy, Administration, and Institutions*, 26, 449–471.

Olken, B.A., & Pande, R. (2012). Corruption in developing countries. *Annual Review of Economics*, 4, 479–509.

Oswald, A. (1982). *The history and practice of falconry*. Jersey: Neville Spearman.
Pfaff, A., Amacher, G. S., & Sills, G. S. (2014). Realistic REDD: Improving the forest impacts of domestic policies in different settings. *Review of Environmental Economics and Policy*, 7, 114–135.
Platt, J. R. (2010). Fished out: Wildlife group objects as South Africa lifts abalone ban. Retrieved from http://blogs.scientificamerican.com/WSS/post.php?blog=46&post=777
Raemaekers, S., & Britz, P.J. (2009). Profile of the illegal abalone (*Haliotis midae*) fishery in the Eastern Cape, South Africa: Organised pillage and management failure. *Fisheries Research*, 97, 183–195.
Raemaekers, S., Hauck, M., Burgener, M., Mackenzie, A., Maharaj, G., Plagányi, É.E., & Britz, P.J. (2011). Review of the causes of the rise of the illegal South African abalone fishery and consequent closure of the rights-based fishery. *Ocean & Coastal Management*, 54, 433–445.
Richards, M., Wells, A., Del Gatto, F., Contreras-Hermosilla, A., & Pommier, P. (2003). Impacts of illegality and barriers to legality: A diagnostic analysis of illegal logging in Honduras and Nicaragua. *International Forestry Review*, 5, 282–292.
Robbins, P. (2000). The rotten institution: Corruption in natural resource management. *Political Geography*, 19, 423–443.
Rothstein, B., & Torsello, D. (2014). Bribery in preindustrial cultures: Understanding the universalism-particularism puzzle. *Journal of Anthropological Research*, 70, 263–282.
Siebert, U., & Elwert, G. (2004). Combating corruption and illegal logging in Bénin, West Africa: Recommendations for forest sector reform. *Journal of Sustainable Forestry*, 19, 239–261.
Smith, J., K. Obidzinski, S., Wood, M., & Suramenggala, S.I. (2003). Illegal logging, collusive corruption and fragmented governments in Kalimantan, Indonesia. *International Forestry Review*, 5, 293–302.
Sundström, A. (2012). Corruption and regulatory compliance: Experimental findings from South African small-scale fisheries. *Marine Policy*, 36, 1255–1264.
Sundström, A. (2013). Corruption in the commons: Why bribery hampers enforcement of environmental regulations in South African fisheries. *International Journal of the Commons*, 7, 454–472.
Sundström, A. (2014). Not to be used during fire: Performance-related pay for civil servants as an anticorruption tool. *Quality Of Government Institute Working Paper*, 2014, 11. Gothenburg, Sweden: University of Gothenburg.
Sundström, A. (2016). Violence and the costs of honesty: Rethinking bureaucrats' choice to take bribes. *Public Administration*. Retrieved from http://onlinelibrary.wiley.com/doi/10.1111/padm.12242/epdf
Sundström, A. (2015). Covenants with broken swords: Corruption and law enforcement in governance of the commons. *Global Environmental Change*, 31, 253–262.
Treisman, D. (2007). What have we learned about the causes of corruption from ten years of cross-national empirical research? *Annual Review of Political Science*, 10, 211–44.

U4. (2008). Organized crime and corruption: U4 expert answer. Christian MichelsenInstitute:Bergen.Retrievedfromhttp://www.u4.no/publications/organised-crime-and-corruption/

U.N. Convention on the International Trade in Endangered Species of Fauna and Flora. (2014). *What is CITES?* Retrieved from http://cites.org/eng/disc/what.php

van Duyne, P. (1997). Organized crime, corruption and power. *Crime, Law & Social Change*, 26, 201–238.

van Rijckeghem, C. & Weder, B. (2001). Bureaucratic corruption and the rate of temptation: Do wages in the civil service affect corruption, and by how much?' *Journal of Development Economics*, 65, 307–331.

Wyatt, T. (2013). *Wildlife trafficking: A deconstruction of the crime, victims and offenders*. Basingstoke, United Kingdom: Palgrave Macmillan.

Wyatt, T. (2012). *Green criminology & wildlife trafficking: The illegal fur and falcon trades in Russia Far East*. Saarbrücken, Germany: LAP Lambert Academic Publishing.

7

Problem-Oriented Policing for Natural Resource Conservation

Mark C. G. Gibson

Non-compliance with laws is widely recognized as a major challenge to the effective management and conservation of natural resources at local, regional, and global scales (Nellemann, Henriksen, Raxter, Ash, & Mrema, 2014). This is problematic, as more restrictive laws and regulations, not less, are needed to ensure long-term sustainability (Millennium Ecosystem Assessment, 2005). One opportunity to address this present and emerging "compliance crisis" would be to implement a best-practice theory and method of policing—problem-oriented policing (POP)—for possible use in the context of natural resource management. The four sections that follow provide (a) background information on the theory and practice of POP among mainstream policing agencies; (b) an evaluation of the opportunity for POP in natural resource management; (c) a case study of POP being applied in Australian Commonwealth fisheries; (d) consideration of how POP might be modified for use in other natural resource management contexts.

7.1 What is Problem-Oriented Policing?

POP is a progressive policing paradigm that aims to treat crime problems with highly tailored interventions. The central premise is that illegal behaviors may be analyzed to identify similar, related, or recurring crime incidents, or problems, and that addressing these specific problems will increase police effectiveness (Goldstein, 1990; Scott, 2000). Although this approach to policing may seem almost common-sensical for consideration among academic and professional communities, decades of research now indicates that the application of POP can lead to meaningful crime reductions (Weisburd, Telep, Hinkle, & Eck, 2010). Because of this, POP has been recommended for widespread adoption by an expert panel on policing convened by the U.S. National Research Council (National Research Council, 2004), and has also been adopted by national policing agencies in the United Kingdom (U.K.), Norway, and Sweden (Knutsson, 2003).

The reason POP has relevance for modern policing agencies is that most appear to direct their resources to the detection and deterrence of general incidents of crime (Figure 7.1) rather than the identification and treatment of specific crime problems (Figure 7.2). As a result, many policing agencies prioritize practices that

Conservation Criminology, First Edition. Edited by Meredith L. Gore.

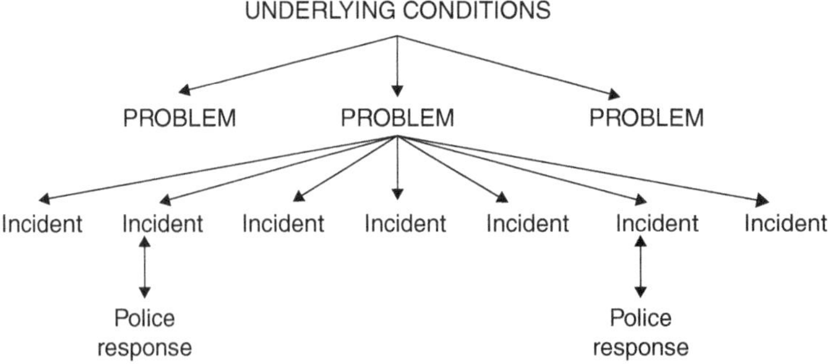

Figure 7.1 Incident-based policing conceptual diagram. Adapted from Eck & Spelman (1987).

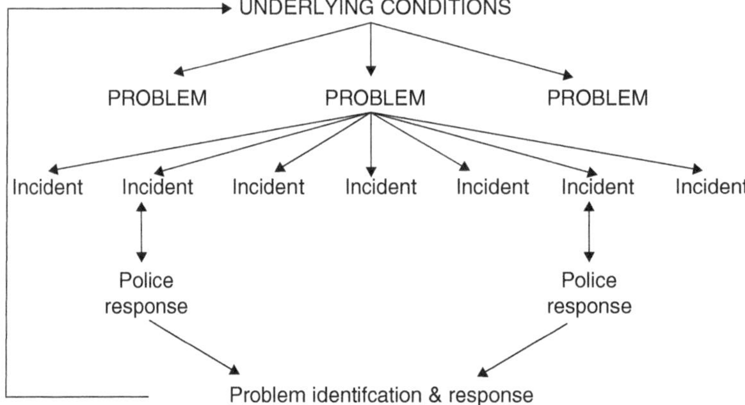

Figure 7.2 Problem-oriented policing conceptual diagram. Adapted from Eck & Spelman (1987).

have been found to have only minor impacts on crime. Such practices may include increasing the size of police agencies, random patrols across all parts of the jurisdiction, rapid response to calls for service, generally applied follow-up investigations of suspected incidents, and generally applied intensive enforcement and arrest policies (National Research Council, 2004). According to POP advocates, there are at least four reasons why these practices produce limited results among most police agencies (Clarke & Eck, 2003). First, police typically operate over large geographic areas, so only substantial increases in police force size would meaningfully alter their coverage. Second, police often obtain little useful information to prevent future crimes from calls for service and follow-up investigations. Third, offenders often act according to short-term interests, since the penalties imposed by the justice system are typically incurred at a far later date. Finally, intensive enforcement and arrest policies can easily overwhelm the capacities of the courts, making the overall justice system less effective. Given this, incident-based policing practices are best understood as generally necessary, but insufficient to achieve meaningful reductions in crime.

In contrast to incident-based policing, POP, by its very nature, has no set of typical real-world practices. In other words, POP is not so much an enforcement

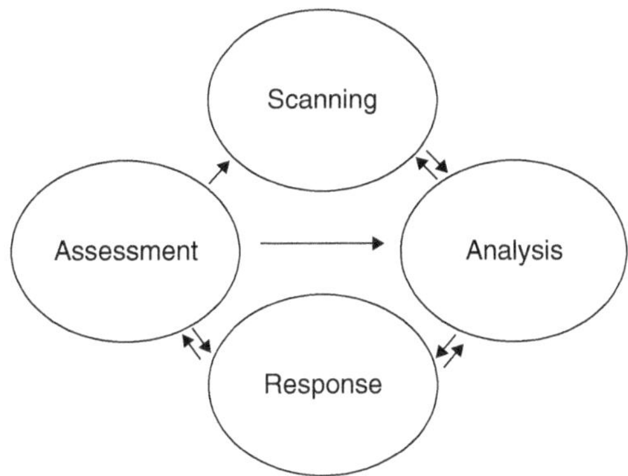

Figure 7.3 The SARA model of problem-oriented policing.

strategy as a strategy to design and evaluate enforcement strategies. As such, there exists a diverse literature on how to practice POP. To navigate this diversity, existing theory can be categorized as pertaining to one of three conceptual domains (a) implementation frameworks; (b) problem analysis tools; (c) problem response strategies. Each of these categories is briefly described in the remainder of this section.

Implementation frameworks may be defined as conceptual constructs that provide abstract guides to implement POP from start to finish. When policing agencies use of one of these frameworks to identify and treat one or more crime problems, it can be said that they are engaging in a POP project. The most popular implementation framework today is the Scanning, Analysis, Response, and Assessment (SARA) Model (Figure 7.3), although it is possible this framework is most well-liked because it was the first POP implementation framework to be described (see Eck & Spelman, 1987). Other possibly useful implementation methodologies include Clients, Acquire/Analyze information, Partnerships, Response, and Assessment (CAPRA); Intelligence, Intervention, Implementation, Involvement, and Impact (5Is); and Problem, Cause, Tactic or Treatment, Output, and Result (PROCTOR) (see Sidebottom & Tilly, 2010 for additional discussion).

Problem analysis tools are sets of theoretical concepts and their interrelationships that facilitate critical thinking about crime problems. In general, these tools assist police as they seek to identify and analyze the causes of crime problems. In this domain of POP theory, most of the constructs have in fact been borrowed from environmental criminology, which concerns itself with how everyday built environments (e.g., neighborhoods, street corners, transit stations) shape crime opportunities. For instance, the Problem Analysis Triangle (Figure 7.4) was developed on the basis of Routine Activities Theory, one of the main theories of environmental criminology. Other tools for problem analysis include the CHEERS criteria (i.e., Community, Harmful, Expectation, Event, Recurring, Similarity), CRAVED criteria (i.e., Concealable, Removable, Available, Valuable, Enjoyable, Disposable), and 80/20 Rule which reminds crime analysts that a small proportion of offenders, targets, and places typically produce most incidents of crime (see Clarke & Eck, 2005).

Finally, response strategies may be defined as generic plans consisting of one or more policing practices that serve to address crime problems. POP practitioners

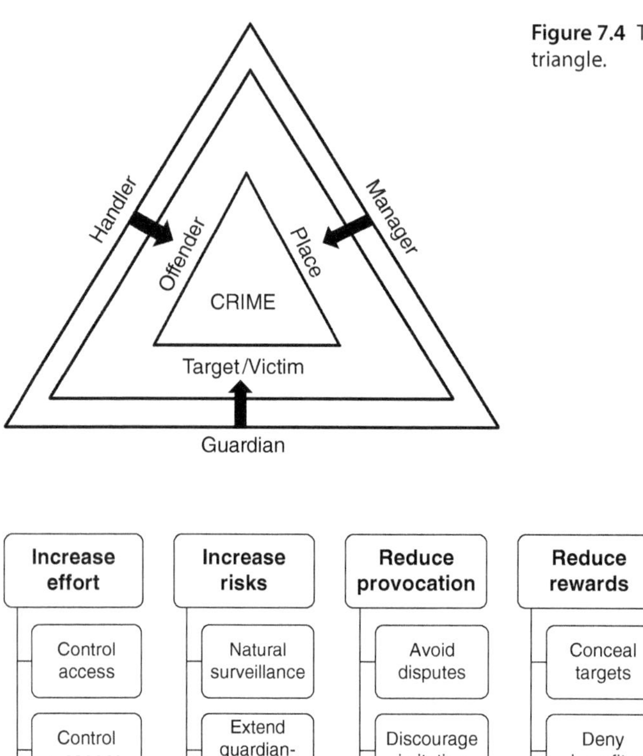

Figure 7.4 The problem analysis triangle.

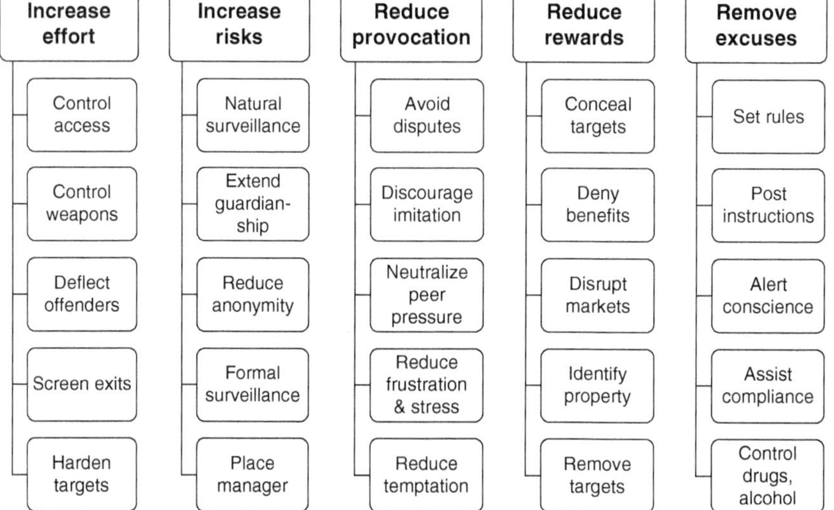

Figure 7.5 Twenty-five techniques of situational crime prevention.

have identified various response strategies that may be applied once problems have been identified and analyzed. One widely regarded response strategy is Situational Crime Prevention (SCP), which was designed as a way to apply environmental criminological theory in real-world settings (Clarke, 1997). After over two decades of development, SCP now consists of 25 practices that may be categorized according to five intended impacts on potential offenders: increase the effort, increase the risks, reduce the rewards, reduce provocations, and remove excuses (Figure 7.5; Cornish & Clarke, 2003). Meanwhile, the Center for Problem-Oriented Policing, in collaboration with the Office of Community Oriented Policing Services of the U.S. Department of Justice, has produced a series of best-practice documents for both responding to common problems and applying specific practices that might be effective in reducing crime problems. The former Problem Guide series covers such problems as assaults in and around bars (Scott & Dedel, 2001), drug dealing in privately owned apartment complexes (Sampson, 2001), and spectator violence in stadiums (Madensen & Eck, 2008). The latter Response Guide series covers such practices as video surveillance of public places (Ratcliffe, 2006), crime prevention publicity campaigns (Barthe, 2006), and sting operations (Newman & Socia, 2007).

7.2 The Opportunity for POP in Natural Resource Management

A review of literature suggests, but does not clearly indicate, a need for more POP in natural resource management. This may be reasoned on the basis of three general findings. First, relatively little research appears to have been conducted into policing of natural resource management laws and regulations in general. This view has been explicitly expressed in regards to policing for terrestrial wildlife management (Eliason, 2011), and is implied by the limited information on policing practices in technical documents for the management of other resources, including forests (e.g., FAO & ITTO, 2005; 2010), fisheries (e.g., Bigue *et al.*, 2015; Flewwelling *et al.*, 2002), and flora and fauna sold in international markets (Reeve, 2002). This finding alone suggests an opportunity for POP. Although it may be possible that natural resource enforcement agencies are more progressive than mainstream policing agencies, a precautionary approach cautions researchers to assume these agencies face similar bureaucratic incentives to direct their attention to the detection and deterrence of incidents, rather than identification and treatment of specific crime problems.

The limited technical guidance for policing natural resources primarily focuses on incident-based policing practices rather than practices that might facilitate more POP. For instance, although the Food and Agriculture Organization has produced a technical fisheries management document recommending policing practices such as at-sea patrols, logbooks, and permits (Flewwelling *et al.*, 2002), the document does not discuss how fisheries enforcement agencies may strategically assign their resources or address common compliance problems. Similarly, the wildlife and forest crime analytic toolkit developed by the International Consortium on Combating Wildlife Crime (ICCWC, 2012) advises how enforcement agencies might develop their human resources, conduct investigations, and evaluate the appropriateness of existing legislation but offers little insight into how enforcement agencies might conduct the recommended proactive investigations, scholarly and independent research and diagnostic surveys to identify the most important compliance problems when trade and law enforcement statistics are limited and low quality.

Finally, although there is widespread recognition that innovation in natural resource enforcement is needed to address the compliance crisis, the focus of conservation organizations has centered on the development of novel compliance monitoring technologies, rather than more effective practices for enforcement agencies. For instance, Global Fishing Watch, a collaboration between Sky Truth, Oceana, and Google, offers a platform to identify illegal fishing vessels through compilation of GPS information that is publically broadcasted by certain fishing vessels. Similarly, the Spatial Monitoring and Reporting Tool (SMART), developed by a variety of conservation organizations including CITES, Frankfurt Zoological Society, and Wildlife Conservation Society, has enabled improved collection and analysis of spatial data for the policing of terrestrial wildlife reserves. Although such technologies may facilitate POP, adoption of these or similar technologies does not necessarily require or encourage comprehensive problem scanning or analysis of the conditions underlying compliance problems.

In sum, these three findings suggest that incident-based policing remains the primary approach to policing natural resources among most governments of the world, and that natural resource management may benefit from problem-oriented practices. This possibility is further explored in the next section with a case study of how POP can benefit fisheries management.

7.3 A Case Study of Australian Commonwealth Fisheries Management

A useful case study of POP for natural resource management is offered by the Australian Fisheries Management Authority (AFMA). AFMA is responsible for management of Australian Commonwealth fisheries, or those fisheries generally occurring from three nautical miles offshore to the limit of the Australian Fishing Zone, and offers a rare example of POP in natural resource management. Specifically, AFMA as an organization underwent reform in the 2000s and, as a result, staff made use of POP theory through study of the published works of and direct teaching of Malcolm Sparrow of Harvard University (e.g., Sparrow, 2000). Furthermore, the quasi-experimental results of AFMA's problem-oriented operations suggest that POP may benefit other agencies managing fisheries and other natural resources.

This case study is presented below in five sub-sections. The first sub-section provides background on Australian Commonwealth fisheries and AFMA's operational structure, while the remaining four sections outline AFMA's use of POP to address a variety of compliance problems. In order to simplify the presentation of AFMA's POP practices, the remaining four sub-sections are structured according to the steps of the SARA methodology, though this implementation framework was not purposefully used by AFMA staff.

7.3.1 The Australian Fisheries Management Authority

AFMA is responsible for the management of commercial fishing in the Australian Fishing Zone (AFZ), which is the world's third largest national fishing zone and extends from 3 to up to 200 nautical miles offshore. Australian states and territories, meanwhile, manage fisheries in inland and coastal waters up to 3 nautical miles offshore and typically assume responsibility for recreational fishing in the entirety of the AFZ. Commercial fisheries occurring within the AFZ are typically referred to as Commonwealth Fisheries and yield an estimated 15% of annual fishery landings worth approximately AU$ 320.4 million. Approximately 320 vessels operate across this large geographic area and land their catch at as many as 75 ports.

Presently, AFMA actively manages 13 distinct Commonwealth Fisheries. These fisheries include the Bass Strait Central Zone Scallop Fishery, Coral Sea Fishery, Eastern Tuna and Billfish Fishery, Heard Island and McDonald Islands Fishery, Macquarie Island Toothfish Fishery, Northwest Slope Trawl Fishery, Northern Prawn Fishery, Small Pelagic Fishery, Southern and Eastern Scalefish and Shark Fishery, Southern Bluefin Tuna Fishery, Southern Squid Jig Fishery, Western Deepwater Trawl Fishery, and Western Tuna and Billfish Fishery. As suggested by their names, these fisheries represent a variety of different target species, gears, and locations in the AFZ. In general, AFMA regulates access to these fisheries through the assignment of fishing concessions; application of input restrictions, like gear prohibitions and season limits; and the application of output restrictions, mainly total allowable catch (TAC) limits and quotas that assign fixed portions of the catch limits to rights holders. All fishing vessels operating in Commonwealth Fisheries are also required to have satellite-based vessel monitoring systems (VMS) installed, and a portion of the total fleet is also required to have on-board sensor and video recording packages, otherwise known as electronic monitoring systems (EMS). Finally, Commonwealth Fisheries are subject to a network of spatial closures. Collectively, these measures are used to ensure that Commonwealth Fisheries are managed to provide maximum economic yield and do not cause significant adverse impacts to vulnerable marine ecosystems, as required under Commonwealth law.

As of 2015, AFMA enforces Commonwealth Fisheries law and regulations through four different operational programs with approximately 70 full-time staff members involved in compliance programs to some extent. The Communication and Education Program aims to increase voluntary compliance and deter potential offenders by sharing information through media and meetings with fishers. The General Deterrence Program consists of a series of patrols and vessel inspections targeted at high risk ports, boats, and fish receivers. The Targeted Risk Program involves identifying, prioritizing, and treating compliance risks. The Maintenance Program continues the monitoring of compliance risks previously treated by the Targeted Risk Program. Noticeably, these programs represent a stark departure from AFMA enforcement operations in the 2000s, which oriented primarily around contracting out services to state and territory fisheries management agencies. A central government audit of this enforcement approach suggested performance outcomes could be improved. AFMA responded by shifting toward more centralized, risk-based operations in 2009. As part of the revised centralized compliance model, a new organizational structure was implemented with separate Intelligence, Planning and Operations units (Figure 7.6). As a result

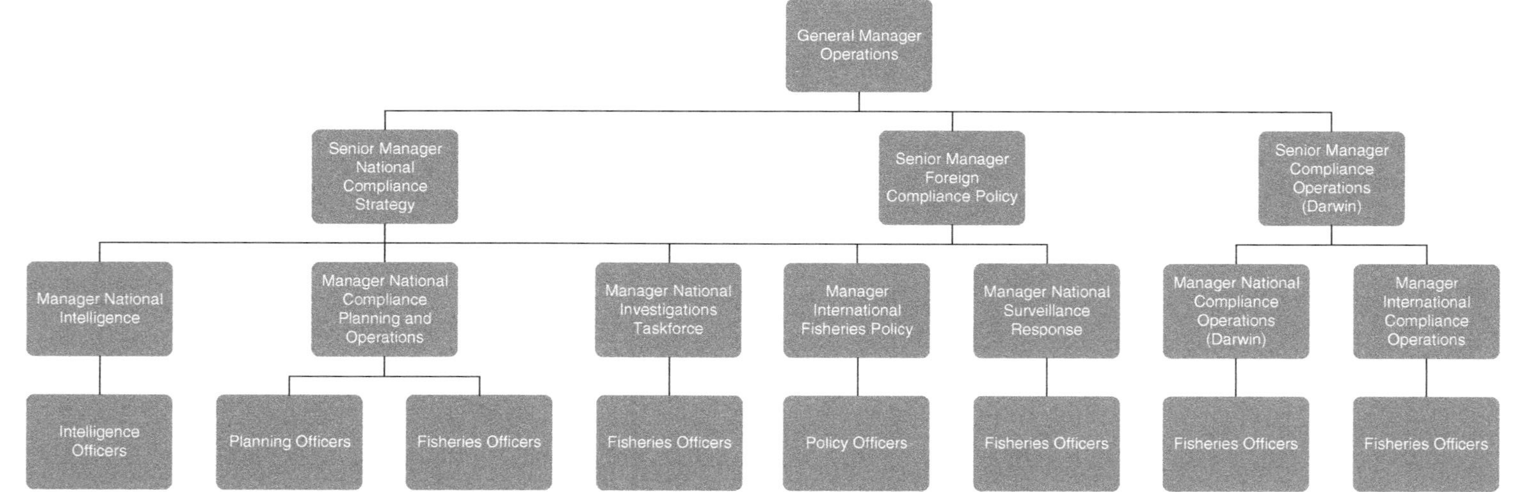

Figure 7.6 National compliance structure for Australia's Commonwealth Fisheries.

of these reforms, AFMA's enforcement operations can now be understood to operate according to key principles of POP. Four principles—problem scanning, problem analysis, problem response, and impact assessment—are further considered below.

7.3.2 Scanning

As noted above, AFMA's operations were reformed such that enforcement operations are now guided by key principles of POP. A first principle that may be considered is that AFMA analysts now regularly engage in problem scanning. This principle is notably institutionalized as formal, systematic compliance risk assessments that are conducted every two years. In order to ensure effective scanning, these assessments are guided by a formal compliance risk assessment methodology (see AFMA, 2013) that was designed in accordance with the risk standard established by the International Standards Organization (see ISO, 2009). Furthermore, in order to efficiently evaluate compliance risks, the risk assessments are only carried out for the seven major Commonwealth Fisheries or fishery sectors. These are the Eastern Tuna and Billfish Fishery, Western Tuna and Billfish Fishery, Southern Bluefin Tuna Fishery, Bass Strait Central Zone Scallop Fishery, Northern Prawn Fishery, Gillnet Hook and Trap Sector Fishery, and Great Australian Bight sectors of the Southern and Eastern Scalefish and Shark Fishery. Other fisheries are excluded from formal risk assessment because they comprise a small percentage of the Commonwealth catch, have a small number of license holders, or present a low set of risks due to 100% on-board observer coverage. It has generally been the case that treatments to improve compliance in the seven major Commonwealth fisheries or fishery sectors are also implemented in these other fisheries.

Under the AFMA compliance risk assessment methodology, problem scanning is undertaken through two broad steps. First, a set of potential risks is identified. Although the precise list of potential compliance risks for each assessed fishery is never publically released due to the sensitivity of the assessments, a generic assessment document has been released that offers a set of common compliance risks that are likely quite representative of risks that are identified in the assessments. These risks may be grouped into nine categories (Table 7.1).

Second, information on the scale of these risks is solicited from both AFMA staff and fishery stakeholders. This information pertains to both to the "inherent risk," or the risk of a compliance problem that naturally exists in a fishery, and the "residual risk," or the risk of a compliance problem that remains given existing enforcement activities. The evaluation of inherent risks proceeds through internal consultation and analysis according to standardized scales by AFMA observer section staff, fisheries managers, domestic compliance staff, and intelligence officers. The evaluation of residual risk, meanwhile, also includes standardized inputs from fishing industry associations and management advisory councils, in which industry representatives actively participate.

Table 7.1 Potential Compliance Risks in Australia's Commonwealth Fisheries.

Compliance Risk	Example
Breaking TAP regulations	Breaching threat abatement plan regulations
Breaking trip, size, & jurisdictions	Breaching trip and/or species size limits
Bycatch & other species interactions	Failure to report interaction/retention of protected or prohibited species; shark finning and not retaining carcasses
Logbook misreporting	Failure to accurately complete or submit logbooks; completion of logbooks by unauthorized representative
Processing catch at sea	Processing catch at sea; high grading of quota species; landing and selling catch to unauthorized receiver
Quota and Catch Disposal Record offences	Taking in excess of allocated quota an failing to reconcile within required timeframe; deliberate unreported take of quota species and/or misreporting catch disposal records to avoid quota decrementation
Sale to unlicensed fish receiver	Landing and selling catch to unauthorized receiver
Unauthorized fishing	Not carrying required documents on board vessel
VMS & position reporting	Failure to fit approved Vessel Monitoring System on board or having it operating at all times

7.3.3 Analysis

A second POP principle that guides AFMA operations is that the agency engages in the analysis of compliance problems, both in terms of their impacts and causes. These activities are notably institutionalized as part of the biannual compliance risk assessment as well as AFMA's subsequent selection of key compliance problems for specialized treatment. A final step in the compliance risk assessment methodology is that AFMA staff calculate standardized residual risk scores for each fishery and for the AFZ as a whole. Importantly, these scores are not simply a function of the residual risk data provided by AFMA staff and fishery stakeholders, but are weighted through in-depth evaluation of available compliance data. Essentially, this means that if risks are ranked as low by stakeholder input, they may still be assigned a relatively higher residual risk score if information indicates that there is a high rate of detected offences. Based on these risk scores, certain compliance problems are assigned for specialized treatment by AFMA's Operational Management Committee (OMC). The OMC includes the General Manager of the Fisheries Operations Branch, the senior managers of the National Compliance Strategy Section, and the National Compliance Operations Sections from the cities of Canberra and Darwin. Due the sensitivity of the information AFMA does not release the full results of compliance risk assessment to the public, however those risks selected for treatment are typically disclosed through the AFMA's published annual compliance program documents. To date, seven risks have been identified in public documents: breaches of area closures, failure to have an operational VMS at all times while at sea, failure to have a functioning Electronic Monitoring System (EMS) on-board, failure to purchase or otherwise obtain enough quota within the required time period, failure to report interactions with specially protected species, late logbook reporting, and misreporting catches to avoid the use of quota catch allocations.

7.3.4 Response

A third POP principle that guides AFMA operations is that the agency specially assigns resources to respond to compliance problems identified through formal scanning and analysis activities. Although a range of treatments have been employed, including new investigation taskforces and interagency collaborations, AFMA has perhaps most notably responded to compliance problems through the establishment of specialized Compliance Risk Management Teams (CRMTs). These teams are multidisciplinary, if not multi-agency, with their composition determined by the nature of the risk being addressed. Furthermore, every CRMT must develop specific objectives, which may include information analysis, inspections, and special operations, such as surveillance of individual vessels or concession holders, as well as a variety of associated performance measures. The broad range of objectives and measures that may be developed by the CRMTs may be evidence by the following examples:

- **Logbook Returns CRMT**. Established as part of 2010–2011 annual Targeted Risk Program, this CRMT focused on reducing risks of non-compliance with logbook reporting requirements. This team focused on monitoring the submission of logbooks and proceeding with follow-up communications and, possibly, disciplinary actions for tardy logbook submissions. A key performance target of the CRMT was to reduce late logbooks to 3% or less of all submitted logbooks.
- **Misreporting CRMT**. Established as part of the 2013–2014 annual Targeted Risk Program, this CRMT focused on reducing the risk of fishers misreporting or not reporting a catch to avoid use of allocated quota. The team was charged with reviewing academic literature to identify the drivers that motivate operators to commit quota evasion, developing a baseline measure of misreporting on official catch disposal records (CDRs), and examining novel data sets and collections methods that could provide further intelligence capacities. Key performance measures were a soon-to-be created measure of misreporting on CDRs, a qualitative survey of AFMA on-board observers on fishers' reporting behaviors, and the number of desktop audits conducted.
- **VMS and EMS CRMT**. First established as part of the 2011–2012 annual Targeted Risk Program, this CRMT focused on reducing the risk of non-compliance with VMS requirements. The team's focus was then modified to also treat the risk of non-compliance with EMS requirements as part of the 2015–2016 annual Targeted Risk Program. To address VMS and EMS non-compliance, the

CRMT is charged with daily monitoring of active vessels which are identified through the submission of logbooks within three days after landing at a port and then crosschecking these records with submitted VMS and EMS data. Beyond this routine monitoring the CRMT is also charged with conducting periodic, short-term zero tolerance programs during which time at-sea failures of VMS or EMS result in vessels returning to port. Key performance targets for this CRMT are for 100% of active boats to be fully compliant with VMS and EMS requirements.

7.3.5 Assessment

A fourth and final POP principle that guides AFMA operations is that the agency assesses the impact of its tailored compliance risks treatments and—depending on the results—either completes or revises the risk treatments. This is operationalized through the monthly and annual reports of the Targeted Risk Program, which evaluate CRMTs, taskforces, and other formal responses according to previously assigned performance targets and measures. Although experimental examinations have yet to be conducted, the most recent publicized assessment data indicate meaningful reductions in compliance problems. Key successes from past CRMTs include the following:

- **Large reduction in late logbook submissions**. The activities of the Logbook Returns CRMT from 2009 to 2011 was found to be associated with a significant reduction in the number of late logbook submissions. The overall percentage of logbooks returned late to AFMA fell from 5.5% in 2009 to 1.4% in 2010 and remained at a similarly low level thereafter. This met the CRMT's target of 3% and as a result, the CRMT ended in 2011. Regular monitoring of logbooks has since continued as part of ordinary operations.
- **Large reduction in late quota reconciliations**. The activities of the Quota Reconciliation CRMT from 2012 to 2013 were associated with meaningful reductions in the number of quota reconciliation matters to which AFMA staff had to attend. The number of quota matters declined from 133 in 2012 to 41 in 2013 and as a result the CRMT was ended in 2013. Regular monitoring of quota non-reconciliation has since continued as part of ordinary operations.
- **Large reduction in suspected breaches of area closures**. The activities of the Closures CRMT from 2009 to 2013 were associated with reductions in suspected area closure violations. The number of suspected breaches fell from an average of 17 each month during the 2009–2010 period to an average of 2 suspected breaches during the period ending June 2013. As a result the Closures CRMT was ended in 2013. Regular monitoring of closure violations has since continued as part of ordinary operations.
- **Improvement in compliance with VMS requirements**. The activities of the VMS CRMT from 2008 to 2015 have been associated with improvements in the number of active vessels complying with VMS requirements. Specifically, VMS compliance rates have increased from an average of 87.5% of active vessels in the

2008–2009 period to 97.9% in the 2014–2015 period. In spite of this success, VMS compliance remains the focus of an on-going CRMT because the risk of non-compliance associated with VMS requirements continues to be assessed as high.

Beyond these successes, AFMA has demonstrated it can and will revise its approach to treating compliance risks when CRMTs are unsuccessful. Most notably, AFMA has significantly revised its approach to reducing the risk of quota evasion in recent years. This risk was first selected for treatment with a Quota Evasion and Avoidance CRMT in the 2011–2013 period. After further assessment the CRMT was replaced by the Misreporting CRMT (see above) in 2013, a Fish Receiver Fraud CRMT which primarily undertook audits of fish receivers, and Substitution/Concealment CRMT which identified species of higher substitution/concealment risks, conducted educational workshops with fishers, and inspected vessels of concern or special interest. Furthermore, in 2014, a Quota Evasion Tools CRMT was established to develop tools that automatically crosscheck CDRs with logbooks.

7.4 Adapting POP for More Effective Conservation

The preceding sections suggest that POP may, in at least some circumstances, be an effective way for governments and other conservation actors to improve compliance with natural resource management laws, regulations, and rules. The question then becomes can and how may POP be adapted for other natural resource management contexts? This section explores suggestions for expanded trial of POP through consideration of (a) how the Australian POP model may be replicated by other national management agencies responsible for offshore fisheries; (b) possible challenges to adapting the Australian POP model for use by agencies responsible for other types of fisheries; and (c) barriers that may exist for successful use of POP in the management of natural resources generally.

With regards to replicating the Australian compliance risk assessment and treatment model, it is possible AFMA represents a special case that has limited implications for other national fisheries agencies with responsibility for offshore fisheries. That is, while another national agency can surely embrace the Australian POP model for offshore fisheries management it is possible that it will have less success unless it also receives a special mandate to improve overall agency performance from its national legislative or executive body. In Australia's case, the national government had previously embraced a program of microeconomic reform so that the public sector could better foster economic competition in the early 1990s; the program was further revised and strengthened in the mid-2000s. One of the many results was introduction of strong principles of government accountability with respect to Commonwealth fisheries management. For instance, AFMA's fisheries management functions were subjected to a full audit by the Australian National Audit Office in 2009, and were partially audited as part of a follow up review in 2013. Prior to 2009 the compliance monitoring programs for Commonwealth Fisheries had been internally reviewed six times since 1988.

It is unlikely the Australian compliance risk assessment and treatment model will be wholly useful to the management of nearshore marine fisheries or freshwater inland fisheries unless managing agencies either engage in similarly comprehensive intelligence gathering and analysis activities or obtain information on potential compliance problems through more resource-limited monitoring methods. Although mentioned peripherally above, AFMA's use of VMS, EMS electronic reporting technologies and deployment of a large number of regular on-board observers is an integral component of its enforcement activities. Unfortunately, these technologies and strategies may be more difficult to implement in other types of fisheries that (a) produce lower profits, thus limiting cost-recovery; (b) employ a relatively greater number of vessels and fishers, which can raise the transaction and financial costs of intelligence gathering; (c) are less easily subject to port and processor inspections due to their multiple landing sites. These characteristics are common among near-shore and inland fisheries. Instead, it is likely compliance examiners will need to parallel stock assessment researchers (e.g., Apel, Fujita, & Karr, 2013) in the development of less rigorous compliance assessment methods when resources are limited. Although additional evaluation is needed, one such opportunity is the use of qualitative approaches to compliance assessment, such as by using semi-structured interviews and purposive sampling to collect compliance data from fishers themselves (e.g., Gibson & Gore, unpublished data).

Finally, the experiences of implementing POP in mainstream policing suggests there are a number of organizational and political factors that should be generally considered when implementing POP principles in the management of natural resources. Specifically, in recognition of the fact that POP has not been more widely embraced by police agencies, the intellectual father of POP—Dr. Herman Goldstein of the University of Wisconsin—has identified five factors that inhibit more widespread use of POP:

1) Lack of a long-term organizational commitment.
2) Lack of skilled staff.
3) Lack of clear academic connection.
4) Absence of informed outside pressures.
5) Lack of financial support (Goldstein, 2003).

Although more research is needed, one may speculate as to how these obstacles might be overcome in natural resource management settings. It is possible AFMA overcame the challenge of long-term organizational commitment by adopting formal policy to assess compliance risks every two years; similar policies could be adopted by other agencies. A lack of skilled staff among management agencies, meanwhile, might be addressed through efforts to develop publically available problem analysis tools and response strategies for common problems, such as those that have been created and disseminated by the Center for Problem Oriented Policing (see above). Finally, academic research support, outside pressure, and overall financial support could be provided by environmental nonprofit organizations or multilateral agencies with natural resource management responsibilities or interests, provided that these organizations are more experienced with the opportunity for POP in natural resource management.

7.5 Conclusion

This chapter has explored POP as a way that the conservation and enforcement communities may better address the present and emerging compliance crisis in natural resource management. It is likely POP represents a new opportunity to improve natural resource management through the reform of enforcement activities to more proactively identify and analyze compliance problems, respond to problems with tailored interventions, and adjust enforcement practices based on results. As the case of Commonwealth Fisheries management in Australia suggests, POP can be effectively tailored to natural resource management contexts, though this success may be particularly tied to the characteristics and environments of the management agencies themselves. It now remains to scientists and practitioners in the field of natural resource management to further evaluate this opportunity for advancing conservation and, where necessary, develop new theory and tools for its realization.

References

AFMA. (2013). National compliance 2013-15 risk assessment methodology. Retrieved from http://www.afma.gov.au/wp-content/uploads/2010/06/2013-15-RA-Methodology-accessible-version.pdf

Apel, A. M., Fujita, R., & Karr, K. (2013). *Science-based management of data-limited fisheries: A supplement to the catch share design manual.* Environmental Defense Fund.

Barthe, E. (2006). *Crime prevention publicity campaigns.* Response guides series, No. 5. Problem- oriented guides for police. Washington D.C.: U.S. Department of Justice, Office of Community Oriented Policing Services.

Bigue, M, Bravo, M., Rosero, O., Arnold, R., Revenga, C. & Rude, J. (2015). *Enforcement guide: Nearshore artisanal fisheries.* The Nature Conservancy and WildAid.

Clarke, R. V. (1997). *Situational crime prevention: Successful case studies.* 2nd Edition. New York, NY: Harrow and Heston.

Clarke, R. V., & Eck, J. (2003). *Become a problem solving crime analyst in 55 small steps.* London, England: Jill Dando Institute of Crime Science.

Cornish, D. B., & Clarke, R. V. (2003). Opportunities, precipitators and criminal decisions: A reply to Wortley's critique of situational crime prevention. *Crime Prevention Studies,* 16, 41–96.

Eck, J. E., & Spelman, W. (1987). *Problem-solving: Problem-oriented policing in Newport News.* Washington D.C.: Police Executive Research Forum.

Eliason, S. L. (2011). Policing natural resources: Issues in a conservation law enforcement agency. *Professional Issues in Criminal Justice,* 6, 43–58.

FAO & ITTO. (2005). *Best practices for improving law compliance in the forest sector.* FAO *Forestry Paper 145.* International Tropical Timber Organization and the Food and Agriculture Organization of the United Nations.

FAO & ITTO. (2010). *Forest law compliance and governance in tropical countries: A region-by-region assessment of the status of forest law compliance and governance, and recommendations for improvement.* International Tropical Timber Organization and the Food and Agriculture Organization of the United Nations.

Flewwelling, P., Cullinan, C., Balton, D., Sautter, R.P., & Reynolds, I.E. (2002). Recent trends in monitoring, control and surveillance systems for capture fisheries. *FAO Fisheries Technical Paper, No. 415*. Rome, Italy: FAO.

Gibson, M. C. G., & Gore, M.L. (unpublished data). *Toward improved management of data-limited fisheries: A mental models approach to fisher compliance assessment.*

Goldstein, H. (1990). *Problem-oriented policing.* Philadelphia, PA: Temple University Press.

Goldstein, H. (2003). On further developing problem-oriented policing: The most critical need, the major impediments, and a proposal. *Crime Prevention Studies*, 15, 13–47.

ISO. (2009). *Risk management –principles and guidelines.* ISO 31000, 2009.

ICCWC. (2012). Wildlife and forest crime analytic toolkit. Brussels: United Nations.

Madensen, T.D., & Eck, J.E. (2008). *Spectator violence in stadiums.* Problem-specific guides series, No. 54. Problem-oriented guides for police. Washington D.C.: U.S. Department of Justice. Office of Community Oriented Policing Services.

Millennium Ecosystem Assessment. (2005). *Ecosystems and human well-being: Policy responses, Volume 3.* Washington, DC: Island Press.

Knutsson, J. (2003). Introduction. *Crime Prevention Studies*, 15, 1–11.

National Research Council. (2004). Fairness and effectiveness in policing: The evidence. committee to review research on police policy and practices. Skogan, W., & Frydl, K. (Eds.). Committee on Law and Justice, Division of Behavioral and Social Sciences and Education. Washington, DC: The National Academies Press.

Nellemann, C., Henreiksen, R., Raxter, P., Ash, N., & Mrema, E. (2014). *The environmental crisis-threats to sustainable development from illegal exploitation and trade in wildlife and forest resources.* United Nations Environment Programme: Gland Switzerland.

Newman, G.R., & Socia, K. (2007). *Sting operations.* Response guides series, No. 6. Problem-oriented guides for police. Washington D.C.: U.S. Department of Justice. Office of Community Oriented Policing Services.

Ratcliffe, J. (2006). *Video surveillance of public places.* Response guides series, No. 4. Problem-oriented guides for police. Washington D.C.: U.S. Department of Justice. Office of Community Oriented Policing Services.

Reeve, R. (2002). *Policing international trade in endangered species: The CITES treaty and compliance.* New York, NY: Earthscan.

Sampson, R. (2001). *Drug dealing in privately owned apartment complexes.* Problem-specific guides series, No. 4. Problem-oriented guides for police. Washington D.C.: U.S. Department of Justice. Office of Community Oriented Policing Services.

Scott, M. S. (2000). *Problem-oriented policing: Reflections on the first 20 years.* Washington D.C.: U.S. Department of Justice, Office of Community Oriented Policing Services.

Scott, M. S., & Dedel, K. (2001). Assaults in and around bars. Problem-specific guides series, No. 1. 2nd Edition. Problem-oriented guides for police. Washington D.C.: U.S. Department of Justice. Office of Community Oriented Policing Services.

Sidebottom, A., & Tilley, N. (2010). Improving problem-oriented policing: The need for a new model? *Crime Prevention & Community Safety*, 13, 79–101.

Sparrow, M. K. (2000). *The regulatory craft: Controlling risks, solving problems, and managing compliance*. Washington, DC: The Brookings Institution.

Weisburd, D., Telep, C.W., Hinkle, J.C., & Eck, J.E. (2010). Is problem-oriented policing effective in reducing crime and disorder? Findings from a Campbell systematic review. *Criminology & Public Policy*, 9, 139–172.

8

Exploring the Sociology of Wildlife Tourism, Global Risks, and Crime

Jessica Bell Rizzolo

Tourism with the purpose of encountering wildlife is hugely popular, expanding rapidly and can both prevent and promote crime. Wildlife tourism includes a range of experiences and activities involving wildlife viewing and photography, the use of wildlife for entertainment, transportation and trekking, hunting and fishing, visiting protected areas, and managed encounters. Globally, wildlife tourism has an annual growth rate of 10% and is valued at approximately $ U.S. 45 billion (Newsome & Rodger, 2013). The industry is expected to continue growing alongside increases in global education and income (Newsome, Dowling, & Moore, 2005). Wildlife tourism is often promoted as a mechanism for raising the socioeconomic value of wildlife as well as enhancing awareness of and support for conservation. Although tourism does have the potential to promote conservation and generate local economic benefits, it can also produce negative socio-cultural outcomes, harm wildlife, and facilitate environmental crime (Duffy, 2010). Since tourists overwhelmingly engage in wildlife tourism in new and unfamiliar social contexts, exploring the intersection of sociological theory and wildlife tourism can enhance understanding and management of myriad conservation crimes in cross-cultural contexts (Botterill & Jones, 2010). Sociology provides insights into the supply and demand dimensions of wildlife tourism and crime and the motivations behind tourists' preferences for particular tourism ventures. This information can enhance the composition, evaluation, and implementation of tourism and wildlife policies.

This chapter synthesizes insights from conservation, criminology, and sociological theory. The chapter profiles different forms of wildlife tourism and the associated benefits and risks. It then examines how criminology, natural resources management, and risk and decision science are integral to examining the links between wildlife tourism and conservation crime. Next, the chapter describes how sociological work on power relations and authenticity can further enhance analysis. Finally, a case study of elephant tourism, crime, and conservation in Thailand is presented, based on two months of observational and interview data gathered by the author. This case illustrates how sociology contributes to thinking about conservation crime as well as builds theory to examine questions about the use of wildlife tourism for conservation and the reduction of risks associated with wildlife tourism.

Conservation Criminology, First Edition. Edited by Meredith L. Gore.

8.1 Wildlife Tourism

8.1.1 Types of Wildlife Tourism

Wildlife tourism is often classified by three typologies. First, wildlife tourism can occur in captive, semi-captive, or wild environments (Orams, 2002; Tisdell & Wilson, 2012). Second, wildlife tourism can be related to conservation or entertainment (Shackley, 1996). Although most wildlife tourism ventures include a combination of conservation and entertainment, they differ in the relative emphasis they place on these two goals. For example, circuses are primarily an entertainment venue whereas nature reserves prioritize conservation (Fennell, 2012; Shackley, 1996). Third, wildlife tourism can be consumptive or non-consumptive. Non-consumptive wildlife tourism involves human recreation that does not remove or permanently affect wildlife (Duffus & Dearden, 1990).

Truly impact-less tourism is unattainable. Tourism scholars focus on determining what constitutes acceptable tourism-related modifications to the environment and how to minimize, rather than eliminate, environmental risks (Tisdell & Wilson, 2012). The environmental impacts are highly specific to the location, species of interest, and structure of the tourist program. Since wildlife tourism encompasses so many different settings and markets, the motivations, intentions, and attitudes of wildlife tourists are highly variable. The tourist base of wildlife attractions changes over time. When a site is new it tends to attract more knowledgeable, specialized tourists; as word of the tourist site grows the visitor base becomes more generalized (Fennell, 2012). This has implications for the environmental impacts of wildlife tourism because generalized tourists are typically less aware of how their behavior impacts wildlife and require more conservative management to minimize environmental risks (Tisdell & Wilson, 2012).

8.1.2 Benefits of Wildlife Tourism Link Biodiversity Conservation and Livelihood Preservation

Wildlife tourism can have many biodiversity conservation and livelihood preservation benefits. When wildlife tourism includes education and interpretation of wildlife behavior, it can affect tourists' attitudes and perceptions of conservation. For example, after visiting the Elephant Nature Park in Chiang Mai, Thailand, tourists reported they were less likely to participate in elephant trekking, attend elephant shows, and feed street elephants; they were more likely to visit a national park or elephant sanctuary (Rattan, Eagles, & Mair, 2012). Certain forms of tourism can increase concern for wildlife and fuel demand for ethical and sustainable tourism. Many wildlife tourism ventures include research and captive breeding components, which can enhance conservation by promoting scientific knowledge and genetic diversity (Fennell, 2012).

Wildlife tourism can also promote conservation though raising the socioeconomic value of wildlife; this can result in both direct and indirect benefits. Successful wildlife tourism provides the local community with direct economic benefits of tourism such as fees and tour-related employment and can also lead to indirect economic benefits from tourists purchasing food, lodging, transportation, or souvenirs (Archer, 1982; Newsome *et al.*, 2005). Unique or emblematic species, such Indonesia's Komodo dragon, can be especially important for generating economic benefits for local communities (Walpole & Goodwin, 2000; Walpole & Leader-Williams, 2002). In theory, if wildlife provide economic benefits the local community is more likely to tolerate the costs of human-wildlife conflict, to value wildlife, and to protect wildlife habitat (Wilson & Tisdell, 2003;). Thus, providing an economic incentive for the conservation of wildlife is considered a crucial requisite for counteracting the economic rewards that can be reaped from poaching, logging of wildlife habitat, or agricultural expansion (Tisdell & Wilson, 2012). Importantly, when local communities are excluded from the planning and profits of wildlife tourism, negative perceptions associated with human-wildlife interactions and poaching rates may actually increase (Duffy, 2010; Scheyvens, 1999).

8.1.3 Risks Associated with Wildlife Tourism

There are negative effects associated with wildlife tourism, including ideological effects, alteration of animals' natural behaviors, growth of infrastructure, depletion of natural resources, and wildlife trafficking. Introducing wildlife tourism to an area can promote and amplify the idea that wildlife are exploitable resources and alter their eating and sleeping patterns. Wildlife tourism is also typically accompanied by construction of hotels and roads, which sometimes requires deforestation or the filling of wetlands. With more tourists, there are also more consumers available to purchase illegal wildlife products in local markets as souvenirs or novelty items; illegal non-wildlife activities may also increase (e.g., prostitution), which can negatively impact local communities.

Negative ideological effects of wildlife tourism on conservation primarily stem from entertainment-based endeavors. Wildlife entertainment settings such circuses can pose risks to wildlife by reinforcing an ideology that emphasizes humans' power and dominion over animals; these venues can also promote valuing ex-situ (i.e., captive) over in situ (i.e., wild) sites as being superior for conservation, which is not always the case (Bell, 2015; Fennell, 2012). For example, circuses can espouse the notion that the wild is a dangerous and undesirable place for wildlife and frame natural processes, such as predation and drought, as more harmful to wildlife than captive conditions (Bell, 2015). Zoos often present themselves as providing people with superior access to and a greater variety of animals than in the wild (Malamud, 1998). Sometimes, this ideology contradicts the goal of preservation of wildlife habitat (Malamud, 1998).

Wildlife tourism frequently alters animal behavior, even when it is unintended. Although viewing animals in the wild does not require them to perform tricks or live in artificial environments, wild animals often respond to tourists' presence through avoidance, attraction, or food conditioning. All of these changes can expose the animals to new forms of predation or other ecological risks or lead to new human-wildlife conflicts (Newsome *et al.*, 2005). Many forms of wildlife tourism take place in previously undisturbed habitats. Wildlife tourism that occurs in wild lands or national parks can be accompanied by growth in tourist-related infrastructure, which can have detrimental environmental impacts (Fennell, 2012; Tisdell & Wilson, 2012). These impacts include the construction of roads, noise disturbances, vehicle strikes, migration barriers, pollution, and the degradation of sensitive habitats (Newsome *et al.*, 2005).

Since tourists often spend a relatively short amount of time in any given area, they are often unaware of, and unaffected by, the long-term environmental effects of their tourism activities. Seemingly trivial and ephemeral activities, such as posing with an endangered animal for a photograph or collecting a shell, can have cumulatively dramatic effects on wildlife when performed by many tourists over time. For example, tourists may be offered the opportunity to take a photograph with a marmoset in Mexico or a slow lorys in Thailand; these animals have often been taken from the wild as infants, an act that requires killing the mother (Duffy, 2010). Cumulatively, tourists' payment for these photographs can help drive illegal wildlife trafficking and threaten species' survival. The perception of wildlife tourism photography as being benign for wildlife may be helping to fuel the practice of photo documenting chance encounters with wildlife for social media; some animals have died after being handled by too many people. For example, in 2016, a 7.5 meter reticulated python was found at a construction site in Malaysia. Civil Defense Forces moved the animal, thought to be the second largest python ever found, and posed for countless photos. Many people can be seen holding the snake, taping its mouth shut, and making a noose around its neck. The animal died 2 days later; some speculated the snake died from the stress of being handled (Howard, 2016). In Argentina, a rare juvenile La Plata dolphin died after being removed from the water for "selfies" with beachgoers, who continued to take photographs even after the animal had died (Venkat, 2016).

Importantly, wildlife tourism can have negative economic effects on local communities. These effects include economic stratification and a rise in the cost of living for local people in areas where tourism is introduced. When the profits of wildlife tourism ventures primarily benefit corporations based in the global North, or the elite rather than local communities, tourism can perpetuate unequal power relations and yield exploitative practices (Duffy, 2002). Marketing often relies on myths about developing countries that reinforce colonial notions of people of the global South as being exotic, inferior, uncivilized, and unrestrained (Echtner & Prasad, 2003; d'Hauteserre, 2004) which can result in negative impacts on the national identity of host countries (Palmer, 1994).

8.2 Conservation Criminology and Wildlife Tourism

The knowledge base from natural resource management, risk and decision science, and criminology holds a number of implications for wildlife tourism policy and practice. This section profiles wildlife tourism issues from the perspective of each.

8.2.1 Natural Resources Management and Conservation Biology

Research on how tourism influences wildlife physiology, behavior, population levels, reproduction, and species composition contributes to the evidence base upon which to implement effective tourism policy (Rodger & Calver, 2005). Natural scientists have examined the effects on wildlife populations of consumptive tourism practices such as sport hunting, and the barriers to sustainability of these practices. The costs and benefits to local people from trophy hunting have also been explored by conservation social scientists. For example, the trophy hunting of predators such as African lions and leopards has been linked to declines in populations of these species in some contexts (Packer *et al.*, 2009; Packer *et al.*, 2011; Lindsey *et al.*, 2013). Biological studies exploring the impacts of tourism have indicated that non-consumptive wildlife tourism can also affect wildlife, particularly through trampling of sensitive habitat (e.g. Boyle & Samson, 1985). Human presence at nest sites has increased the stress physiology of Magellanic penguins, which in turn increases disease susceptibility and yields reduced fertility (Fowler, 1999). Humpback whales observed for long periods of time by whale-watching boats have altered their normal behavior (Corkeron, 1995) and night-time visits by tourists to see Green turtle nesting has altered nesting behaviors (Jacobson & Lopez, 1994). These types of data help decision-makers calculate the risks and benefits of tourism development and evaluate the legality of tourism practices. Ecological data on patterns of when, how, and why disturbances to wildlife occur can be integrated with data on human systems (e.g., attitudes and expectations) to inform policy decisions about what limits to set on wildlife tourism practices and also to set realistic expectations for biodiversity conservation and livelihood preservation (Cater, 1995; Reynolds & Braithwaite, 2001). Policy instruments can be used to minimize the environmental effects of tourism. These include motivational tools such as education and awards, self-regulatory mechanisms like guidelines and eco-labeling, economic tools such as fees and licenses, and enforcement of regulatory instruments (Newsome *et al.*, 2005). However, choosing between these policies involves assessing and characterizing the source of the environmental risk. The negative environmental consequences of a tourism practice may be due to lack of compliance or enforcement, market forces, consumer behavior, or a combination thereof; ideally, successful tourism practices are matched to the source of the risk (Newsome *et al.*, 2005). These risks include both objective risks to the environment as well as tourists' perceptions of and behavioral responses to these objective risks.

8.2.2 Risk and Decision Science

Risk and decision science helps explain and predict assessed and perceived risks associated with wildlife tourism. Assessed risk is the product of the probability of an event and its severity; perceived risk, on the other hand, is the judged and intuitive nature of a risk. Tourism and crime involves both of these risk dimensions. Stakeholders' perceptions of crime types and rates are just as predictive of patterns in tourist behavior as assessed risks of crime (Selby, Selby, & Botterill, 2010). Perceptions can be linked to tourists' place image of a particular location

(Selby *et al.*, 2010). African elephant poaching for the global commercial black market provides an example of assessed and perceived risks. This illegal killing poses an assessed risk to the survival of the species; African elephants are being decimated at a rate that exceeds their capacity to reproduce (Wittemyer *et al.*, 2014). The violence and militarization under which elephant poaching often occurs perpetuates a place image of Africa as dangerous and politically unstable, which curbs tourism (Tairo, 2012). The illegal killing of African elephants therefore affects tourism in two ways. First, it reduces the number of elephants in the landscape available to be seen by tourists (i.e., objective risk). Second, it increases the perceived risk among tourists (i.e., subjective risk). In addition to exploring risks on tourism associated with criminal activity itself, the risks tourists create can also be considered. Decision-makers can measure, weigh, and minimize the objective risks that tourists pose to a community, the environment, and wildlife. Wildlife tourism can result in, among other costs, increased water consumption, pollution, the disturbance of natural areas and wildlife, and increased access to wildlife that can facilitate poaching. These risks must be weighed against the economic and conservation benefits of tourism.

8.2.3 Criminology

The mobile and transitory nature of tourists provides opportunities for criminal offending (Botterill & Jones, 2010). Criminologists have demonstrated that tourism growth can increase community crime rates and lead to parallel growth in industries such as gambling and prostitution to meet tourist demand. A culture of reduced responsibility and decreased moral concern in areas with large numbers of tourists can contribute to increased criminal activity (Brunt & Hambly, 1999). The tourism industry, especially in developing nations with weak central governments, has also proved to be a place where illicit businesses can easily form connections with corrupt politicians. For example, tourism development in Belize has been linked to expansion of the cocaine trade. Tourism ventures can provide a way to launder money and to access valuable trade routes (Duffy, 2010). Wildlife tourism ventures can offer a front for illicit activities, or may also themselves incorporate illegal actions; some legal elephant tourism ventures in Thailand have links to the illegal ivory and live animal trades (Nijman, 2014). There are three main ways wildlife tourists may perpetuate crime. First, the crime in itself may be a tourist attraction. For example, taxi hunting of Oribi in KwaZulu-Natal involves groups of urban poachers who hire taxis to transport poachers and hunting dogs to private lands in surrounding rural areas to illegally trespass and hunt the small antelope, which is an endangered and therefore protected species. The poachers typically gamble over the outcome. Second, since tourism involves the global movement of people, tourism provides trade routes for purposeful crime for economic gain. Tourists traveling to remote regions of Madagascar's Masoala Peninsula have been known to ask guides to help them find Mantella frogs, which are extremely colorful, rare and prized in the reptile trade; tourists often return at night to collect the animals local guides helped them locate during the day. Third, tourists sometimes hold different cultural norms about crime than those present in the region they are visiting and thus

Figure 8.1 A poster in Bangkok Airport, Thailand aimed at informing Asian tourists about the illegality of ivory souvenirs.

may either cognitively neutralize their violations as not constituting a real crime or be unaware that their behavior is against the law. Tourists may eat endangered and protected animals in restaurants adjacent to a protected area simply because it is a novelty; they may be unaware of local laws protecting such species. Criminology offers important insights into these dimensions of wildlife tourism and crime; sociological theory help contextualize the problem within larger power, economic, and value systems.

8.3 Theoretical Insights on Wildlife Tourism from Sociology

8.3.1 Wildlife Tourism and Power

Examining power relations and inequality is central to most sociological theories. Although initially these theories were applied to human social systems, sociology increasingly recognizes that power analysis can also be applied to human-animal interactions (Peggs, 2012). Sociology provides theory and tools for analyzing global power relations, stratification within social systems, and the role of ideological and discursive power. The interactions and power dynamics that structure global North-South relations are the focus of World Systems Theory (WST). This theory explicates how power inequalities influence the supply and demand dimensions of both tourism and crime. WST views the world as being comprised of three types of nations: core, semi-periphery, and periphery (Wallerstein, 1974). Core nations have the most power and periphery nations the least. Nations are classified depending upon the presence within their borders of particular products and industries, which impact how states interact in the global system. Core states focus on maintaining their control over profitable and desired industries and products whereas periphery states are pressured to accept unequal benefits and lower wages. Peripheral countries are often rich in natural resources, including wildlife, but are forced to accept economic conditions set by core countries. In the context of wildlife tourism, tourists often come from the global North and visit local communities in the global South. Communities in the global South provide tourists with resources such as wildlife, but are often compelled to conform to tourist demand and to accept whichever economic conditions tourists view as appropriate. The power imbalances explored by WST also relate to conservation crimes. Globalization facilitates the ability of transnational corporations headquartered in core nations to export environmental effects, such as toxic waste, air pollution, or deforestation, to periphery nations. The economic, political, and institutional weaknesses of periphery countries reinforce tolerance of environmental practices outlawed in core countries (Frey, 2003). Because the demand for an illegal wildlife product generally originates with tourists from core countries, it can be difficult for host periphery countries to exert the political and economic power needed to cease this trade.

WST promotes thinking about wildlife tourism policies. By definition, tourists within core countries have some proportion of income beyond what is necessary for shelter and sustenance, which they have chosen to invest in a host country. Individuals in and the economies of host countries may be highly dependent on tourism for income. For this reason, some scholars contend that the focus should be on reducing tourist demand for activities and products that harm the environment rather than on outlawing these practices. If tourism-dependent communities are not provided with alternative, sustainable sources of income and tourist demand remains high, policies will be ineffective (Duffy, 2010). Currently, such policies designed to regulate touristic ventures are often written from the perspective of global North, or core, countries (Duffy & Moore, 2011). This reinforces the power inequalities between core and periphery countries. WST is part of a broader intellectual tradition of postcolonial scholarship that examines how dynamics of exploitation continue to function in the contemporary global system. Tourism can be considered a postcolonial system in that it perpetuates the notion of periphery countries as both exotic and inferior (d'Hauteserre, 2004) and is a vehicle for exporting global North ideologies such as neoliberalism and capitalism (Duffy, 2002). Colonial practices, such as the sport hunting of wild animals in Africa and Asia by wealthy tourists and the naturalization of certain geographic areas as leisure spots for the elite, are sometimes supported under the pretense of tourism.

Designing sustainable and equitable wildlife tourism requires an understanding of how tourism exploits marginalized groups. The Theory of Oppressions (ToP) posits that oppression of humans and animals is interlinked and is produced by three factors: economic exploitation, unequal power, and ideological control (Nibert, 2002). Economic exploitation refers to the designation of one population as a mere resource for another, unequal power denotes the ability of one group to coerce and control another group and ideological control designates how oppression is legitimized through ideologies such as racism, classism, and speciesism that serve to devalue the oppressed. ToP can be applied to wildlife tourism ventures that exert power over human and nonhuman marginalized groups, such as elephant riding camps in Thailand that economically exploit both elephants and mahouts (i.e., elephant handlers). Whereas WST and ToP focus on global and societal stratification, sociological work on authenticity and discursive power offers insight into tourists' individual motivations to engage in wildlife touristic ventures that harm animals.

8.3.2 Authenticity as a Sociological Aspect of Tourism

A key premise that emerges from sociological work on tourism is that tourists seek, in various degrees, an authentic experience. Social spaces have "front rooms," where experiences are available to anyone, and "back rooms," where experiences are accessible only to insiders or members of the community (MacCannell, 1973). Tourists often try to participate in activities they see as part of the back room, because they perceive these activities as intimate, more authentic, and thus most desirable. In many cases, tourism operators purposefully create staged experiences to appear authentic (MacCannell, 1973). Tourists who take part in these activities are made to feel that they are being granted access to the back room when in fact they are merely engaging with an artificial environment created for them. A veneer of authenticity ensures tourists stay interested.

Staged authenticity occurs frequently in wildlife tourism. Curators at zoological parks use various architectural techniques to give the illusion that an animal's habitat is natural. Circus-type shows frequently frame culturally induced behaviors, such as animals performing tricks, as natural behaviors in an attempt to promote these behaviors as ethical and morally legitimate (Bell, 2015). One example that has received widespread media attention is Thialand's Wat Pha Luang Ta Bua Yanasampanno Temple. This Buddhist temple provided tourists with opportunities to pose with Indochinese tigers. Although the temple existed to generate revenue from tourism and maintained control over the tigers through drugging and physical force, many tourists perceived it as an authentic Thai and Buddhist experience and a must-see attraction (Cohen, 2013). Accusations of animal abuse and illegal wildlife trafficking at the infamous "Tiger Temple" led Thai authorities to raid this facility in June 2016, where they uncovered the bodies of 40 tiger cubs in a freezer and other evidence of illegal wildlife trade. Despite the closure of this temple, similar attractions, such as "Tiger Kingdom," remain popular, with staged authenticity central to their appeal.

Sociological work on ideological and discursive power sheds light on the intersection of staged authenticity, media exposure, and tourist expectations. According to Critical Discourse Analysis (CDA) (Fairclough, 1993), oppression often occurs through hegemony, or the domination of people or animals through ideological means. Through different forms of discourse such as language and media, hegemony produces "common sense in the service of sustaining unequal power relations" (Fairclough, 1989, p. 70). By framing certain wildlife tourism practices as germane and inevitable, discourse can be used as a tool of legitimation and naturalization. This in turn can produce consent or socialization for such practices. For example, discourse that frames circus animals as willing performers naturalizes the notion of animals in circuses, conceals the latent domination inherent in such practices, and produces consent for the continued use of animals in entertainment (Bell, 2015).

Media exposure is a primary mechanism by which people form an image of what is authentic for a particular context. Experiences with wildlife through the media's virtual landscape primes people to approach live encounters with wildlife in tourist destinations with certain preconceptions and expectations (Bentrupperbaumer, 2005). The expectation of gaining proximity to wildlife creates false expectations among tourists, who after viewing animals up close for hours on television easily believe that their wildlife experience can and will include frequent proximity to animals. These tourists also may believe that being closer to animals is the best type of experience (Fennell, 2012). Wildlife tourism ventures often use public relations and advertising to promote themselves as authentic and reinforce the notion that proximity to wildlife is preferable. For example, pamphlets advertising "be a mahout" programs in Thailand promote the notion that closeness to elephants through riding them is natural and desirable. Tourists are told that participation in the programs leads to an authentic immersion in mahout culture (Figure 8.2). However, these programs are staged for tourists and, according to some mahouts interviewed by the author, can minimize and denigrate the skills of mahouts. Some mahouts have noted that this staging is disrespectful to their deep-seated cultural traditions that rely on years of developing a relationship with an elephant. Providing tourists with a few hours of "training" is both insulting to mahouts and can pose risks to elephants. Since tourists rarely have any prior knowledge of either the individual elephant or elephant behavior, and elephants do not willingly allow strangers to ride on their backs, "be a mahout" programs can facilitate conditions for the elephant that, according to the mahouts, are stressful and often abusive.

Tourists' expectations and search for authenticity can produce new environmental risks and sometimes crimes. The desire to see animals at close range can prompt tour operators to engage in baiting and food conditioning wildlife. Such operators may follow wildlife for great distances (e.g., humpback whales, spinner dolphins), sometimes violating regulations governing interactions with wildlife (Fennell, 2012). Images of pristine beaches and unpeopled wilderness are common in both tourism promotional materials and wildlife media. Unbeknownst to many tourists, tour operators catering to these expectations

Figure 8.2 A brochure for a "be a mahout" program available at hotels in Chiang Mai, Thailand.

can engage in practices that have far-ranging environmental impacts. For example, tourists' desire for wide, sandy beaches has led to the practice of beach building, which involves transferring sand from the seabed to the shore, in areas such as Playa Del Carmen, Mexico. Although beach building produces scenery that meets tourists' expectations and thus positive reviews that fuel future tourism revenue, the extraction process damages coral reefs and can pollute the marine ecosystem. Beach building is one example of a tourism-based practice that can sacrifice long-term sustainability for short-term economic gain. Although tour operators often attempt to meet tourist expectations, in some instances cultural differences yield conflicting value systems and dissimilar beliefs about the impacts of tourism on wildlife and the environment (Cohen, 2013). Crafting policies that are reflexive with the cross-cultural context of wildlife tourism and encourage tourists to engage in responsible practices can also benefit from these sociological theories. In the following section the sociological concepts and theoretical frameworks discussed above are applied to the case study of elephant tourism and crime in Thailand.

8.4 Elephant Tourism and Crime in Thailand

8.4.1 Elephant Tourism in Thailand

The capture and use of elephants for domestic uses, particularly logging, has a long history in Thailand. After logging was federally banned in 1989, commercial use of elephants shifted to the tourist industry (Lair, 2004; Rattan, Eagles, & Mair, 2012). Thailand now has multiple forms of elephant tourism including elephant riding, elephant painting shows, volunteering at elephant sanctuaries, and circus-type elephant performances. Tourism is Thailand's largest industry and elephant tourism in particular is a growing market. Elephant tourism in Thailand is dominated by entertainment over education. In 2010, an estimated 106 elephant tourism venues held 1,688 elephants (Nijman, 2014; Schmidt-Burbach, Ronfot, & Srisangiam, 2015). The vast majority of these venues (90%) provided elephant riding and almost a third (28%) included circus-type elephant shows. Slightly over 5% of these tourism sites offered "be a mahout" programs, and 3% did not use elephants for any entertainment activities (Schmidt-Burbach *et al.*, 2015). Conservation education at captive wildlife tourism sites in Thailand is rare; 71% of these sites offered no education and only 6% provided comprehensive education (Schmidt-Burbach *et al.*, 2015). "Be a mahout" programs, in which tourists ride on an elephant's neck rather than back and learn to give commands to the elephant, have expanded in the past five years due in part to marketing programs advertising them as being less cruel to elephants. These programs represent a diversification rather than a diminishment of the elephant tourism industry in Thailand, and elephant riding and elephant shows remain popular (J. Schmidt-Burbach, personal communication, February 13, 2016). Although tourism provides a livelihood for mahouts and generates revenue for communities impacted by the national logging ban, the elephant tourism industry in Thailand has been linked to several criminological issues: the illegal smuggling of elephant calves captured from the wild, the ivory trade, and animal welfare problems such as violent training methods and the splitting of highly social elephant families (Cohen, 2015; Nijman, 2014; Stiles & Martin, 2002).

8.4.2 Wild Live Elephant Trafficking

Populations of wild endangered Asian elephants have decreased over 50% in the past 75 years due to a combination of deforestation, poaching, and capture for human uses such as tourism (Choudhury *et al.*, 2008). Thailand has more Asian elephants in captivity than in the wild (Sukumar, 2006). The demand for young elephants is partially met by poaching live elephants in Myanmar and trafficking them across the Thailand-Myanmar border (Nijman, 2014; Figures 8.3 and 8.4). Illegal trafficking of live elephants into and out of Thailand is partially completed through legal channels. The certification program that registers Thai elephants as captive-born contains loopholes and is susceptible to corruption, fraud, and forgery (Nijman, 2014).

Figure 8.3 A juvenile Asian elephant caught in a pit trap in Myanmar. © TRAFFIC

8.4.3 Illegal Ivory Trade

There is an enormous and relatively unregulated market for ivory in Thailand (Doak, 2014). Ivory from captive-held elephants and antique ivory can be legally traded within Thailand. This legal domestic market provides infrastructure through which illegally obtained elephant ivory from wild elephants is smuggled in and out of the country (Doak, 2014). Since enforcement authorities cannot visually differentiate between ivory from captive-held versus wild elephants, they rely on paperwork that can easily be forged to determine the conservation status of the ivory. Traffickers are known to use various techniques to make newly harvested ivory appear older in order to escape suspicion and confiscation, such as submerging ivory in Coca-Cola to give it an aged appearance. Tourists from the United States, Europe, Japan, China, and Taiwan are the main buyers of Thai ivory (Stiles & Martin, 2002). Tourists who purchase ivory in Thailand are typically incorrectly informed that it is legal to transport it back to their home countries (Naylor, 2004). A geographic hub of elephant tourism in Thailand, Surin province, is also a primary site for the illegal trafficking of live elephants and elephant parts (Figure 8.4). Surin hosts the annual Surin Round Up, one of Thailand's largest elephant festivals, at which ivory and other elephant products, such as elephant hair, skin, tails, trunks, teeth, and bones, are widely available for sale (Nijman, 2009).

8.4.4 Animal Welfare

Although several of the animal welfare issues associated with elephant tourism remain legal, criminological notions of harm can be expanded beyond legalistic definitions to incorporate notions of species justice, or legal harms toward animals (White, 2008). In Thailand, training young elephants to be ridden and

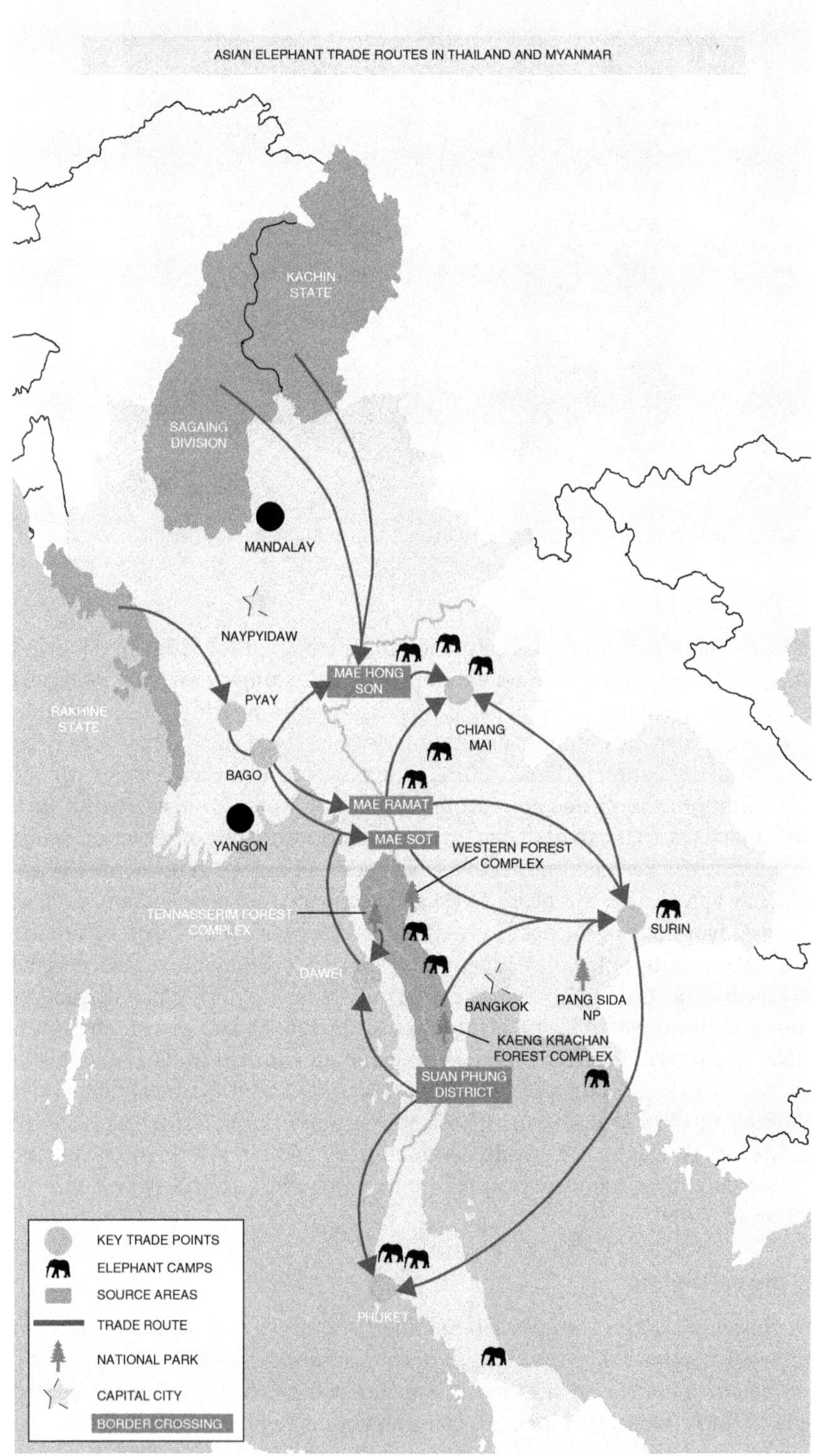

Figure 8.4 A trade route map of elephant trafficking in Thailand and Myanmar. © TRAFFIC

perform tricks is commonly accomplished via the phajaan, or "crush" method (Cohen, 2015). There are variations of the phajaan that depend upon the age and sex of the elephant, what actions the elephant is being trained to do, the philosophy of elephant training endorsed by the mahout, and the location of the training; however, training elephants to perform abnormal behaviors, such as riding bicycles and painting, cannot be accomplished without force. Such behaviors are often produced by placing an elephant calf in a cage only slightly larger than his body and engaging in relentless and unpredictable punishment with nails and other sharp objects until the calf submits to commands (Cohen, 2015). Practices such as the premature separation of calves from their mothers, forcing elephants to ingest amphetamines to work longer hours, continuous chaining, and prohibiting social interaction between conspecifics are common (Lohanan, 2002; Schmidt-Burbach *et al.*, 2015). Additional welfare problems can arise as the unintentional results of environmental conditions, with eye, foot, and spine problems particularly prevalent (Mandal & Khadka, 2013). Elephant spines have sharp, bony protrusions that are very sensitive to weight, and elephants ridden by tourists often suffer from deformed spines and lesions. Elephants used in urban street begging commonly experience foot injuries from prolonged walking on hot concrete and blindness from repetitive exposure to flash photography.

In addition to physical ailments, elephants used in tourism can show signs of psychological distress. Stereotypic behaviors associated with psychological distress in elephants used in circuses (Garrison, 2008), such as repetitive head bobbing and trunk biting are commonly displayed by elephants used in tourism (Schmidt-Burbach *et al.*, 2015). Many elephants used for riding and elephant shows exhibit symptoms such as hyper-vigilance, aggression, impaired social functioning, unpredictable reactions to stress, avoidance and social withdrawal, self-injury, and anxiety; these are symptoms of Complex Post-Traumatic Stress Disorder (c-PTSD), a condition seen in human and nonhuman survivors of prolonged trauma and captivity, such as prisoners of war and torture survivors (Bell Rizzolo & Bradshaw, 2016b; Bradshaw, Capaldo, Lindner, & Grow, 2008; Herman, 1997). Thailand has begun to address risks to animal welfare by outlawing elephant street begging and passing the nation's first animal welfare law in November of 2014. Prior to 2014, harming or killing a captive-held elephant was legal. The efficacy and enforcement of the law as it stands today remains untested, and numerous practices that violate elephants' species-specific needs, such as social deprivation, remain legal.

Although elephant tourism in Thailand contributes to illegal wildlife trafficking and the ivory trade as well as animal welfare problems, tourist dollars have the potential to help overcome risks vis a vis funding conservation and supporting local communities in Thailand. The risks and crimes associated with elephant tourism arise from tourist demand for illegal and unsustainable elephant products and activities. An analytical lens that draws from both conservation criminology and sociological theory serves to map the impacts of elephant tourism and crime within larger power, economic, and value systems. Such knowledge is key for mitigating the negative impacts of elephant tourism and amplifying its potential conservation benefits.

8.4.5 Elephant Tourism and Crime: Insights From Conservation Criminology and Sociological Theory

Conservation criminology and sociology can be synthesized to inform policies and practices that might contribute to more sustainable elephant tourism in Thailand. Conservation criminology presents three different components for analyzing the question of elephant tourism: natural resource management, risk and decision science, and criminology and criminal justice. The first aspect of conservation criminology is natural resource management. Scholarship in this area has examined how tourism impacts the population dynamics and viability of wild elephant populations in Southeast Asia. Ecologists quantified the number of wild-caught elephants trafficked for the tourism trade, finding that at a single Thailand-Myanmar border site, 240 elephants were trafficked over the course of a year and half. Coupled with other ecological data, there is evidence that this trade poses risks to the Asian elephant population (Shepherd & Nijman, 2008). Behavioral and physiological effects of tourism practices on captive-held elephant populations are quantifiable. A recent study evaluated the conditions of elephants in Thai tourism ventures on several variables essential to elephant wellbeing: mobility, hygiene, shelter, environmental noise quality, naturalness of environment, social interaction, diet, entertainment intensity and animal management techniques. Overall, 86% of elephants were kept in severely inadequate conditions (Schmidt-Burbach *et al.*, 2015). The majority (54%) of elephants in Northern Thailand were kept in severely inadequate conditions and the proportion of elephants experiencing these conditions increased to 92% and 93%, respectively, in Southern and Central Thailand. These differences may be due to the fact that, compared to other regions, Northern Thailand tends to have elephant tourism sites that are less transitory and less focused on circus-type shows. Further, mahouts from Northern Thailand draw from the Karen tribal traditions of elephant training, whereas mahouts from other regions tend to use methods developed in Surin. Ultimately, these are empirical questions that when answered, could have theoretical and practical implications for policy. Assessing the impact tourism has on wild and captive-held elephant populations aids calculating objective risk, and examining regional differences in the welfare impacts of elephant tourism can inform the design, implementation, and evaluation of policies designed to maximize elephant welfare and concomitantly contribute to local livelihood preservation.

Risk and decision science can be used to compare tourists' risk perceptions associated with elephant tourism with the assessed risks posed by this industry. Green washing, or portraying elephant tourism as more environmentally friendly than it is, is a common tactic in industry marketing (e.g., Figure 8.2). Tourists are often unaware of the risks their actions pose to wild and captive-held elephants and many tourists are even led to believe that their attendance at elephant trekking camps or shows actually aids conservation. One study compared tourist reviews of wildlife tourism ventures with the assessed risks the sites posed to conservation and animal welfare; unsurprisingly the majority of tourists were unable to accurately assess risks (Moorhouse, Dahlsjö, Baker, D'Cruze, & Macdonald, 2015). Results suggested that relying on a free market model, in which tourists self-select sustainable wildlife tourism ventures and do not attend ones with negative conservation or animal welfare impacts, is insufficient for reducing risks posed by wildlife tourism. External policy instruments such as regulation or certification are often suggested as alternative mechanisms for reducing risks (Moorhouse *et al.*, 2015).

Criminological scholarship on illegal ivory and live elephant trafficking can help direct policy decisions for elephant tourism. TRAFFIC International, the wildlife trade monitoring network, has mapped illegal trade routes through which wild elephants are smuggled into Thailand (Nijman, 2014; Figure 8.3) and analyzed how legal trade of ivory from captive-held Asian elephants contributes to illegal poaching and the sale of tusks from African elephants (Stiles, 2009; Doak, 2014). Criminologists discussed a role for legal and policy changes such as closing loopholes allowing wild-caught elephants to be certified as captive-born, increasing cross-border cooperation and enforcement of existent conservation laws, and modifying the legal system so as to more adequately protect elephants held in tourist camps (Nijman, 2014). The supply and demand functions of elephant tourism and crime can be contextualized within larger power, economic, and value systems. Sociological scholarship on power relations within tourism, staged authenticity, and environmental values contributes such insight.

WST's sociological perspective on global power relations may inform thinking about elephant tourism and crime in Thailand. For example, the standards of elephant welfare in the tourism industry have been critiqued in part because they have been defined by animal welfare non-governmental organizations (NGOs) based in the global North (Duffy & Moore, 2011). In this regard, the decision-making system perpetuates unequal power relations by framing the global North as the "agents" and the global South as the "objects" of ethical tourism standards, and by overlooking cultural variations in tourism practices and conceptualizations of captivity (Duffy & Moore, 2011). Specifically, the NGOs are criticized for failing to wholly understand the barriers to moving elephants from tourist camps in Thailand into the wild; including partners from the global South as agents of change would theoretically help overcome these obstacles. Further, and consistent with WST, tourists from core countries such as the United States, Europe, Japan, and China are the main consumers of Thai ivory (Stiles & Martin, 2002), and demand from tourists based in these core countries drives the illegal elephant trafficking trade (Nijman, 2014). Thus, although regulations in the peripheral countries are necessary, core countries must also address the consumer side of these markets.

ToP offers insight about how the subjugation of mahouts and elephants in tourism camps is coupled and functions through unequal power, economic exploitation, and ideological control. The owners of the tourist camps receive the majority of the economic benefits of elephant riding. In many camps, mahouts receive no salary or food for the elephant; they are paid by the ride and even then receive only a small portion of the fee. It is common practice for the mahouts who live at these camps to have no electricity, running water, or hygienic facilities and to receive no compensation in the case of elephant illness or death. As a result, many elephants in camps are forced to work long hours and receive inadequate nutrition and care. This system is maintained by ideologies of speciesism, classism, and racism toward elephants and mahouts, particularly mahouts from the Karen ethnic group, a population known for working with elephants. Mahouts have a low social status in Thailand and Karen mahouts in particular are particularly devalued and discriminated against. A common theme expressed by mahouts is that infusing the mahout profession with economic empowerment and social status is essential for improving the joint wellbeing of elephants and mahouts (Bell Rizzolo & Bradshaw, 2016a).

Understanding tourist demand is essential for mitigating the risks associated with elephant tourism. Sociological scholarship on staged authenticity and discursive power offers a perspective on why particular forms of elephant tourism have such appeal. Numerous tourism providers use media advertisements to promote elephant riding as the most authentic way to experience Thailand. For example, a brochure shows tourists riding elephants like a "real" mahout (Figure 8.2). From a sociological perspective (MacCannell, 1973), the promotion of elephant riding as authentic is directly linked to its desirability. Although captive-held Asian elephants are biologically identical to their wild counterparts, elephants used in tourism are framed as domesticated animals with whom tourists can safely play and cuddle with (Figure 8.2). From the standpoint of sociological scholarship, discourse frames certain practices as common and inevitable, which in turn produces consent for such practices (Fairclough, 1993). Collapsing the difference between domesticity and wildness, framing elephants as willing performers eager to interact with humans, and promoting the notion of a docile, domesticated elephant are all discursive maneuvers used to legitimate the use of wild elephants for entertainment (Bell, 2015). Disrupting the framing of elephant riding as authentic and natural may be one way to reduce demand for this practice.

8.5 Conclusion

The science of conservation crime is a mostly uncharted domain; human behavior that results in or contributes to environmental change can substantially harm environmental and human health. Wildlife tourism is a globally distributed behavior that is growing in scale and scope; the activity is predicated on direct human-environment relationship and interactions. Along with growth in the industry is the potential for wildlife tourism to raise the socioeconomic value of wildlife and enhance conservation awareness. However, wildlife tourism also poses risks, including social inequality and increased demand for unsustainable or illegal wildlife products and activities. Wildlife tourism carries with it diverse risks at the intersection of human and natural systems. This chapter aims to enhance understanding about, and potentially change, human and organizational behaviors that pose risks to the environment within the wildlife tourism sphere. Synthesizing conservation criminology and sociological theory reveals diverse linkages between wildlife tourism and environmental crime and provide insights on how to reduce the crimes and risks associated with wildlife tourism. Sociological scholarship on power relations and staged authenticity provides insights into the supply and demand dimensions of tourism and crime, tourists' motivations to attend particular tourism ventures, and the opportunities and challenges of promoting pro-environmental behavior in tourists. Ultimately, this information may be used to enhance the composition, evaluation, and implementation of tourism and wildlife policies.

References

Archer, B. H. (1982). The value of multipliers and their policy implications. *Tourism Management*, 3, 236–241.

Bell, J. (2015). There is no wild: Conservation and circus discourse. *Society & Animals*, 23, 462–483.

Bell Rizzolo, J. & Bradshaw, G. A. (2016a). Elephant culture, psychology, and trauma in Asia's tourism industry, presented at Eastern Sociological Society, Boston, MA.

Bell Rizzolo, J. & Bradshaw, G. A. (2016b). Prevalence and patterns of complex PTSD in Asian elephants (*Elephas maximus*), presented at International Conference on Asian Elephants in Culture and Nature, Kelaniya, Sri Lanka.

Bentrupperbaumer, J. (2005). Human dimension of wildlife interactions. In Newsome, D., Dowling, R.K., & Moore, S.A. (Eds.). *Wildlife tourism*. Clevedon, NY: Channel View Publications.

Botterill, D., & Jones, T. (2010). Introduction: Tourism studies and criminology. In Botterill, D., & Jones, T. (Eds.). *Tourism and crime: Key themes*. Mesa, AZ: Goodfellow Publishers Limited.

Boyle, S. A., & Samson, F. B. (1985). Effects of nonconsumptive recreation on wildlife: A review. *Wildlife Society Bulletin*, 13, 110–116.

Bradshaw, G. A., Capaldo, T., Lindner, L., & Grow, G. (2008). Building an inner sanctuary: Complex PTSD in chimpanzees. *Journal of Trauma & Dissociation*, 9, 9–34.

Brunt, P., & Hambly, Z. (1999). Tourism and crime: A research agenda. *Crime Prevention and Community Safety: An International Journal*, 1, 25–36.

Cater, E. (1995). Environmental contradictions in sustainable tourism. *Geographical Journal*, 21–28.

Choudhury, A., Lahiri Choudhury, D.K., Desai, A., Duckworth, J.W., Easa, P.S., Johnsingh, A.J.T., ... Wikramanayake, E. (IUCN SSC Asian Elephant Specialist Group). (2008). Elephas maximus. *The IUCN Red List of Threatened Species 2008*. Retrieved from http://www.iucnredlist.org/details/714

Cohen, E. (2015). Young elephants in Thai tourism: A fatal attraction. In Markwell, K. (Ed.), *Animals and tourism: Understanding diverse relationships*. Clevedon, NY: Channel View Publications.

Cohen, E. (2013). Buddhist compassion and animal abuse in Thailand's tiger temple. *Society & Animals*, 21, 266–283.

Corkeron, P. J. (1995). Humpback whales (*Megaptera novaeangliae*) in Hervey Bay, Queensland: Behaviour and responses to whale-watching vessels. *Canadian Journal of Zoology*, 73, 1290–1299.

D'Hauteserre, A. (2004). Postcolonialism, colonialism, and tourism. In Lew, A. A., Hall, C. M., & Williams, A.M. (Eds.). *A companion to tourism*. Malden, MA: Blackwell Publishing.

Doak, N. (2014). *Polishing off the ivory trade: Surveys of Thailand's ivory market.* Cambridge, UK: TRAFFIC International.
Duffus, D.A., & Dearden, P. (1990). Non-consumptive wildlife-oriented recreation: A conceptual framework. *Biological Conservation*, 53, 213–31.
Duffy, R. (2002). *A trip too far: Ecotourism, politics, and exploitation.* London, UK: Earthscan.
Duffy, R. (2010). *Nature crime: How we're getting conservation wrong.* New Haven, CT: Yale University Press.
Duffy, R., & Moore, L. (2011). Global regulations and local practices: The politics and governance of animal welfare in elephant tourism. *Journal of Sustainable Tourism*, 19, 589–604.
Echtner, C. M., & Prasad, P. (2003). The context of third world tourism marketing. *Annals of Tourism Research*, 30, 660–682.
Fairclough, N. (1989). *Language and power.* London, U.K.: Longman.
Fairclough, N. (1993). *Discourse and social change.* Cambridge, U.K.: Polity Press.
Fennell, D. A. (2012). *Tourism and animal ethics.* London, U.K.: Routledge.
Fowler, G. S. (1999). Behavioral and hormonal responses of Magellanic penguins (*Spheniscus magellanicus*) to tourism and nest site visitation. *Biological Conservation*, 90, 143–149.
Frey, R. S. (2003). The transfer of core-based hazardous production processes to the export processing zones of the periphery: The maquiladora centers of northern Mexico. *Journal of World-Systems Research*, 9, 317–354.
Garrison, J. (2008). The challenges of meeting the needs of captive elephants. In Wemmer, C., & Christen, C.A. (Eds.). *Elephants and ethics: Toward a morality of coexistence.* Baltimore, MD: The Johns Hopkins University Press.
Herman, J. L. (1997). *Trauma and recovery.* New York, NY: Basic Books.
Howard, B.C. (2016). A colossal snake dies under mysterious circumstances. National Geographic. Retrieved from http://news.nationalgeographic.com/2016/04/160412-reticulated-python-killed-malaysia/
Jacobson, S. K., & Lopez, A. F. (1994). Biological impacts of ecotourism: Tourists and nesting turtles in Tortuguero National Park, Costa Rica. *Wildlife Society Bulletin*, 22, 414–419.
Lair, R. C. (2004). *Gone astray: The care and management of the Asian elephant in domesticity (4th ed.).* Bangkok: FAO Regional Office for Asia and the Pacific.
Lindsey, P. A., Balme, G. A., Funston, P., Henschel, P., Hunter, L., Madzikanda, H.,...Nyirenda, V. (2013). The trophy hunting of African lions: Scale, current management practices and factors undermining sustainability. *PLOS One*, 8. Retrieved from doi:10.1371/journal.pone.0073808.
Lohanan, R. (2002). The elephant situation in Thailand and a plea for co-operation. In Baker, I., & Kashio, M. (Eds.). *Giants on our hands: Proceedings of the international workshop on the domesticated Asian elephant.* Bangkok, Thailand: FAO Regional Office for Asia and Pacific.
Mandal, R. K., & Khadka, K. K. (2013). Health status of captive Asian elephants in Chitwan National Park, Nepal. *Gajah*, 39, 37–39.
MacCannell, D. (1973). Staged authenticity: Arrangements of social space in tourist settings. *American Journal of Sociology*, 79, 589–603.

Malamud, R. (1998). *Reading zoos: Representations of animals in captivity.* New York, NY: New York University Press.
Moorhouse, T. P., Dahlsjö, C. A., Baker, S. E., D'Cruze, N. C., & Macdonald, D. W. (2015). The customer isn't always right - Conservation and animal welfare implications of the increasing demand for wildlife tourism. *PLOS One*, 10. Retrieved from doi:10.1371/journal.pone.0138939.
Naylor, R.T. (2004). The underworld of ivory. *Crime, Law and Social Change*, 42, 261–295.
Newsome, D., Dowling, R.K., & Moore, S.A. (2005). *Wildlife tourism*. Clevedon, NY: Channel View Publications.
Newsome, D. & Rodger, K. (2014). Wildlife tourism. In Holden, A., & Fennell, D. (Eds.). *The Routledge handbook of tourism and the environment.* New York, NY: Routledge.
Nibert, D. (2002). *Animal rights/human rights: Entanglements of oppression and liberation.* Lanham, MD: Rowman & Littlefield Publishers.
Nijman, V. (2014). *An assessment of the live elephant trade in Thailand.* Cambridge, UK: TRAFFIC International.
Orams, M. B. (2002). Feeding wildlife as a tourism attraction: A review of issues and impacts. *Tourism Management*, 23, 281–293.
Packer, C., Kosmala, M., Cooley, H. S., Brink, H., Pintea, L., Garshelis, D., … Nowell, K. (2009). Sport hunting, predator control and conservation of large carnivores. *PLOS One*, 4. Retrieved from doi:10.1371/journal.pone.0005941
Packer, C., Brink, H., Kissui, B. M., Maliti, H., Kushnir, H., & Caro, T. (2011). Effects of trophy hunting on lion and leopard populations in Tanzania. *Conservation Biology*, 25, 142–153.
Palmer, C. A. (1994). Tourism and colonialism: The experience of the Bahamas. *Annals of Tourism Research*, 21, 792–811.
Peggs, K. (2012). *Animals and sociology.* New York, NY: Palgrave Macmillan.
Rattan, J. K., Eagles, P. F. J., and Mair, H. L. (2012). Volunteer tourism: Its role in creating conservation awareness. *Journal of Ecotourism*, 11, 1–15.
Reynolds, P. C., & Braithwaite, D. (2001). Towards a conceptual framework for wildlife tourism. *Tourism Management*, 22, 31–42.
Rodger, K., & Calver, M. (2005). Natural science and wildlife tourism. In Newsome, D., Dowling, R.K., & Moore, S.A. (Eds.). *Wildlife tourism.* Clevedon, NY: Channel ViewPublications.
Scheyvens, R. (1999). Ecotourism and the empowerment of local communities. *Tourism Management*, 20, 245–249.
Schmidt-Burbach, J. (2016, February 13). Personal communication.
Schmidt-Burbach, J., Ronfot, D., & Srisangiam, R. (2015). Asian elephant (Elephas maximus), pig- tailed macaque (Macaca nemestrina) and tiger (Panthera tigris) populations at tourism venues in Thailand and aspects of their welfare. *PLOS One*, 10, e0139092.
Selby, M., Selby, H. & Botterill, D. (2010). Tourism, image and fear of crime. In Botterill, D., & Jones, T. (Eds.). *Tourism and crime: Key themes.* Mesa, AZ: Goodfellow Publishers Limited.
Shackley, M. L. (1996). *Wildlife tourism.* London, UK: International Thomson Business Press.

Shepherd, C. R., & Nijman, V. (2008). *Elephant and ivory trade in Myanmar*. Petaling Jaya, Malaysia: TRAFFIC Southeast Asia.

Stiles, D. (2009). *The elephant and ivory trade in Thailand*. Petaling Jaya, Malaysia: TRAFFIC Southeast Asia.

Stiles, D., & Martin, E. (2002). The trade in African and Asian ivory in South and South East Asia. *Pachyderm*, 33, 74–87.

Sukumar, R. (2006). A brief review of the status, distribution and biology of wild Asian elephants Elephas maximus. *International Zoo Yearbook*, 40, 1–8.

Tairo, A. (2012). Poaching threatens Africa elephants and tourism. ETN Global Travel Industry News. Retrieved from http://www.eturbonews.com/31557/poaching-threatens-africa-elephants-and-tourism

Tisdell, C., & Wilson, C. (2012). *Nature-based tourism and conservation*. Northampton, U.K.: Edward Elgar Publishing.

Venkat, A. (2016). Selfish selfies kill rare baby dolphin. Asia Times. Retrieved from http://www.newsjs.com/url.php?p=http://atimes.com/2016/02/sel-fish-selfies-kill-rare-baby-dolphin/

Wallerstein, I. (1974). The rise and future demise of the world capitalist system: Concepts for comparative analysis. *Comparative Studies in Society and History*, 16, 387–415.

Walpole, M. J., & Goodwin, H. (2000). Local economic effects of dragon tourism in Indonesia. *Annals of Tourism Research*, 27, 559–576.

Walpole, M. J., & Leader-Williams, N. (2002). Tourism and flagship species in conservation. *Biodiversity and Conservation*, 11, 543–547.

White, R. (2008). *Crimes against nature: Environmental criminology and ecological justice*. Cullompton, UK: Willan Publishing.

Wilson, C., & Tisdell, C. (2003). Conservation and economic benefits of wildlife-based marine tourism: Sea turtles and whales as case studies. *Human Dimensions of Wildlife*, 8(1), 49–58.

Wittemyer, G., Northrup, J. M., Blanc, J., Douglas-Hamilton, I., Omondi, P., & Burnham, K. P. (2014). Illegal killing for ivory drives global decline in African elephants. *Proceedings of the National Academy of Sciences*, 111, 13117–13121.

Part III

Models and Innovations

9

Technological Innovations Supporting Wildlife Crime Detection, Deterrence, and Enforcement

Heidi Kretser, Emma Stokes, Serge Wich, David Foran, and Alexa Montefiore

Wildlife crime constitutes a major global threat to wildlife populations; it includes trade in commercial products derived from threatened and endangered wild animal populations around the world. Detection, deterrence, and enforcement of wildlife crime at a scale sufficient to improve the protection of wildlife populations requires cooperation and coordination across many government jurisdictions and among numerous organizations. Part of this cooperation and coordination includes testing and deploying approaches that might assist with securing wild animal populations and bringing perpetrators of crime to justice. These approaches ideally address fundamental elements of criminology including situational crime prevention, market reduction approaches, and enforcement (Pires & Moreto, 2011; Schneider, 2008; Wellsmith, 2008).

Situational crime prevention (SCP) refers to the manipulation of environments to disrupt opportunities for a crime to take place. This is achieved by preventing the right factors (e.g. target animal, offender, weapon) from being in the right place for the crime to happen (Clarke, 2009; Pires & Moreto, 2011). SCP seeks to discourage would-be offenders from committing crimes by creating sufficient risk deterrents. Additionally, would-be offenders can be given opportunities to engage in alternative behaviors that yield a similar outcome, for example by providing economic incentives (Wellsmith, 2008). Market reduction approaches increase the risk of selling or buying products and specifically focus on those transporting goods (i.e., handlers) and consumers. Market reduction approaches are data-driven and place an emphasis on market analysis to understand trade routes (Schneider, 2008; Wellsmith, 2008). Enforcement consists of two central components: monitoring adherence to existing regulations, laws, or agreements; and ensuring perpetrators are punished for infractions and given meaningful penalties (Keane, Jones, Edwards-Jones, & Milner-Gulland, 2008). Enforcement overlaps with both SCP and market reduction approaches to act as a deterrent. In reality, improvements in all of these areas are needed for better management of wildlife crime and its associated risks.

Different strategies can be employed to achieve SCP, market reduction strategies, and enforcement within wildlife crime. These may include but are not limited to building resources and capacity for traditional surveillance

Conservation Criminology, First Edition. Edited by Meredith L. Gore.

of poachers by patrols (e.g., park rangers) in source countries (Hilborn *et al.*, 2006), documenting trade chains and connecting consumer markets to source countries, implementing campaigns to reduce demand for wildlife products (e.g., WildAid, 2015), monitoring vendors in actual and online marketplaces, strengthening penalties for those engaged in illicit behavior and non-compliance with wildlife trade laws, and supporting diplomacy across countries from source to market.

Technological advances have enabled offenders to organize more complicated and successful covert operations. This has contributed to a dramatic rise in poaching and trade and has made situational crime prevention, market reduction approaches, and enforcement more challenging (The Economist, 2014). Modern weapons and technologies for locating wildlife enable illegal killing to occur at much higher success rates than in the past. Modern criminals can more effectively disguise wildlife parts for consumption (Emslie, Milliken, & Talukdar, 2013). In some cases, criminals employ sophisticated, encrypted online communications to plan illicit activities as well as coordinate and maintain networks (Lavorgna, 2014; Warchol, 2004). Individuals, loosely associated groups, and organized criminals use the internet to build a vibrant marketplace for connecting buyers to suppliers and suppliers to new sources (Lavorgna, 2014). Although technology can be used to facilitate the illegal activities of global wildlife trade, technological innovations also have the potential to contribute to documenting and resolving wildlife crimes by creating more efficient ways to address situational crime prevention, initiate market reduction approaches, and improve enforcement.

In this chapter, we present four case studies on different technologies: the Spatial Monitoring and Reporting Tool (SMART), conservation drones, mobile applications, and genetic forensic science. These technologies are examples of innovative tools that assist with decreasing risks of illegal wildlife trade when deployed in conjunction with traditional approaches. We examine how these relatively recent advances can positively contribute to conservation crime monitoring, detection, and enforcement. We explore how these technologies have been deployed in the field and discuss the limitations of implementing these technologies across many scales. Finally, we recommend how the technologies themselves and their implementation might need to evolve in order to create larger-scale improved outcomes for solving wildlife crimes and protecting species in the wild.

9.1 Challenges for Wildlife Crime Detection and Enforcement

Many challenges plague governments, organizations, and individuals working to reduce risks to people and wildlife from wildlife crimes. Foremost may be the lack of political will and resources to address many facets of the problem. Until recently, wildlife crime received less notice compared to other transitional crimes such as drug and human trafficking (Nellemann, Henriksen, Raxton,

Ash, & Mrema, 2014; Wellsmith, 2008). This may be because wildlife crime was considered a topic more appropriately addressed within the environmental and conservation field, and therefore infractions were not necessarily addressed as crimes and criminal activity (Wellsmith, 2008). However, we now understand that wildlife crimes occur at three levels:

1) The micro level, such as killing an individual animal for subsistence purposes.
2) The meso level, such as killing animals as part of an organized network for financial gain.
3) The macro level, such as importing and exporting wildlife over international borders (Wellsmith, 2008).

The recent increase in macro level infractions, coupled with severe wildlife population decline, has brought increased attention to the criminology of wildlife crimes. Even with this attention, wildlife crimes pose dramatically little risk for criminals because the penalties are not severe compared with the very high gains that can be made from successful transactions (The Economist, 2014; Schneider, 2008). Law enforcement officers penalizing micro and meso offenders may be perceived as creating undue hardships on a neighbor or community member. In part because of this, many crimes go unreported and unpunished (Infield & Namara, 2001; Pires & Clarke, 2012). Additionally, source countries for many species facing threats from wildlife crime often have pressing socioeconomic and political concerns ranging from communicable disease and poverty to war and corruption. These issues often receive greater attention and resources compared to issues related to the environment or wildlife and specifically environmental crimes. In some cases, government involvement in such crimes may be the origin of apathy toward or lack of political will to address wildlife crime (Bennett, 2011). A lack of political will translates to insufficient resources available for addressing the full scope of the problem at all levels.

At the micro and meso levels, parks and protected areas are notoriously understaffed, rangers are often underpaid, and they lack the equipment and training necessary to adequately patrol and detect wildlife crimes (Bennett, 2011; Kaaria & Muchiri, 2011; Warchol, 2004). Responsibility for enforcement rests mostly with these individuals. It also spans those working at different points along supply chains including transportation and border guards. Resources to support staff, training, and equipment at each of those points are insufficient for adequate enforcement and disrupting opportunities for crimes to occur. At the meso and macro levels, the ability to coordinate evidence and link individuals to secretive trade chains becomes increasingly difficult without structured systems for data management in place and effective communications across local, national, and international jurisdictions. Resources and capacity building are needed to coordinate enforcement efforts and communicate data to disrupt movement of illicit items. At the macro level, where wildlife crimes extend beyond country boundaries and demand markets flourish, resources and capacity are needed to raise awareness of wildlife crime, document evidence in a manner suitable for prosecution, bolster support systems for managing information across jurisdictions, and facilitate the dismantling of supply chains and end markets.

Implementing innovative technologies provides opportunities to counter challenges at each level and within every step of the crime process by providing those individuals, organizations, and governments working to dismantle illegal wildlife trade the tools and sophisticated structures necessary for a more holistic and integrated approach to address these problems (Cress & Zommers, 2014).

9.2 Technological Advances in Conservation

Technological advances provide tools to assist with documenting global biodiversity worldwide. Programs such as eBird, iNaturalist, and Reef Life Survey are some among many examples of large scale, big-data datasets being used to answer conservation questions (Pimm *et al.*, 2014; Pimm *et al.*, 2015). Additionally, field equipment such as camera traps, GPS wildlife collars, and acoustic monitors are transforming how we understand wildlife use of habitats (Depraetere *et al.*, 2012; Kays & Slauson, 2008; Matthews *et al.*, 2013). Researchers and programs can use these tools, and others, to document illegal poaching and wildlife trade activities (Cress & Zommers, 2014). One of the potentially most significant benefits that modern technology can contribute to the fight against wildlife crime is the ability to coordinate huge amounts of data over space and time more efficiently. This benefit extends across many facets of the wildlife trade chain from patrolling for poaching activity in the field to customs clearance in consumer countries. Previously, the seemingly simple task of entering paper records into computerized databases often taxed the already overworked park rangers collecting information. Systems allowing direct entry of data into a computer format are more efficient. Similarly, large scale and centralized databases documenting customs seizures assist enforcement agents with understanding trade routes (Chandran, Krishana, & Nguyen, 2011). Centralized databases containing DNA markers of wild species populations aid enforcement efforts as scientists can match DNA sequences to source locations, map potential routes that products take from source to market, and target surveillance in efficiently (Wasser *et al.*, 2008). The ability to access these large databases remotely can facilitate the capture of illegal items moving across borders and potentially the apprehension of suspects involved in that trade. Many of the technologies now available to use in the field have become more cost-effective to implement.

Below we introduce several technologies that can be used within a criminology framework to facilitate collection of data at different levels, assist with linking movements of animals and products from sources to markets, and contribute to improved enforcement at all scales. First, the Spatial Monitoring and Reporting Tool (SMART) measures, evaluates, and can improve the effectiveness of wildlife law enforcement patrols and site-based conservation activities. SMART directly links to situational crime prevention by ensuring wildlife law enforcement effectively monitor assigned territories and provide more of a strategic deterrent for potential criminals as patrols more effectively cover their assigned areas. Even with adequate staff, detection of bushmeat hunters or poachers has proven to be difficult in large expanses of forest or other habitat with limited accessibility.

Provision of sufficient resources, including funding and equipment, to anti-poaching units has been linked to a decline in the rates of poaching within specific areas (Hilborn *et al.*, 2006). However, bushmeat hunting and poaching are currently at extremely high levels and novel techniques might help to reduce this threat. Second, conservation drones are relatively inexpensive autonomous unmanned aerial vehicles, capable of surveying and scanning the forest for wildlife and for criminal activity. Drones are one asset for situational crime prevention. Third, risk and decision-tree style mobile applications can be used by law enforcement officers, as well as the general public, along trade routes, checkpoints and in markets to assist with the preliminary identification of suspicious products or wildlife (Kretser *et al.*, 2015, WildScan, 2014). Although mobile apps provide a market reduction approach in situ, details to the species level will ultimately frame tactical decisions made by law officers by developing a more complete understanding of the traded goods, the markets, and the sources (Schneider, 2008). Finally, in many cases confirmation of species and links to source countries will need to be achieved through genetic forensic analysis that can assign DNA to a particular region within a species' range (Wasser *et al.*, 2008).

9.3 Spatial Monitoring and Reporting Tool (SMART)

To improve monitoring and management of site-based protection efforts, a global partnership of conservation organizations developed and launched SMART in 2013. The SMART Partnership currently includes the Convention on International Trade in Endangered Species of Wild Fauna and Flora-Monitoring Illegal Killing of Elephants Programme(CITES-MIKE), Frankfurt Zoological Society, North Carolina Zoo, Panthera, Peace Parks Foundation, Wildlife Conservation Society, World Wildlife Fund, and Zoological Society of London. SMART responds to two fundamental needs repeatedly identified by protected area managers and field-based users: first, the need for up-to-date, standardized and cost-effective information on threats in a protected area; and second, the need to track, evaluate and guide performance of protection staff like rangers in responding to those threats. The tool functions in austere environments with relatively low technical, management, or financial capacity; it provides the means to rapidly convert field data into useful information in a highly visual and spatially explicit format with maps and diagrams. SMART is a unique example of a global collaborative conservation NGO partnership—its ability to focus on a clear goal that responds to a pressing conservation need has been fundamental to its success to date.

SMART consists of a software application that enables standardized collection, storage, communication, and evaluation of ranger-based data (Figure 9.1). The software application documents patrol efforts, including time spent on patrols, areas visited, and distances covered. It also documents patrol results, including, for example, how many snares were removed or how many arrests were made on each patrol. Threat levels are captured by measuring signs of poaching or poachers. Mobile data collection is enabled through a CyberTracker

Figure 9.1 SMART users in Cambodia and Nigeria. © Wildlife Conservation Society

plug-in that simplifies and speeds up the collection and entry of field data (Pimm *et al.*, 2015). SMART has powerful analytical, mapping and reporting functionality that enables rapid conversion of patrol data to information for park management, such as patrol coverage and location of threat hotpots. This information highlights coverage gaps and identifies key areas where patrol deployment should be intensified. The process can improve direct management of protection staff by reporting on individual performance, which can help reward success, remedy failure, and boost the morale and motivation of front-line rangers.

Although a number of software-based data collection tools exist (e.g., ODK, Observer), none are conservation law enforcement-specific and designed explicitly to reduce wildlife crime. SMART builds upon other, existing information management systems used for law enforcement monitoring but has enhanced usability, functionality, and scalability to ensure relevance in a range of languages and contexts around the globe. The technology has been built with a plug-in architecture that facilitates development and integration of new components.

SMART is one of the few law enforcement monitoring solutions being built to perform in both connected and disconnected environments. The application is open source and freely available to the entire conservation community. Being embedded within a partnership has enabled SMART to develop a business and governance model that ensures both the financial and technical sustainability of the tool.

Beyond development of SMART technology, the SMART Partnership supports efforts to improve the global deployment of the tool in wide range of different regions. The Partnership helps develop human capacity to capitalize on the tool and emphasize the importance of adaptive management practices for site-based conservation (see also Stokes, 2010). The combination of monitoring, patrolling and protection efforts, results, and threats to inform and adapt management practices is collectively termed the SMART Approach.

The Approach supports a wide range of protected area or site-based management, improving detection and enforcement at a micro and meso scale. It helps address challenges in both the terrestrial and marine realms and is scalable to a variety of applications, from helping to decide where patrolling resources need to be deployed, to evaluating and improving ranger performance, to assessing impact and success of law enforcement strategies. At the request of protected area and wildlife agencies, SMART is increasingly scaled up from individual sites to entire protected area networks around the world. Information collected via SMART is secured through a granular security system, with different access permissions, restrictions and password requirements for different levels. One step in the implementation of the technology is to secure the networks and infrastructure deploying. Through SMART, database administration and management protocols can be put in place to ensure data security. By documenting patrolling effort and results SMART can also promote transparency and improved governance. The ability to collate standardized and timely information on pressing threats at relatively little additional cost is also becoming increasingly attractive to donors and partners in understanding how their investments are being used. In this way, adoption and implementation of SMART can sustain opportunities for maintaining management and enforcement.

9.3.1 Limitations of SMART Technology and Opportunities for Future Improvements

SMART technology alone will not improve protection of species, increase deterrence or reduce crime. Basic enforcement capacity, equipment (e.g., computers, GPS) and infrastructure (e.g., communications infrastructure, offices) must also be in place to supplement SMART technology. The SMART Approach helps define these additional needs. Although SMART software and tools are free, additional operational resources, skills, and activities are required to employ effective adaptive patrol management practices. Among the necessary additions to SMART are strong leadership, feedback mechanisms between managers and rangers, and in some cases ranger performance-based incentives.

Although SMART was designed operate in environments with low technical or management capacity it does require technical support for set up and design, which has created a gap between the willingness to deploy SMART and the ability to do so. It is therefore recommended that site-based staff receive training from and work with experienced SMART experts in the introduction of the SMART Approach at a site. To address this need, the Partnership is building capacity through a training of trainers approach to ensure more people are trained and a cadre of conservation professionals is created who can themselves provide instruction and support to their peers in the use of SMART. An online SMART Forum with over 100 members provides a platform for users to post problems and share experiences is available on the website to facilitate information sharing and problem solving.

The growing user group has played and will continue to play a critical role in the development of SMART, their feedback ensures the approach continues to meet expanding technology needs and stays grounded in the needs of field practitioners. SMART recently added a plug-in to collate, manage and visualize systematic ecological survey and monitoring data, extending its application beyond law enforcement to include other types of data key for protected area management—a sort of 'one-stop shop' for protected area managers. Having already implemented SMART for ranger-based monitoring at a site, the ability to extend its functionality is much more appealing to most users than having to manage multiple different systems.

SMART is still a relatively new tool despite its rapid global uptake. At the time of writing, SMART has been implemented in more than 150 sites in almost thirty countries worldwide in under three years. This vindicates the core need for the tool and lends considerable potential to have real impact. In many sites and in many countries, SMART is the only source of regular information flow from field staff to decision-makers. A comprehensive monitoring and evaluation plan is now needed to determine under what contexts SMART is best able to deliver in improving site-based conservation efforts.

9.4 Conservation Drones

Autonomous unmanned aerial vehicles (UAVs), colloquially called drones, are another technology being newly employed to further conservation goals. Drones can be inexpensive to design and operate and have been used successfully for surveying and mapping forests, land-use change, and wildlife populations of orangutans, elephants, whales, and birds, among others (Hodgson, Kelley, & Peel, 2013; Koh & Wich, 2012; Vermeulen, Lejeune, Lisein, Sawadogo, & Bouché, 2013). Conservation drones have wide ranging potential for use in wildlife crime prevention and enforcement (Figure 9.2).

Detection of bushmeat hunters or poachers has proven to be difficult in large expanses of forest or other habitat. Providing sufficient resources to anti-poaching units has been linked to a decline in poaching (Hilborn *et al.*, 2006). Current levels of bushmeat hunting and poaching are extremely high and novel detection techniques might help to reduce this threat in addition to providing money and equipment to agencies. Given that logging roads facilitate access to forested areas and are often associated with increased hunting (Laurance, Goosem, &

Figure 9.2 Conservation drones can detect wildlife crimes. © Conservation Drones

Laurence, 2009), detecting illegal logging and forest conversion can assist with poaching prevention by directing enforcement officers to areas prone to wildlife crimes.

Freely available low-resolution satellite-based remotely sensed images (e.g., Landsat, MODIS) have limited utility for tracking land-cover change at small scales. This is particularly true in the tropics where frequent cloud cover prevents real-time deforestation information. Sub-meter resolution images (from, e.g., QuickBird, IKONOS) can be prohibitively costly. Conservation drones, however, can provide reasonably priced high-resolution data critical for accurately detecting and tracking land-cover transitions at a smaller scale. These high-resolution video or still images allow for easy discrimination of land uses including oil-palm plantations, maize fields, human habitation, forests, logged areas, and forest trails. They also enable detection of activities associated with hunting such as people, cars, car tracks, animal carcasses, fire, smoke, tents and huts. Video footage obtained in Indonesia and Congo allowed for the detection of smoke plumes that can be the sign of fresh forest clearing or of bushmeat hunters drying animals on racks in the forest (conservationdrones, unpubl. data). The geo-tagged images can be combined into a high resolution georeferenced mosaic and superimposed on geographical information system (GIS) software packages such as ArcGIS. Such information could facilitate more targeted deployment of local rangers to increase their success in intercepting bushmeat hunters or people clearing forests.

Conservation drones can use low-cost autopilots, including those developed by online communities (e.g., diydrones.com). Drones usually include a computer processor, GPS, data logger, pressure sensor, airspeed sensor, triple-axis gyro, and accelerometer. By combining the autopilot with ground control software, most remote control model airplanes and multi-rotors can be converted to an autonomous drone. Basic small fixed-wing systems can fly up to ~50 km during a single flight, whereas small multi-rotor systems can fly up to ~3km during a single flight. A variety of still and video cameras can be used with these platforms. In addition to standard color cameras, thermal imaging cameras can also be used to detect heat signals from humans, fires, and cars.

Using ground control software, flight paths can be programmed in a satellite map interface. Such software allows for flexible mission planning, acquisition of high-resolution maps, reconnaissance flights or straight transects for wildlife counts. Drones can be programmed to take off and land autonomously, circle over any waypoint for specified number of turns or duration, and a number of other flight options. Users can also program other flight parameters such as ground speed and altitude along the flight route. Drone takeoff and landing depends on whether the system deployed is a fixed-wing or a multi-rotor. Take-off for fixed wings is achieved by either a light toss into the air or by using a bungee cord that is attached to the plane's fuselage. Fixed wing landings can be programmed to be semi or fully autonomous. Fully autonomous landings for fixed-wing drones require a relatively large flat space (at least 100x100m) depending on the system. Multi-rotor systems can takeoff and land fully autonomous and in much smaller spaces.

Despite the relative ease of use, operating drones successfully requires training. Many drones feature a telemetry system connecting a laptop/tablet/smartphone and the drone, allowing for direct viewing of the drone's location within the software program during flight. Software allows users to monitor flight parameters such as ground speed, elevation, battery voltage. The range of the drone and the range of the telemetric connection are functions of the terrain, flight parameters, and the battery in the drone. Drones are also subject to special laws in some countries, which managers and researchers must be aware of and abide by.

9.4.1 Limitations of Drone Technology and Opportunities for Future Improvements

Although drones are an innovative technology for monitoring land-use change and human activity in potential poaching hot spots, some limitations exist for the proper usage of these systems in crime prevention and enforcement. These limitations also present some opportunities for future improvements. Conservation projects that currently deploy drones mostly have one drone in the air at a time operating as part of a single mission planning control system thus limiting the coverage capabilities. Future efforts that aim to implement drones to reduce wildlife crime can potentially benefit from having multiple drones in the air simultaneously to constantly monitor key areas. Such multiple drone monitoring can combine short and long-duration fixed wings and multi-rotor systems. User-friendly mission planning and control systems that can integrate drone systems with different control hardware will minimize operational complexity. Drone usage may also be subject to regulation, making coordination with local officials and potentially with national governments needed.

Although the cost of the actual drones is relatively low, associated costs can be very high. Traditional ground surveys can be time-consuming, financially impracticable, and logistically challenging in remote areas (Gardner *et al.*, 2008), but drones come with their own challenges. The cost of maintaining drone technology, as well as training of local personnel to use the equipment and to download and manually process and analyze thousands of images and hundreds of hours of video, may be a barrier for many source sites in developing countries (Chen *et al.*, 2014). These longer-term costs need to be considered when setting up a drone system for monitoring wildlife crimes.

An essential step for making drone deployment relevant to situational crime prevention and enforcement is the conversion of drone mission plans and information gathered during flight into actionable data for wildlife managers and patrol teams on the ground. Because of this, efforts to improve the efficacy of drone systems in the field of wildlife crimes include designing software to make data analyses automated; these efforts could potentially integrate data from drone missions into software packages like SMART. Drones can be very useful in collecting relevant data, but these data will only improve conservation if organized into a format which can be acted upon by conservation area managers, patrol teams, law enforcers, and other relevant parties.

The usefulness of drones in conservation and research is rapidly spreading and several organizations now use drones as part of their standard conservation research and management practices. Given this expansion, the conservation community now has options to carefully assess whether use of drones leads to significant savings of time or human and financial resources for local conservation workers and researchers. These assessments help determine if drones can be efficiently used to prevent crimes by identifying areas prone to poaching and deploying patrols to intercept would-be criminals, and what improvements to drone deployment systems and methods will enable more efficient enforcement of critical source sites for wildlife.

9.5 Mobile Device Applications

Mobile applications (apps) are software programs designed for use on mobile devices such as smartphones, tablets, and even some desktop computers. Apple initiated development of mobile apps in 2008 and by 2013 app stores operated by Apple and Google had more than 1.4 million apps available for download (Lessen & Ante, 2013). Worldwide usage of smartphones has surpassed one quarter of the world's human population in 2015 and is expected to climb to one third of the population by 2017 (eMarketeer, 2014). With their increased popularity and ever-increasing processing power of mobile devices, applications are a technology that can play an important role in fighting wildlife crimes.

Several mobile apps exist that could contribute to market reduction approaches, though to date, data on actual impacts of mobile apps are now available. Wildlife Witness (Taronga, 2014) allows users to report suspicious activity involving the poaching, smuggling, or selling of wildlife. The features include geolocation capability and opportunity to provide detailed information about the incident. Reports are sent to TRAFFIC, a wildlife trade monitoring network, which coordinates with authorities to investigate reports (Taronga, 2014). The app does not currently have a system to enable users to identify the animal, but it is designed for use by travelers as well as local citizens and is available in English on iOS and Android platforms.

Three additional apps include a decision-tree approach to enable preliminary identification of species in the field (Kretser *et al.*, 2015; Murphy & Olsen, 1996; Rosen & Smith, 2010). Wildlife Guardian assists with the identification of 475 species of mammals, birds, and reptiles. It does so by asking users up to five multichotomous questions about body parts and features and matching responses with the database. Wildlife Guardian specializes in the identification of whole animals but it is also possible to identify parts of 358 species with this app (Kretser *et al.*, 2015; Wildlife Conservation Society, 2013; 2016). A forthcoming update of Wildlife Guardian will include geolocation function as well as the ability to query local experts about the animal or product in question. Wildlife Guardian was designed specifically for use by Chinese law enforcement but is available to the general public. It is currently available in Mandarin and English and available on iOS and Android platforms.

Wildlife Alert, released in December 2014, is another decision-tree style tool. Wildlife Alert was designed specifically to assist United States military police stationed in Afghanistan to identify the most commonly traded species available for purchase by U.S. military personnel and U.S. contractors. These species are available at local on-base markets and identification at the site prevents transport of products made from potentially threatened or endangered species across international borders (Kretser *et al.*, 2015; Kretser *et al.*, 2012). The app focuses entirely on the identification of species from parts of the animal such as fur, horns, antlers, and shells rather than the whole animal because military personnel often purchase products made from wildlife rather than whole animals. The app lacks geolocation or reporting capabilities in its present iteration; it is in English and is available on iOS and Android platforms.

WildScan, released in September 2014, uses a decision-tree style approach to identify whole animals and parts of animals typically traded in Southeast Asia through a series of questions to narrow choices. It also features a comprehensive reporting function that includes the ability to take a photo and submit a report to central law enforcement. Wildscan is presently available in English for Android platforms (WildScan, 2014).

9.5.1 Limitations of Mobile App Technology and Opportunities for Future Improvements

Major challenges to overcome with mobile apps include misidentifications, equipment ownership and coordination across multiple tools. Even with the applications that employ decision-tree tools to facilitate identification, misidentification may result, particularly when trying to identify a species from only a part of an animal, such as a piece of fur. Multiple matches may be a common output of the programs. False negatives and false positives may also be prevalent as the databases are parameterized and questions are being field tested and refined. False negatives, or allowing items through when confiscation should happen, could be detrimental to wildlife, while false positives, or

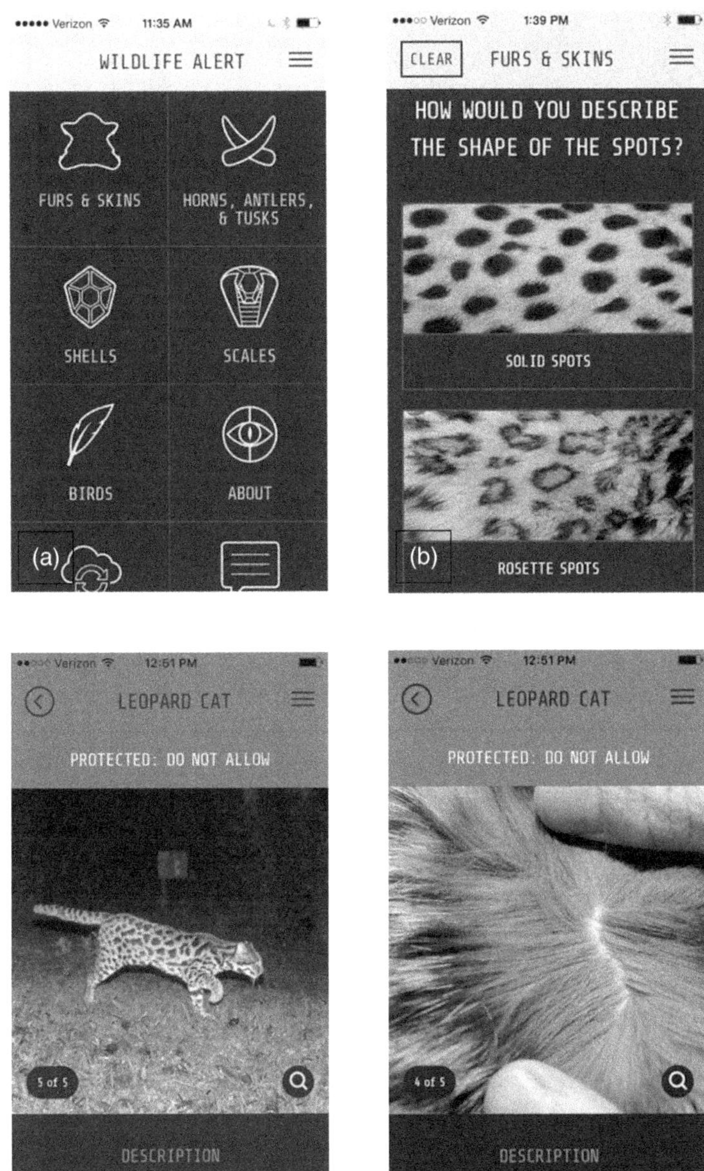

Figure 9.3 Decision-tree apps facilitate identification through a step-wise process: (a) app product interface, (b) question interface, (c) and (d) matching animal interface. © Wildlife Alert

confiscating when a product meets country regulations, could negatively impact individuals or local economies (Bowen-Jones, Brown, & Robinson, 2003). In instances where app-based identifications will ultimately be used for prosecution via the criminal justice sector, multiple confirmations may be needed (e.g., from genetic analysis).

Although global trends indicate one-third of the world's population will own smartphones by 2017, issues may arise as organizations juggle whether to invest in dedicated mobile devices for enforcement personnel to use only while working or have employees use personal devices. Investing in dedicated devices would represent a significant financial hurdle for many organizations. However, failing to make that investment assumes individuals will have compatible phones and possess some media literacy. Consistent access to mobile devices could improve detection of potential items and also deter movement of products across checkpoints and borders. However, consistent use may depend upon whether individuals, local organizations, and governments can provide equipment as well as support for ensuring the equipment has the latest updates. Further, staff using programs need to be trained on software as well as hardware. Access to the internet or satellites may be a further consideration particularly if programs require frequent updates.

Given the release of three apps employing the decision-tree style approach within a two-year period, future work may need to involve better coordination across all app development. The databases, including images used as back-end materials for the mobile identification keys, should be shared to facilitate efficient use of funding and materials. Different interfaces, or front-end styles, should be rigorously tested to understand what features and improvements can minimize the potential for user errors yet maintain a positive app experience. Testing should also account for cultural sensitivities based on who the target audience might be. For example, U.S. military personnel, Chinese forestry police, and Australian travelers may have very different reactions to a particular front-end style, yet regardless of style sharing the back-end data could yield a larger conservation benefit. True decision-tree algorithms assign weights to responses for each diagnostic question. Future improvements to apps might explore weighting responses depending on how critical a question is to the identification of an actual species as well as the severity of implications associated with a false negative. For example, a false negative that could allow rhino horn or elephant ivory to pass through a checkpoint would constitute a severe mistake; questions leading to identification of endangered or critically endangered species might be weighted more heavily to avoid this situation.

Despite some of these limitations, mobile apps have the potential to disrupt wildlife crime activities throughout supply chains and contribute to market reduction approaches. Crowd sourcing mobile app code creation may help overcome some of the current limitations discussed above. Further, crowd sourcing may be an interesting alternative to the "Ask an Expert" element for confirmation of species. The ability to geolocate an incident and simultaneously submit a report to a centralized database (Chandran *et al.*, 2011), will allow the law enforcement community to map the dynamics of supply chains and use a data-driven approach to inform actions. Investing in coordinated mobile app development can best enable the technology to fit within crime prevention approaches; standardizing types of information collected as well as level of detail on purported incidents can engender confidence in collating intelligence from both the law enforcement and public sectors. Such comprehensive datasets can facilitate targeted education to recommend alternative choices for consumers and ultimately assist with dismantling supply chains (Schneider, 2008).

9.6 Conservation Forensics

Technological advancements within the field of forensic science have increased capacity to identify whole animals and animal parts; in some cases forensics can link those animals to specific geopolitical regions of the world. This capability facilitates enforcement by providing scientific data indicating whether an animal was harvested from a protected population, and enabling data to bolster criminal prosecutions. The opportunities for utilizing forensic science in the enforcement side of wildlife crime prompted the U.S. Fish and Wildlife Service to open a full service forensic laboratory in Ashland, Oregon in 1989. This laboratory, along with its National Oceanic and Atmospheric Administration marine counterpart in Seattle, Washington, a small number of State laboratories, and numerous scientists based in academia, use diverse methods to investigate traded animals and animal parts from around the world to determine whether or not a wildlife crime has occurred.

Almost any tool used in crime laboratories that focuses on human criminal activity can be used in wildlife forensics. One of the most powerful tools is deoxyribonucleic acid (DNA) analysis. DNA has several strengths forensically, foremost of which is the large amount of variation that exist in it among species, populations, and individuals, making it extremely useful for identification. The explosive growth of online DNA databases enables any species that has already been identified to serve as a forensic baseline to which any questionable unknown sample can be compared. DNA is a relatively stable molecule and can often be obtained from extremely old specimens or ones that have been mechanically or chemically treated or otherwise adulterated. DNA is the same in every cell of an individual, thus even highly disparate samples (e.g., a tusk, a tail) can be compared to see if they originated from the same animal. The fact that forensic DNA analysis is well established and is practiced by most public crime laboratories and many private laboratories means it is widely accepted throughout the criminal justice system. And finally, unlike any other form of forensic evidence, statistical likelihoods can be determined for forensic DNA analysis, providing a powerful evidentiary tool for prosecutors in their efforts to move offenders through a criminal justice system.

Animal DNA is found in two forms: nuclear and mitochondrial (mtDNA); in addition to these, plants also contain chloroplast DNA, which has similar forensic uses to the mtDNA of animals. Nuclear DNA is inherited from both parents, and is unique among individuals (except for identical twins), whereas mtDNA is inherited via the egg, and therefore is shared among maternal relatives (chloroplast DNA is also generally inherited maternally). The different modes of inheritance allow for different forensic uses of the DNA types, along with different methods of analysis.

The individualizing characteristics of nuclear DNA can be used to match two specimens, such as animal parts or products to each other, or to a specific carcass. Today, the most common forensic method for analyzing nuclear DNA is via microsatellites, known as short tandem repeats in human forensics. As the latter name implies, these markers are small segments of DNA, generally 2 to 7 bases in length, that are repeated several times (e.g., GATTGATTGATTGATT).

The number of repeats is determined based on size—more repeats results in a longer stretch of DNA—and a specimen produces results inherited from both parents. For example, a specimen might type as a 7/8, meaning 7 GATT repeat units were inherited from one parent and 8 from the other. If another specimen types as a 6/9, it did not originate from the same individual. If, however, that specimen also types as a 7/8, not only are the two consistent with one another, we can also explore the chances that the two specimens did not actually originate from the same individual. It is possible that 7 and 8 repeats are common, or that they are rare. To determine this, and to put a statistical value on the 7/8 "match" a database of unrelated but geographically similar individuals is needed. Related individuals would tend to share 7/8 s, whereas geographically 7/8 s may be somewhat common in one location and uncommon in another. Once the frequency of a 7/8 in a population is calculated, a second microsatellite marker can be examined and its frequency determined.

Purposefully, markers are tested that are not inherited as a unit (they are 'unlinked') so their frequencies can be multiplied together. If, for instance, the frequency of a 7/8 for one marker is 1 in 10, and the frequency of a 11/14 for another is 1 in 12, then the chance of both existing in an individual is 1 in 120. By examining several more markers, match probabilities in the 1 in millions, billions, or beyond can be obtained. Such risk assessments are extremely powerful and are unique to DNA evidence; even specimens widely considered individualizing, such as fingerprints or other pattern evidence, lack, at least currently, any methodology for statistically proving such uniqueness.

Nuclear DNA can also be used to ascertain the regional origins of a specimen, owing to variable frequencies of microsatellites, or other DNA markers, among populations. At a local level (e.g., different regions of a province or state), some combination of results for multiple microsatellites can be used to statistically estimate a specimen's origin, which is of clear use when taking of an animal may be permitted in one location, while illegal in another. On a larger scale, (e.g., continental), the same factors can be examined to determine, for instance, if a specimen was acquired from a legal source country, or was taken in violation of local or international law; this approach can be particularly useful for addressing criminal infractions at a macro-level.

MtDNA is not individualizing. Owing to its maternal mode of inheritance, individuals can be identical (e.g., siblings), however, it still has forensic utility. As with nuclear DNA, within-species variability in MtDNA sequences can be used to assess the geographic origin of a sample, wherein the sequence GGA<u>A</u>CATTC might be found in a species from one region of the world (e.g., sea turtle in Caribbean Sea), whereas the sequence GGA<u>G</u>CATCC exists in another (e.g., sea turtle Mediterranean Sea). Examining sequences associated with adjoining regions for a questioned animal product or part can help pinpoint its geographic origin. MtDNA is an invaluable tool for species identification, which can be critically important in determining if an animal or plant product is protected or is legally traded. MtDNA-based species identification, sometimes called DNA barcoding, takes advantage of small regions of mtDNA that are conserved among all animal species, even those as evolutionarily distant as insects and mammals. The conserved sites act as anchor points, between which the DNA sequence is determined. That sequence can be searched online against the long-established DNA database GenBank, housed by the U.S. National Institutes of Health, into which researchers deposit plant, animal, and other DNA sequences as they are obtained. Today the number of GenBank sequences is approaching 200 million, including very rare and threatened or endangered species. A series of identical or highly similar sequences is quickly displayed, beginning with those most similar (often 100%) to the queried sequence. Exact or near exact matches indicate that the unknown species has been identified, or minimally a very closely related species. In this way, the biological source of legally or illegally possessed or traded skins, feathers, or sundry other items can be objectively determined.

The strategy of using mtDNA for species and population identification as a conservation tool is exemplified by the early work of Baker and Palumbi (1994) through mtDNA analysis of whale meat ("kujira") obtained from markets in Japan. In theory, all such meat should be from allowed 'scientific whaling' of common species, particularly minke whales, which are broadly dispersed across the globe. Because it is illegal to transport whale products across borders, scientists traveled to Japan with their equipment and processed samples in a hotel room. Using the species strategy outlined above, whale meat purchased from markets was identified as being from minke whales, as well as fin whales, humpback whales, and dolphins. Subsequent studies have uncovered numerous other protected species whose meat is for sale in many different countries. DNA testing has also been used to show that expensive restaurant cuts of seafood are sometimes cheap fakes, that the purported (and expensive) health enhancer bear bile sometimes comes from pigs, and that supposed aphrodisiacal seal penises originate from dogs.

9.6.1 Limitations of Forensic Technology and Opportunities for Future Improvements

The incredible statistical power of DNA analysis in informing enforcement of wildlife trade laws is somewhat offset by its technical complexity. In an ideal world, a wildlife sample would be quickly tested on site and the species or origin determined. In situ testing would have another notable advantage, given that transporting all or parts of protected species, even DNA purified from them, is often illegal, regardless of intent. Forensic laboratories are highly regulated in regards to personnel qualifications, quality control, chain of custody, laboratory standards, equipment and sundry other factors that make shifting the technology to the field, particularly for legal purposes, difficult. Therefore, samples are overwhelmingly currently transported to forensic laboratories for testing. There is a strong push in human forensics for fast, on site technology that yield a minimal wait time in determining a suspect's true identity or if he might be related to other crimes for which DNA evidence already exists. Such technology would readily translate to wildlife testing and would allow a laboratory to be taken to the evidence, instead of the evidence to a laboratory.

Other potentially limiting factors in wildlife DNA analysis include the fact that DNA can degrade over time, and may not be obtainable from old, putrefied, or chemically treated materials like tanned hides and processed foods. As important, the sensitivity of DNA testing means that contamination can be problematic; which can occur in the field or the laboratory. Although the smallest of samples can generally be analyzed (e.g., a single hair, a feather, a scale) being able to retest an item as needed, or potentially different parts of an item, is advantageous, thus having access to the entire specimen in the laboratory is useful. DNA testing in general can be time consuming, and backlogs often exist, particularly given that automation is difficult with samples from myriad species in so many different forms. Finally, DNA testing can be expensive compared to other types of analyses; testing an item may cost hundreds of dollars or more given personnel, supplies, and equipment requirements. Regardless of all these caveats, however, the advantages that DNA profiling introduces to the realm of wildlife crime are immense, and as prices continue to go down and speed continues to increase, its utilization and outcomes will only improve.

9.7 Conclusion

Technology has great potential to assist with disrupting and uncovering covert operations in the field, in transit, and in markets. Technologies will also aid wildlife investigations and prosecutions through the collection of information and intelligence. Cases studies detailed in this chapter demonstrate how technology can contribute to situational crime prevention, that is the killing of animals in the field—the ultimate goal for conservation. At the micro and meso level, SMART facilitates a more strategic and accountable ranger presence in the field and allows coordination of enforcement activities across shifts and geographies to deter deleterious activities. Conservation drones can assist rangers in the field by monitoring areas difficult to access by foot or vehicle. Drones also offer the potential for large scale monitoring and feedback to enforcement on the ground (Wilkie & Rose, 2013). At the meso and macro level, mobile technologies can coordinate and provide intelligence at markets to inform future actions within market reduction approaches (Kretser *et al.*, 2015). These tools have the potential to capture evidence on which to base prosecutions and ultimately punishments. Genetic forensic science can further link that which is captured along trade chains and in markets to source countries thus directing scant resources to the areas facing the largest pressure from poachers and subsequently supporting situational crime prevention (Wasser *et al.*, 2008). This tool has important ramifications for improving crime prevention—particularly if future innovations and capacity building can enable DNA analysis to occur across the areas where supply chains and markets exist. These may ultimately improve deterrent effects particularly if forensic evidence contributes to prosecutions and more effective criminal case management.

Despite these implications for conservation, positive impacts from these tools are unlikely to be realized unless implemented alongside a cadre of trained law enforcement authorities monitoring parks and stationed at customs, immigration, police, military, agricultural, and transportation checkpoints. Additionally, governments must be willing to leverage resources, take action and levy severe punishments that will effectively deter crimes from happening in the first place. Combined, willing governments, trained authorities, and innovative technologies will improve detection, deterrence and enforcement of wildlife crimes.

References

Baker, C. S., & Palumbi, S. R. (1994). Which whales are hunted? Molecular genetic evidence for illegal whaling. *Science*, 265, 1538–1539.

Bennett, E. L. (2011) Another inconvenient truth: The failure of enforcement systems to save charismatic species. *Oryx* 45, 4, 476–479.

Bowen-Jones, E., Brown, D., & Robinson, E. J. Z., (2003) Economic commodity or environmental crisis? An interdisciplinary approach to analysing the bushmeat trade in central and west Africa. *Area*, 35, 4, 390–402.

Chandran, R., Krishana, P. & Nguyen, K. (2011). Wildlife enforcement monitoring system (WEMS): A solution to support compliance of multilateral environmental agreements. *Government Information Quarterly*, 28, 231–238.

Chen, Y., Shioi, H., Montesinos, C. F., Koh, L. P., Wich, S. & Krause, A. (2014). *Active detection via adaptive submodularity*. Proceedings of The 31st International Conference on Machine Learning. Pp. 55–63.

Clarke, R. V. (2009). Situational crime prevention: Theoretical background and current practices. In Krohn, M. D., Lizotte, A. J., & Penly, G. (Eds.) *Handbook on crime and deviance*. New York, NY: Springer.

Cress, D., & Zommers, Z. (2014). *Technologies: Smarter ways to fight wildlife crime*. United Nations Environment Programme global environmental alert service. Retrieved fromhttp://na.unep.net/geas/getUNEPPageWithArticleIDScript.php?article_id=13

Depraetere, M., Pavoine, S., Jiguet, F., Gasca, A., Duvaild, S., & Sueura, J. (2012). Monitoring animal diversity using acoustic indices: Implementation in a temperate woodland. *Ecological Indicators*, 13, 46–54.

The Economist. (2014). *Earning with the fishes*. January 18, 2014.

eMarketeer. (2014) Worldwide Smartphone Usage to Grow 25% in 2014. Retrieved from www.emarketer.com/Article/Worldwide-Smartphone-Usage-Grow-25 2014/1010920#sthash.xEUClJUV.dpuf

Emslie, R.H., Milliken T., & Talukdar, B. (2013). African and Asian rhinoceroses – Status, conservation and trade report to the 16th meeting of the CITES conference of the parties, CoP16 Doc. 54.2 (Rev. 1) Annex 2. Retrieved from www.cites.org/eng/cop/16/doc/E-CoP16-54-02.pdf

Gardner, T. A., Barlow, J., Araujo, I. S., Ávila-Pires, T. C., Bonaldo, A. B., Costa, J. E.,&... Peres, C. A. (2008). The cost-effectiveness of biodiversity surveys in tropical forests. *Ecology Letters*, 11,139–150.

Hilborn, R., Arcese, P., Borner, M., Hando, J., Hopcraft, G., Loibooki, M., &...Sinclair, S. (2006). Effective enforcement in a conservation area. *Science*, 314, 1266.

Hodgson, A., Kelly, N., & Peel, D. (2013). Unmanned aerial vehicles (UAVs) for surveying marine fauna: A dugong case study. *PloS ONE*, 8, e79556.

Infield, M., & Namara, A. (2001). Community attitudes and behavior towards conservation: An assessment of a community conservation programme around Lake Mburo National Park, Uganda. *Oryx*, 35, 48–60.

Kaaria, B. I., & Muchiri, N. L. (2011). Enforcement challenges across borders: detecting and prosecuting illegal wildlife trafficking. *Proceedings of The Ninth International Conference on Environmental Compliance and Enforcement*, 204–208.

Kays, R. W., & Slauson, K. M. (2008). Remote cameras. In Long, R. A., MacKay, P., Ray, J., & Zielinski, W. (Eds.). *Noninvasive survey methods for carnivores.* Island Press, Washington D.C., USA.

Keane, A., Jones J. P. G., Edwards-Jones, G., & Milner-Gulland, E.J. (2008). The sleeping policeman: Understanding issues of enforcement and compliance in conservation. *Animal Conservation*, 11,75–82.

Koh, L. P., & Wich, S. A. (2012). Dawn of drone ecology: Low-cost autonomous aerial vehicles for conservation. *Tropical Conservation Science*, 5, 121–132.

Kretser, H. E., Johnson, M. F., Hickey, L. M., Zahler, P., & Bennett, E. L. 2012. Demand for wildlife trade products available to U.S. military personnel serving abroad. *Biodiversity and Conservation*, 21, 967–980.

Kretser, H. E., Wong, R., Roberton, S., Pershyn, C., Huang, J., Sun, F., Kang, A., & Zahler, P. (2015). Mobile decision-tree tool technology as a means to detect wildlife crimes. *Biological Conservation*, 189, 33–38.

Laurance, W. F., Goosem, M., & Laurance, S. G. (2009). Impacts of roads and linear clearings on tropical forests. *Trends in Ecology & Evolution*, 24, 659–669.

Lavorgna, A.(2014). Wildlife trafficking in the internet age. *Crime Science*, 3, 5–17.

Lessin, J. E., & Ante, S. E. (2013). Apps Rocket Toward $25 Billion in Sales. Retrieved from http://www.wsj.com/articles/SB10001424127887323293704578334401534217878

Matthews, A., Ruykys, L., Ellis, B., FitzGibbon, S., Lunney, D., Crowther, M. S., &...Wiggins, N. (2013). The success of GPS collar deployments on mammals in Australia. *Australian Mammalogy*, 35, 65–83.

Murphy, P., & Olson, B.H. (1996). Decision-tree construction and analysis. *American Water Work Association*, 88, 59–67.

Nellemann, C., Henreiksen, R., Raxter, P., Ash, N., & Mrema, E. (2014). *The environmental crisis-threats to sustainable development from illegal exploitation and trade in wildlife and forest resources.* United Nations Environment Programme: Gland Switzerland.

Pimm, S., Jenkins, C., Abell, R., Brooks, T., Gittleman, J., Joppa, L., &... Sexton, J. (2014). The biodiversity of species and their rates of extinction, distribution, and protection. *Science*, 344, 987–997.

Pimm, S. L., Alibhai, S., Bergl, R., Dehgan, A., Giri, C., Jewell, Z., &... Loarie, S. (2015). Emerging technologies to conserve biodiversity. *Trends in ecology & evolution*, 30, 685- 696.

Pires, S., & Moreto, W.D. (2011). Preventing wildlife crimes: Solutions that can overcome the 'Tragedy of the Commons.' *European Journal of Criminal Policy Research*, 12, 101–123.

Pires, S., & Clarke, R. V. (2012). Are parrots CRAVED? An analysis of parrot poaching in Mexico. *Journal of Research in Crime and Delinquency*, 49, 122–146.

Rosen, G. E., & Smith, K. F. (2010). Summarizing the evidence on the international trade in illegal wildlife. *Ecohealth*, 7, 24–32.

Schneider, J.L. (2008). Reducing the illicit trade in wildlife: The market reduction approach. *Journal of Contemporary Criminal Justice*, 24, 274–295.

Stokes, E.J. (2010). Improving effectiveness of protection efforts in tiger source sites: developing a framework for law enforcement monitoring using MIST. *Journal of Integrative Zoology*, 5, 363–377.

Taronga Conservation Society Australia (2014). *Wildlife witness*. Retrieved from http://taronga.org.au/trade

Vermeulen, C., Lejeune, P., Lisein, J., Sawadogo, P., & Bouché, P. (2013). Unmanned aerial survey of elephants. *PloSONE*, 8, e54700.

Wasser, S. K., Clark, W. J., Drori, O., Kisamo, E. S., Mailand, C., Mutayoba, B., & Stephens, M. (2008). Combating the illegal trade in African elephant ivory with DNA forensics. *Conservation Biology*, 22, 1065–1071.

Warchol, G.L. (2004). The transnational illegal wildlife trade. *Criminal Justice Studies*, 17, 1, 57–73.

Wellsmith, M. (2011). Wildlife crime: the problems of enforcement. *European Journal of Criminal Policy Research*, 17, 125–148.

WildAid. (2015). *When the buying stops the killing can too campaign*. Retrieved from http://www.wildaid.org/

Wildlife Conservation Society. (2016). *Wildlife guardian*. Retrieved from http://china.wcs.org/News/LatestNews/articleType/ArticleView/articleId/6692/Wildlife_Guardian_ APP_Version_II.aspx

Wildlife Guardian. (2013). *Wildlife Conservation Society China Program*. Retrieved from http://china.wcs.org/AboutUs/LatestNews/tabid/6788/articleType/ArticleView/a rticleId/953/Wildlife_Guardian_mobile_software.aspx#.VC1OJxZvDfw

WildScan. (2014). Retrieved from http://www.freeland.org/#!wildscan/chp2

Wilkie, D., & Rose. R. (2013). A challenge to the world: Build a better conservation drone. *Policy Innovations*. Retrieved from http://www.policyinnovations.org/ideas/innovations/data/000254

10

PAWS: Game Theory Based Protection Assistant for Wildlife Security

Fei Fang, Benjamin Ford, Rong Yang, Milind Tambe, and Andrew M. Lemieux

This chapter introduces Protection Assistant for Wildlife Security (PAWS) (Yang, Ford, Tambe, & Lemieux, 2014) as a joint effort by computer scientists, conservation researchers, and conservation practitioners from two nongovernmental organizations—Panthera, and Rimba. PAWS is a game theory-based application to assist conservation agency officials in planning wildlife ranger patrols to prevent wildlife crime. Reducing risks to people and wildlife from wildlife crime ideally includes the combined effort of practitioners worldwide and researchers in many different disciplines; PAWS demonstrates the positive impact that research in computational game theory, an important topic within the field of Artificial Intelligence (AI), can have in assisting wildlife conservation agencies to prevent poaching. In recent deployment efforts, patrol planners mentioned that the routes generated by PAWS came close to an actual planner's routes, a promising sign that PAWS can suggest feasible routes and help reduce the significant burden of patrol planning.

Poaching directly threatens some species' survival. For example, tigers, along with many other endangered species, are in danger of extinction because of poaching risks (Global Tiger Initiative Secretariat, 2013; Montesh, 2013). The global population of tigers has dropped over 95% since the 1900s, resulting in 3 out of 9 species going extinct (Global Tiger Initiative Secretariat, 2013) in part to poaching. In 2015, South African rhino poaching reached a rate of approximately 1 death every 8 hours (Save the Rhino International, 2015). Species extinction can destroy ecosystems and weaken the communities and economies that depend on those ecosystems (Global Tiger Initiative Secretariat, 2013). In some cases, such as with the illegal rhino and tiger trades, poachers can be part of well-funded organized crime groups. Many other poachers, however, are not part of organized crime syndicates but still threaten species with over-hunting by snare poaching. Regardless of the scale, wildlife poaching poses negative risks to wildlife and people.

Worldwide, patrols are the most widespread method to combat and prevent wildlife poaching. However, many conservation agencies suffer from a lack of law enforcement resources to conduct these patrols over what are typically vast uninhabited protected areas. One wildlife crime study reported an actual coverage density of 1 ranger per 167 square kilometers (Holmern, Muya, & Roskaft, 2007) while current law enforcement density statistics for New York City show

Conservation Criminology, First Edition. Edited by Meredith L. Gore.

approximately 28 officers per square kilometer (e.g., 34,500 officers over a total land and sea area of 1,213 square kilometers) (City of New York, 2013). It would be impossible to adequately protect the entire protected areas at the same density as in urban areas, increasing the importance and necessity of planning efficient patrols. However, current patrols in many protected or other conservation areas may not make the most efficient use of their limited patrolling resources.

PAWS generates a set of strategically randomized patrol routes, based on a game-theoretic analysis, such that a conservation agency can choose to execute any of these patrols with a given probability. This game-theoretic approach provides a valuable degree of unpredictability, and while this by itself would be useful for assisting agencies with the time-consuming process of patrol route planning, PAWS also formalizes and incorporates two important concepts in patrol planning:

1) Building models of human behavior to better predict where poachers will attack and how they will react to any executed patrol routes.
2) Incorporating domain features such as terrain information into the game-theoretic analysis so that patrollers can easily execute any of the patrols generated by PAWS.

PAWS was first tested at Uganda's Queen Elizabeth National Park (QENP) where poaching is believed to be the most harmful and frequent illegal activity in the park. Now PAWS is regularly deployed in a Southeast Asia protected area in support of tiger conservation. For the security of animals and patrollers, no latitude/longitude information is presented about this site.

10.1 Applying Game Theoretic Analysis to Poaching

Game theory is the study of strategic decision-making and, more specifically, the conflict and cooperation between intelligent decision-makers (Myerson, 1997). In combating poaching, there is a strategic interaction between the conservation agency (or wildlife ranger or other patrollers) and the poachers. In this game, there are two types of players with conflicting interests: the defender (i.e., conservation agency or patrollers) and the poachers. Each player wants to take action(s) so that the outcome is in their best interest. For example, poachers want to place snares and capture wildlife without having their snares confiscated by patrollers, and on the other hand, patrollers want to find snares before they capture any animals. To that end, each player needs to reason about his or her opponent's potential actions and play intelligently. For example, if the patroller always takes the same patrol route every day, the poachers will always be able to avoid the patroller and will always succeed in placing snares in the unpatrolled locations. Thus, it is in the defender's best interest to play unpredictably (i.e., patrol somewhat randomly). Instead of simply "rolling a die" and choosing which patrol route to take in a uniformly random way, a defender should choose patrol routes that visit more important locations (e.g., areas with higher animal densities of key species) more often. Which patrol routes to consider and how to randomly choose among these patrol routes is called the defender strategy or the patrol strategy. Ideally, for the defender, poachers would be deterred from locations with high animal density since they are often patrolled, and the poachers would be reluctant to place snares in areas with low animal density since the chance of successfully capturing an animal in those areas is low.

Even though this ideal case may not be achievable given the defender's limited patrolling resources, it does not mean a game theoretic approach cannot have a positive impact. Indeed, game-theory based decision support systems have been successfully deployed in the real-world to protect critical infrastructure such as airports (Pita *et al.*, 2008), airline flights (Tsai, Rathi, Kiekintveld, Ordonez, Tambe, 2009), seaports (Shieh *et al.*, 2012), and metro trains (Yin, Jiang, Johnson, Kiekintveld, & Leyton-Brown, 2012). In each of these cases, even though the defender also had a limited amount of patrolling resources, these works aided defenders in more efficiently and effectively allocating their resources (Tambe, 2011). PAWS was inspired by these successes and was the first of a new wave of proposed applications in the subarea called Green Security Games (GSGs) (Fang, Stone, & Tambe, 2015; Kar, Fang, Delle Fave, Sintov, & Tambe, 2015), which focus on resource allocation and scheduling problem in domains such as protecting forest, wildlife, and fisheries. PAWS provides quantitative analysis of the game between the defenders and poachers and calculates the optimal patrol strategy.

10.2 Modeling Human Behavior to Create Optimal Patrol Strategies

In generating an optimal patrol strategy (i.e., one that offers the best chance of stopping poaching attacks), modeling poachers' behavior is important. Without an accurate idea of how the poacher is currently planning their attacks and how they will react to the defender's patrols, it is difficult to generate a patrol strategy performs well in practice. Because there is a large number of poachers and poaching data potentially available, we can use this crime data to build a model of the poachers' behavior. In the case of poaching, crime data can be anonymous, or identified if it can be linked to confessed adversaries. Although the latter type of data provides rich information about individual adversaries, it is sparse and hard to collect. Indeed, it is very difficult to catch poachers on site since it requires the patrollers to be at the same location as poachers at the same. The majority of collected data is evidence on crimes committed by anonymous adversaries (e.g., a snare found on a trail). Compared to identified data, anonymous data provides no information about the characteristics of the adversary that committed the crime and therefore cannot be used to build accurate behavioral models on the individual level. The open questions here are then, how do we utilize both types of data to build and learn a better model of the large population of criminals and moreover, how does the learned model help better predict future crime events and thus help law enforcement officials to improve their patrols?

10.3 Domain Feature Modeling

To bring PAWS from theory to real-world deployment, we capture and integrate important domain properties of wildlife crime into PAWS. By doing so, PAWS can generate optimal patrol strategies that accurately reflect many of the factors that influence the creation of patrols. First, we incorporate terrain information (e.g., elevation, ridgelines) and use a novel hierarchical modeling approach to build a virtual street map of the protected area. This virtual street map allows PAWS to scale-up to patrol large areas while simultaneously providing fine-grained guidance. Essentially, the street map connects the whole protected area through easy-to-follow route segments, where each segment could be a ridgeline, stream, river bank, or other geographic feature. The rationale for this approach threefold:

1) Animals use these terrain features and are most easily trapped here.
2) Poachers use these features for trapping and moving about in general.
3) Patrollers can move along these features more efficiently than traversing across ridges.

In other words, animals, poachers, and patrollers all use these features while moving. In addition to incorporating terrain information, PAWS also accounts for incomplete information regarding animal density. Finally, PAWS accounts for real-world patrolling constraints such as time limits on patrolling and needing to start and end at a base camp. In the rest of the chapter we discuss the related work of PAWS and provide a detailed description of the wildlife poaching problem domain. We will then present an overview of the PAWS system and explain how it works, in detail, with respect to game-theoretic analysis, human behavior modeling, and domain feature modeling.

10.4 The Genesis of PAWS from Synthesizing Conservation, Computer Science, and Criminology

Poaching is increasingly studied by criminologists (Montesh, 2013; Pires, 2012) and geographic information systems (GIS) experts (Hamisi, 2008; Ouko, 2013) in addition to conservation practitioners (Wato, Wahungu, & Okello, 2006). A variety of methods are used to identify critical points in the poaching system, such as GIS analysis and interviews with apprehended poachers. In spite of all these efforts, returns on applied research investment can be low because of a lack of law enforcement resources (Hamisi, 2008; Pires, 2012).

Conducting patrols is an important way to combat poaching. In recent years, data collection and aggregation software such as MIST (Stokes, 2010) and SMART (Smart Collaboration, 2015) have enabled conservation managers to more effectively coordinate their protection efforts. These tools are developed to help conservation managers record data and analyze patrols retrospectively. However, these works do not create patrol routes or identify targets to protect; the creation of patrols is still done by an experienced patrol manager. It is well known that humans have an extremely difficult time generating feasible schedules that are also unpredictable (Wagenaar, 1972). In contrast, PAWS builds on concepts and models from game theory, in particular, security games and provides an automated approach that generates efficient and randomized patrol schedules.

Research on security games focuses on overcoming the security and conservation agencies' challenge of limited law enforcement resources. In optimizing security resource allocation, previous work on Stackelberg Security Games (SSGs) has led to many successfully deployed applications to improve the security of airports, ports and flights (Fang, Jiang, & Tambe, 2013; Pita *et al.*, 2008; Tsai, Rathi, Kiekintveld, Ordonez, & Tambe, 2009). Based on the early work on SSGs, recent work has focused on GSGs (Fang, Stone, & Tambe, 2015; Kar *et al.*, 2015) for domains such as protecting forest, wildlife, and fisheries resources (Haskell *et al.*, 2014; Qian, Haskell, Jiang, & Tambe, 2014). Unlike a standard SSG where the attack is assumed to be cross sectional, interactions between the defender and their adversary in GSG are repeated. For example, in the security domain of wildlife protection poachers conduct illegal activities (e.g., place snares in a protected area as shown in Figure 10.1[c]) frequently and repeatedly). Although some GSG research provides conceptual advances in integrating learning and planning (Fang *et al.*, 2015), PAWS

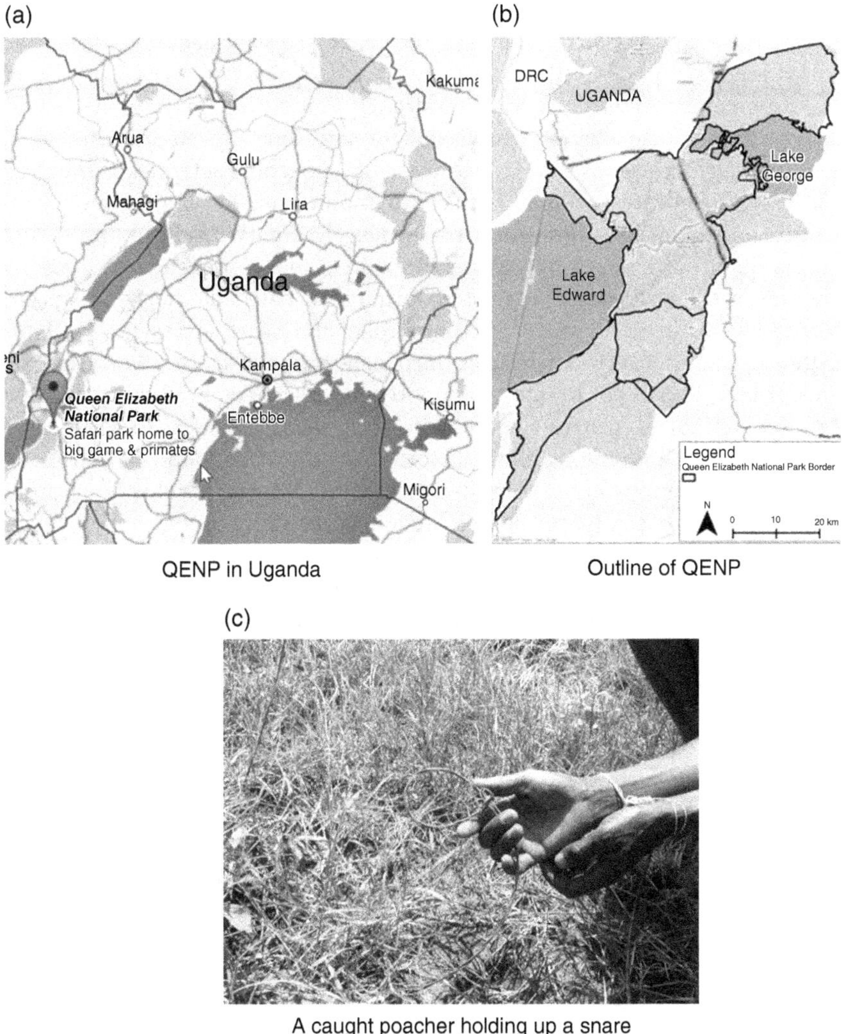

QENP in Uganda

Outline of QENP

A caught poacher holding up a snare (photo taken by Andrew Lemieux).

Figure 10.1 Snare poaching in Queen Elizabeth National Park.

is the first GSG application to combat wildlife crime. PAWS models the interaction between the patroller (i.e., defender) and the poacher (i.e., attacker) as a basic GSG. Every few months, collected poaching data is analyzed, behavioral models of the poacher are updated and reparameterized. Improved patrols are generated.

10.4.1 Describing the Poaching Domain to Create Patrols that Prevent Poaching

Wire snaring, shown in Figure 10.1(c), is one of the main techniques used by poachers. Poachers can set and leave snares unattended and when they think an animal has been captured they will come back and kill the animal. Snares can be designed to target many species. The main targets of snares in Uganda's QENP are hippo, kobs, and antelope. In Southeast Asia where PAWS is now regularly deployed the main targets are elephants, tigers, and Sambar deer (i.e., a key prey species of tigers).

Law enforcement officers, such as park rangers, or patrollers from NGOs and other government agencies are responsible for patrolling a given protected area. One of their primary goals is to reduce successful poaching activities as much as possible so as to protect wildlife in that geographic area. During a given patrol patrollers will typically search for signs of illegal activity inside the protected area, confiscate any poaching equipment found, and apprehend any persons inside the area illegally (e.g., poachers). During their patrol all their findings are recorded in a log book. In most cases, if patrollers find wire snares, they will not find the poacher that set them because the poachers usually leave after setting the snares. If patrollers do encounter and apprehend poachers, however, patrollers are sometimes able to generate confessions from the poachers as to where they set their snares. Thus, among all the records of wire snares found by patrollers, most of them are anonymous. Identified data points, when a poacher is captured and divulges where they placed snares, are inherently more useful as they can be used to obtain a complete behavioral model that can better predict where future poachers will place their traps. If recording and monitoring tools such as SMART and MIST are in use in a protected area, collected data are uploaded to a database after the patrollers return to the outpost. Patrollers usually patrol in teams, and there can be multiple teams of patrollers conducting patrols simultaneously, each team taking a different patrol route.

Poachers can conduct surveillance on patrollers' activities and patrol patterns. Wildlife patrollers are well aware that some neighboring villagers will inform poachers of when patrollers begin their patrols and where they are patrolling (Moreto, 2013). For any number of reasons, such as changes that impact animal migration habits, patrollers may change their patrolling patterns. Poachers, in turn, continually conduct surveillance on the patrollers' changing patrol strategy and adapt their poaching strategies accordingly.

Within a given protected area, different locations may have different importance for animals and people. Locations of high animal density are more important and attractive to poachers. In the case of QENP, areas that contain fresh water (e.g., watering holes, lakes) are known to be high-risk areas for poaching (Montesh, 2013; Moreto, 2013; Wato *et al.*, 2006). In areas with more hilly and complex terrains, such as tropical forests in Southeast Asia, areas along ridgelines or streams serve as natural conduits for wildlife. Despite the available information on animal ecology and ethology from natural science studies, there are still too many areas for patrollers to patrol, and it is a huge cognitive burden to simultaneously account for animal density factors, physical distance constraints and base camp locations while also ensuring that the new patrols are unpredictable. PAWS aims to aid patrol managers by generating an optimal strategy that accounts for all of these factors; PAWS will generate a strategy that enables patrollers to effectively cover these numerous areas with their limited resources.

10.5 The PAWS Model

PAWS is based on game theoretic analyses (Figure 10.2). Input data includes the following information: contour lines that describe elevation, terrain information such as lakes and drainage, base camp locations, previous patrol observations (e.g., animal signs, human activities), and previous patrol tracks. Based on the input data, we estimate current animal population distribution. It is necessary to estimate this distribution because individual sightings of animals are not likely to be spatially representative of the population. To estimate the distribution for tigers, the species of interest in recent deployments, we use Just Another Gibbs Sampler (JAGS) (Plummer, 2003) to produce a posterior predictive density raster derived from a spatially explicit capture-recapture analysis conducted in a Bayesian framework.

Because wildlife patrols and poaching attacks happen frequently, we model this recurrent behavior as a repeated game. PAWS first builds the game model, models the poachers' behavior using wildlife crime data and then calculates the optimal patrol strategy according to the game model, behavior model, and additional patrolling constraints (e.g., contour lines, terrain information). When

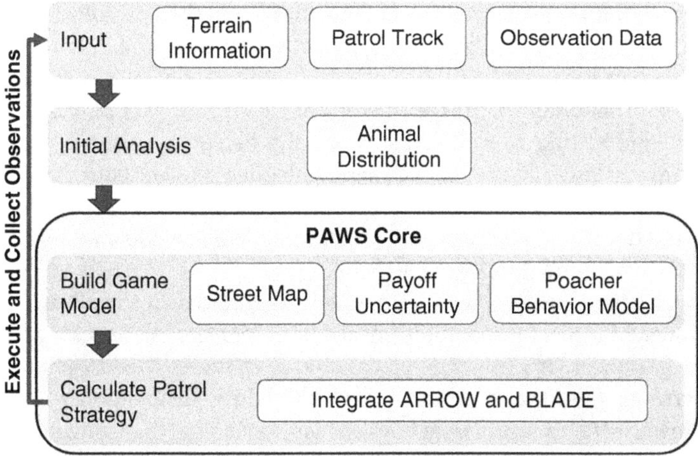

Figure 10.2 PAWS overview.

patrollers execute the PAWS patrols over a period of time, they will collect more crime data and those data are fed into PAWS as inputs for the next set of generated PAWS patrols. In the following sections, we focus on how the game model is built, how the poachers' behavior is modeled, and how the optimal patrol strategy is generated.

10.5.1 The Basis of Game-Theoretic Analysis in PAWS

The problem of combating poaching can be seen as a game with two types of players, the defender (i.e., the conservation agency's wildlife patrollers) and the attacker (i.e., poachers). The players have conflicting interests and there is a strategic interaction between the players. The defender must account for the attacker's actions and vice versa. To reduce successful poaching activities so as to protect wildlife in the area, the defender conducts randomized patrols against poachers while balancing the priorities of different locations with different animal densities. If patrols are not randomized and are deterministic instead (i.e., no randomization), poachers are able to exploit this predictability and thus circumvent any efforts by the defender. To decide which patrol routes need to be considered and how often each of them should be taken so as to provide maximum protection to wildlife, PAWS builds an evidence-based mathematical game model.

In PAWS, a protected area is discretized into a grid (e.g., 1 km by 1 km), where each grid cell is viewed as a target location (i.e., targets) for poachers. The defender tries to protect these T targets from poachers by optimally allocating a set of R patrolling resources (i.e., teams of patrollers, where each team can take a different patrol route). Note that R is typically much less than T; there are typically many more targets to protect than there are resources available to the defender. By executing a patrol route, patrollers can protect the targets along that route. The assignment of resources to patrol routes (i.e., sending out patrollers to patrol) is called the defender's pure strategy. Since our goal is to randomize patrol routes, the defender can choose to execute any of the patrol routes with a certain probability; this probability distribution over pure strategies (i.e., patrol routes) is called the defender's mixed strategy. We compactly represent the defender's mixed strategy as a coverage vector $c = \langle c_i \rangle$ where c_i is the coverage probability for target i (i.e., the probability that target i is protected) (Korzhyk, Conitzer, & Parr, 2010). After committing to a mixed strategy the defender will then randomly select a pure strategy to execute (i.e., send patrollers out on patrol). The adversary observes the defender's mixed strategy through surveillance and then chooses a target to attack (i.e., places snares at a target). We provide an illustrative example of the game model in Figure 10.3.

Each target is associated with payoff values. Higher animal density implies higher payoffs, which indicate separate reward and penalty values for the defender and the poachers. If a poacher places snares in target i, and i is protected by the patroller (i.e., the executed patrol goes through location i), the defender gets a reward $U^d_{y,i}$, and the poacher receives a penalty $U^a_{p,i}$. Conversely, if target i is not protected, the defender gets a penalty $U^d_{p,i}$ and the poacher receives a reward $U^a_{y,i}$.

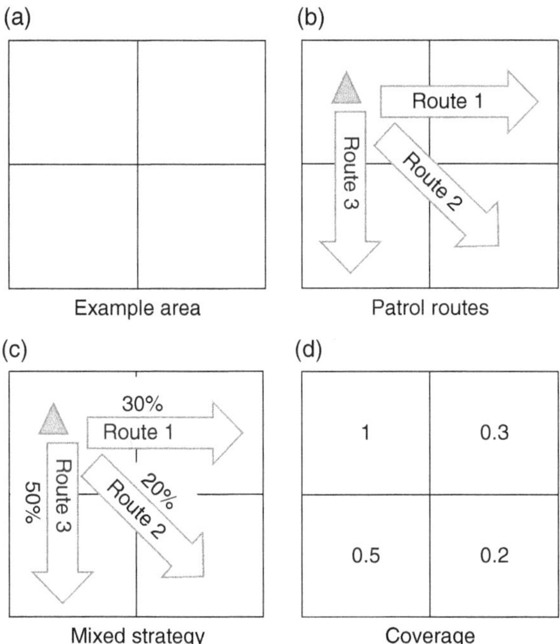

Figure 10.3 Illustrative example for PAWS game model. Figure 10.3(a) shows an example area that is discretized into four cells, that is, four targets. Figure 10.3(b) shows three possible patrol routes for the example area, each of which starts from the upper left cell (base camp location) and protects two targets. Figure 10.3(c) shows a mixed strategy for the example area when there is only one team of patrollers. The compact representation of the mixed strategy in Figure 10.3(c) is shown in Figure 10.3(d).

Given a defender mixed strategy (compactly represented by $c = \langle c_i \rangle$), the probability that target i is protected by patrollers is c_i, and the probability that target i is not protected is $1 - c_i$. Thus, the poacher's expected payoff (also called expected utility) when he chooses target i is

$$U_i^a = c_i U_{p,i}^a + (1 - c_i) U_{r,i}^a$$

On the other hand, the defender's expected utility with respect to target i is

$$U_i^d = c_i U_{r,i}^d + (1 - c_i) U_{p,i}^d$$

Each player in the game seeks to maximize their expected utility; defenders want to stop attacks as much as possible, and attackers want to successfully attack as much as possible. In PAWS, the game is zero-sum, $U_{r,i}^d = -U_{p,i}^a$, $U_{p,i}^d = -U_{r,i}^a$. In other words, whatever the poacher gains by successfully poaching is also how much the defender loses. Since placing snares in a location with high animal density has a higher chance to lead to a successful capture of an animal (and is thus more rewarding to the poacher), the poacher's reward $U_{r,i}^a$ is determined by animal

Table 10.1 Notations used in this chapter.

Notation	Meaning
T	Number of targets
R	Number of defender resouces (teams of patrollers)
$U_{r,i}^{d}$	Reward for defender if target i is selected by poacher and is protected
$U_{p,i}^{a}$	Penalty for poacher if target i is selected by poacher and is protected
$U_{p,i}^{d}$	Penalty for defender if target i is selected by poacher and is not protected
$U_{r,i}^{a}$	Reward for poacher if target i is selected by poacher and is not protected
U_i^a	Poacher's expected utility of selecting target i if strategy c is played by defender
U_i^d	Defender's expected utility of playing strategy c if target i is seclected by poacher
c_i	Coverage probability on target i. Probability that target i is protected by patroller
ω	Parameter of the SUQR model. $\omega = (\omega_1, \omega_2, \omega_3)$ where ω_1, ω_2, ω_3 are the coefficients for c_i, $U_{r,i}^{a}$ and $U_{p,i}^{a}$ respectively

density. When there are multiple poachers, the defender's expected utility is the overall expected utility against all the poachers (see Table 10.1 for notions).

10.5.2 Modeling Human Behavior for PAWS

In SSGs, the adversary's behavior model represents how he will choose a target to attack in response to the defender's mixed strategy. Past work has often assumed that the adversary will act with perfect rationality and will always choose the target with the highest expected utility for him (Pita *et al.*, 2008). However, it is well known that humans do not act in such a way (Camerer, 2003), and bounded rationality models seek to model how humans act (i.e., not always choosing the target with highest expected utility). PAWS is the first deployed application that uses the Subjective Utility Quantal Response model (SUQR), which is aa bounded rationality model. SUQR models the adversary's probabilistic response (i.e., with some probability, attack a target) to the defender's strategy and was shown to perform the best in human subject experiments when compared with other bounded rationality models (Nguyen, Yang, Azaria, Kraus, & Tambe, 2013). SUQR suggest adversaries evaluate targets based on a linear combination of multiple observable features: the probability that a target will be protected and thus the probability that the adversary will be caught, the reward for a successful attack at a target for the adversary, and the penalty for being captured at a target for the adversary. The value of $\omega_1 c_i + \omega_2 U_{r,i}^{a} + \omega_3 U_{p,i}^{a}$ is denoted as the subjective utility where ω_1, ω_2, ω_3 are the parameters indicating the importance of the aforementioned features. The intuition of the SUQR model is that the adversary will, with higher probability, attack targets with higher subjective utility.

10.5.3 Incorporating Learning into the Behavioral Model

Next, we discuss our method for incorporating past crime data to model the poachers' behavior. Each poacher in the population is modeled with the SUQR model, and we use the crime data to learn the values of each poacher's SUQR model's parameters $\omega = (\omega_1, \omega_2, \omega_3)$. Because we are modeling each poacher's preferences individually and we need to create our strategies with a population of poachers in mind, we compute a distribution of the poacher population's SUQR model parameters. We assume the distribution is normally distributed. To learn this distribution, we must incorporate collected crime data. As discussed previously, we have two types of data that are collected by patrollers: identified data and anonymous data. When a poacher is captured, the patrollers question the poacher and get him to confess to any previous attacks that he committed in the protected area. As such, an identified data point can consist of attacks from multiple rounds and can be used to learn an accurate (SUQR) model of the poacher's behavior. Unfortunately, this type of data is sparse, and we thus cannot rely on using only identified data to construct the entire distribution. On the other hand, there are abundant anonymous data. One potential approach is to assume that a new poacher committed this single attack. Because we only have a single attack data point on this "new poacher," it is impossible to learn that poacher's model in the same way we do with identified data. While anonymous data provides a noisy estimation of an individual poacher's behavioral model, it gives a sufficiently accurate measurement of the crime distribution of the poacher population due to its abundance.

Because each type of data has its strengths or weaknesses, we present the PAWS-Learn algorithm that combines both types of data. By doing so, we can obtain a more accurate distribution than if we just used one type or the other. More detailed explanations of the PAWS-Learn algorithm can be found in Yang *et al.* (2014).

10.6 PAWS-Learn

The PAWS-Learn algorithm combines both identified and anonymous data together to obtain a more accurate distribution of the poachers' behavior than if just one type were used. First, a distribution, $f(\omega)'$, is computed using the identified data, and this computation is done via Maximum Likelihood Estimation (MLE). To summarize this process in the form of a question: given the identified data, what distribution $f(\omega)'$ is most likely (as defined by a likelihood function)? Next, we compute the proportion of anonymous crimes committed at each target. Finally, we compute a new distribution, $f(\omega)$, such that the mean squared error (MSE) is minimized between the identified data distribution ($f(\omega)'$) and the proportion of anonymous crimes. This new distribution, $f(\omega)$, is then used by PAWS to compute a new defender strategy for the next round. Combining the two types of data (i.e., identified, anonymous) in a simulation helps the model learn the distribution of poacher behavior faster than using one or the other type of data (Figure 10.4). As can be seen, by combining both types of data with the PAWS-Learn algorithm, we can learn a more accurate model of poacher behavior and thus generate strategies according to that model.

10.6.1 Domain Feature Modeling

PAWS aims to generate optimal patrol strategies that accurately reflect the many factors that influence the creation of patrols. To that end, providing the game-theoretic analysis and modeling the poacher behavior is not adequate. A key missing piece is to capture and integrate important domain features of wildlife crime into PAWS. In this section, we discuss how domain features are incorporated, which leads to the regular deployment of PAWS in the field.

10.6.1.1 Terrain Information

The first important domain feature is the terrain information. The critical importance of topographic information was ignored at the beginning when PAWS was first proposed (Yang *et al.*, 2014) and was identified by patrollers during first tests of PAWS in the tropical forests in Southeast Asia. Topography can affect patrollers' speed in key ways. For example, lakes are inaccessible for foot patrols. Not considering such information may lead to the failure of completing the

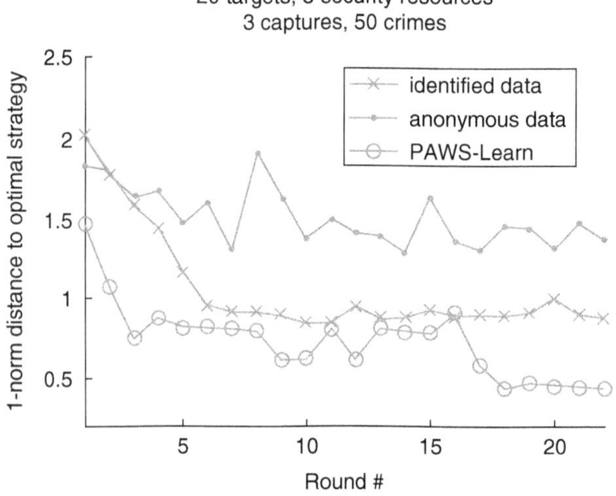

Figure 10.4 Strategy convergence simulation. The X-Axis shows the number of rounds that have elapsed (i.e., the number of interactions between the defender and attacker, and also the number of times a new strategy has been generated). The Y-Axis compares the generated defender mixed strategy in that round to an "optimal" strategy which is generated from the true distribution of poacher behavior (which, outside of a simulation, isn't known); lower values on the axis indicate that the generated strategy is closer to the optimal strategy, indicating that the learned distribution is of higher quality. The first two lines in the figure correspond to learning a distribution with only one type of data available (only identified or anonymous data, respectively) whereas the last line corresponds to the PAWS-Learn algorithm (both data types are combined).

patrol route. Also, changes in elevation require extra patrol effort and extreme changes may stop the patrollers from following a route. In addition, in areas with complex terrain, it is necessary to focus on terrain features such as ridgelines and streams when planning routes for three reasons: (a) they are important conduits for certain mammal species such as tigers; (b) hence, poachers use these features for trapping and moving about in general; and (c) patrollers find it easier to move around here than on slopes. To incorporate terrain information we use a hierarchical modeling approach to build a virtual "street map" of a protected area. This virtual street map allows PAWS to scale-up to patrol large areas while providing fine-grained guidance. We first discretize a protected area into 1 km by 1 km grid cells and treat every grid cell as a target. We further discretize the grid cells into 50 m by 50 m raster pieces and describe the topographic information such as elevation in 50 m scale. The virtual street map is built in the terms of raster pieces while aided by the grid cells in this abstraction as described below. With this hierarchical modeling, the model keeps a small number of targets and reduces the number of patrol routes while allowing for details at the 50 m scale. The street map is a graph consisting of nodes and edges, where the set of nodes is a small subset of the raster pieces and edges are sequences of raster pieces linking the nodes. We denote nodes as Key Access Points (KAPs) and edges as route segments. The street map not only helps scalability but also allows us to focus patrolling on preferred terrain features such as ridgelines. The street map is built in three steps:

1) Determine the accessibility type for each raster piece.
2) Define KAPs.
3) Find route segments to link the KAPs.

10.6.1.2 Patrolling Constraint

In practice, total patrolling time is limited and the patrollers can only move to nearby areas. Also, it is common that there is a base location where patrol routes start from and end with. Such patrolling constraints should be taken into account when designing the patrol routes. Given the street map, these constraints can be easily incorporated to the model by restricting defender's pure strategy to be a patrol route on the street map, starting from the base camp, walking along route segments and ending with base camp, with its total distance satisfying the patrol distance limit.

10.6.1.3 Uncertainty in Animal Distribution

PAWS models a zero-sum game and the reward for the attacker, and the penalty for the defender, is ultimately dictated by animal distribution. However, key domain features such as animal density that contribute to the payoffs are difficult to estimate precisely, leading to uncertainties in the payoff in the game model. Not considering such uncertainty may lead to high degradation in patrol quality. PAWS considers such uncertainty and calculates an optimal patrol strategy that is robust against the uncertainty. In PAWS, the algorithm for calculating the optimal strategy is based on algorithms from the rich security game literature. Specifically, we integrate an algorithm ARROW (Nguyen *et al.*, 2015) with another algorithm BLADE (Yang, Jiang, Tambe, & Ordonez, 2013) to fit the need of the problem: (a) we must generate patrol routes over the street map over the entire conservation area region while; (b) simultaneously addressing payoff uncertainty; and (c) bounded rationality of the adversary. To delineate the algorithm in detail is beyond the scope of this chapter; interested readers may explore the aforementioned references.

10.7 Discussion

Antipoaching patrols, while essential for combating wildlife poaching, are difficult to create and introduce a large cognitive burden on patrol managers due to the large number of factors involved. In addition, it is challenging to create patrols that are randomized, but without doing so, patrols run the risk of becoming predictable and will thus be less effective at deterring and stopping poachers. Resolving these problems requires the efforts of people in many different disciplines; this chapter describes the innovative SSG based application PAWS, the result of joint efforts among computer scientists, conservationists, and criminologists.

PAWS seeks to aid patrol managers by addressing the challenges of creating effective and efficient wildlife patrols; PAWS patrols are intelligently randomized and incorporate many important factors such as terrain information, poacher behavior, and time constraints. Although PAWS cannot completely replace skilled patrol managers' experience and intuition, PAWS provide sufficient aid to conservation agencies in making intelligent decisions. That being said, PAWS represents a novel approach to generating patrols that highlights the importance of: (a) modeling human behavior, so as to better predict where poachers will attack and how they will react to patrols; (b) remaining unpredictable to poachers; (c) modeling the strategic interaction between rangers and poachers.

PAWS poses multiple implications for conservation practice. First, PAWS brings in game-theoretic perspective in designing and analyzing defender's patrol strategy. This proactive information about our adversaries is beneficial because they react to different policies designed to reduce risks to biodiversity and livelihoods and change their behavior accordingly. The overall approach may be applied to diverse conservation policies given the common strategic interaction between conservation policy and noncompliant individuals or groups.

The model emphasizes the importance of human behavior in understanding the effects of conservation policies designed to reduce risk. Human beings are not perfectly rational in most cases and their behavior can affect the effectiveness of conservation policy. PAWS adopts the SUQR model for modeling poachers' bounded rationality and this model may have more general applications in conservation problems. In addition, the method for learning the parameters in SUQR also has broader applications where data is available.

PAWS is the first application of GSG-based research for protecting wildlife and conserving global biodiversity. PAWS has been tested on grassy plains in QENP in Uganda and went through a significant evolution to be deployed in a Southeast Asia protected area with complex terrains; PAWS has proven capable at functioning in areas with diverse terrain, ecosystems, species and human cultures. Based on this success, PAWS shows promise for future deployments to different sites through collaborations with different organizations. It should be noted that future deployments of PAWS will require initial investment by each site and collaborating organization. For past deployments, this investment took the form of aggregating past patrol data, past poaching data, and terrain information for the purpose of training the PAWS models.

PAWS shows the potential that algorithms and techniques in computer science can have in combatting poaching. Indeed, PAWS focuses on one facet of this large, complex problem, namely how to make the most efficient use of foot patrols. AI-based solutions hold promise for addressing additional facets of this issue, such as investigating and interfering with the trafficking of illegal wildlife products.

References

Camerer, C. (2003). *Behavioral game theory: Experiments in strategic interaction.* Princeton University Press.

City of New York (2013). NYPD website- frequently asked questions. *NYPD.* Retrieved from http://www.nyc.gov/html/nypd/html/faq/faq_police.shtml

Fang, F., Jiang, A. X., & Tambe, M. (2013). Optimal patrol strategy for protecting moving targets with multiple mobile resources. In *Proceedings of the 2013 international conference on Autonomous agents and multi-agent systems.* International Foundation for Autonomous Agents and Multiagent Systems.

Fang, F., Stone, P., & Tambe, M. (2015). When security games go green: Designing defender strategies to prevent poaching and illegal fishing. In *International Joint Conference on Artificial Intelligence (IJCAI).*

Hamisi, M. (2008). *Identification and mapping risk areas for zebra poaching: A case of Tarangire National Park, Tanzania* (Doctoral dissertation, Thesis, ITC).

Haskell, W. B., Kar, D., Fang, F., Tambe, M., Cheung, S., & Denicola, E. (2014). Robust Protection of Fisheries with COmPASS. In *Proceedings of the Twenty-Sixth Annual Conference on Innovative Applications of Artificial Intelligence* (pp. 2978–2983).

Holmern, T., Muya, J., & Røskaft, E. (2007). Local law enforcement and illegal bushmeat hunting outside the Serengeti National Park, Tanzania. *Environmental Conservation*, 34, 55–63.

Kar, D., Fang, F., Delle Fave, F., Sintov, N., & Tambe, M. (2015). A game of thrones: When human behavior models compete in repeated Stackelberg security games. In *Proceedings of the 2015 International Conference on Autonomous Agents and Multiagent Systems.* International Foundation for Autonomous Agents and Multiagent Systems.

Korzhyk, D., Conitzer, V., & Parr, R. (2010). Complexity of Computing Optimal Stackelberg Strategies in Security Resource Allocation Games. In *Proceedings of the Twenty-Fourth AAAI Conference on Artificial Intelligence* (pp. 805–810).

Montesh, M. (2013). Rhino poaching: A new form of organized crime. *Technical report, College of Law Research and Innovation Committee of the University of South Africa*, 27, 1–23.

Moreto, W. (2013). *To conserve and protect: Examining law enforcement ranger culture and operations in Queen Elizabeth National Park, Uganda*. Doctoral dissertation, Rutgers University-Graduate School-Newark.

Myerson, R. B. (2013). *Game theory*. Cambridge, MA: Harvard University Press.

National Wildlife Refuge Association. (2015). *Global anti-poaching act seeks to restrict illicit wildlife trade*. Retrieved from http://refugeassociation.org/2015/07/global-anti-poaching-act-seeks-to-restrict-illicit-wildlife-trade/

Nguyen, T. H., Delle Fave, F. M., Kar, D., Lakshminarayanan, A. S., Yadav, A., Tambe, M., ... & Rwetsiba, A. (2015). Making the most of our regrets: Regret-based solutions to handle payoff uncertainty and elicitation in green security games. In Baras, J. S., Katz, J., & Altman, E. (Eds.). In *Decision and game theory for security* (pp. 170–191). Springer International Publishing.

Nguyen, T. H., Yang, R., Azaria, A., Kraus, S., & Tambe, M. (2013). Analyzing the effectiveness of adversary modeling in security games. In *Proceedings of the Twenty-Seventh AAAI Conference on Artificial Intelligence* (pp. 718–724).

Ouko, E. (2013). *Where, when, and why are there elephant poaching hotspots in Kenya*. Doctoral dissertation. Netherlands: University of Twente.

Pires, S. F. (2012). *The illegal parrot trade in the neo-tropics: The relationship between poaching and illicit pet markets*. Doctoral dissertation. Newark, NJ: Rutgers University.

Pita, J., Jain, M., Marecki, J., Ordóñez, F., Portway, C., Tambe, M., ... & Kraus, S. (2008). Deployed ARMOR protection: The application of a game theoretic model for security at the Los Angeles International Airport. In *Proceedings of the 7th international joint conference on Autonomous agents and multiagent systems: industrial track* (pp. 125–132). International Foundation for Autonomous Agents and Multiagent Systems.

Plummer, M. (2003). JAGS: A program for analysis of Bayesian graphical models using Gibbs sampling. In *Proceedings of the 3rd international workshop on distributed statistical computing*. Wien, Austria: Technische Universit at Wien.

Qian, Y., Haskell, W. B., Jiang, A. X., & Tambe, M. (2014). Online planning for optimal protector strategies in resource conservation games. In *Proceedings of the 2014 international conference on Autonomous agents and multi-agent systems* (pp. 733–740). International Foundation for Autonomous Agents and Multiagent Systems.

Save the Rhino International. (2015). *Poaching statistics*. Retrieved from https://www.savetherhino.org/rhino_info/poaching_statistics

Secretariat, G.T.I. (2013). *Global tiger recovery program implementation plan: 2013-14*. Report, The World Bank: Washington, D.C. Retrieved from http://globaltigerinitiative.org/publication/global-tiger-recovery-program-implementation-plan-2013-14/

Shieh, E., An, B., Yang, R., Tambe, M., Baldwin, C., DiRenzo, J., ... & Meyer, G. (2012). Protect: A deployed game theoretic system to protect the ports of the united states. In *Proceedings of the 11th International Conference on Autonomous Agents and Multiagent Systems - Volume 1* (pp. 13–20). International Foundation for Autonomous Agents and Multiagent Systems.

Smart Collaboration (2015). Retrieved from http://www.smartconservationsoftware.org/

Stokes, E. J. (2010). Improving effectiveness of protection efforts in tiger source sites: Developing a framework for law enforcement monitoring using MIST. *Integrative Zoology*, 5, 363–377.

Tambe, M. (2011). *Security and game theory: Algorithms, deployed systems, lessons learned.* Cambridge, United Kingdom: Cambridge University Press.

Tsai, J., Rathi, S., Kiekintveld, C., Ordonez, F., Tambe, M. (2009). IRIS - a tool for strategic security allocation in transportation networks. In *Proceedings of 8th International Conference on Autonomous Agents and Multiagent Systems - Industry Track* (pp. 1327–1334). International Foundation for Autonomous Agents and Multiagent Systems.

Wagenaar, W. A. (1972). Generation of random sequences by human subjects: A critical survey of literature. *Psychological Bulletin*, 77, 65.

Wato, Y. A., Wahungu, G. M., & Okello, M. M. (2006). Correlates of wildlife snaring patterns in Tsavo West National Park, Kenya. *Biological Conservation*, 132, 500–509.

Yang, R., Ford, B., Tambe, M., & Lemieux, A. (2014). Adaptive resource allocation for wildlife protection against illegal poachers. In *Proceedings of the 2014 International Conference on Autonomous Agents and Multi agent Systems* (pp.453–460). International Foundation for Autonomous Agents and Multiagent Systems.

Yang, R., Jiang, A. X., Tambe, M., & Ordonez, F. (2013). Scaling-up security games with boundedly rational adversaries: A cutting-plane approach. In *Proceedings of the Twenty-Third International Joint Conference on Artificial Intelligence* (pp. 404–410).

Yin, Z., Jiang, A. X., Tambe, M., Kiekintveld, C., Leyton-Brown, K., Sandholm, T., & Sullivan, J. P. (2012). TRUSTS: Scheduling randomized patrols for fare inspection in transit systems using game theory. *AI Magazine*, 33, 59.

11

Estimating Poaching Opportunity and Potential

Adrian Treves, Christine Browne-Nuñez, Jamie Hogberg, Jens Karlsson Frank, Lisa Naughton-Treves, Niki Rust, and Zachary Voyles

Most governments today protect wolves, bears, and big cats from unregulated killing (Epstein, 2013). Such protections for large carnivores (LC) can be controversial for people who perceive they are sacrificing safety, recreation, or economic opportunity (Nie, 2003; Treves *et al.*, 2015). Perceptions of these risks appear strongly influenced by both the costs and the benefits of living with LC and other wild animals (Bruskotter & Wilson, 2014). Public discourse and media representations of the balance of benefits with costs may play a large role in diverse audiences' actions and reactions to LC and their management. Opponents of LC protection sometimes aim to reduce LC numbers legally or illegally by poaching (Banse, 2011; St. John *et al.*, 2012; von Essen, Hansen, Kallstrom, Peterson, & Peterson, 2015). Legal opposition to LC protections has been studied extensively; this chapter is focused on lesser known illegal opposition (Gavin, Solomon, & Blank; 2010; Muth, 1998).

Regarding illegal killing of wildlife (i.e., poaching, or the illegal taking of wildlife in violation of a codified law and sometimes a normative rule), we know more about poachers' motivations to poach than we know about the attitudes of poachers and the behaviors they show before, during, and after attempted poaching activities. Motivations for poaching seem to include a complex mix of impulsive and rational factors, including commercial gain, household consumption, recreational satisfactions, trophy poaching, thrill killing, protection of self and property, rebellion, traditional right, disagreement with specific regulations, and gamesmanship (Muth & Bowe, 1998). Kahler and Gore (2012) provided a broader list of motivations which have been empirically tested in Namibia. Although one can debate the utility of these typologies, it is difficult to deny the diversity of motivations. Even for situations involving LC only, people have been documented to kill for profit, as a symbolic protest, to protect livestock or valued game, to gain status, or out of fear or hatred (Kahler, Roloff, & Gore, 2013; Knight, 2003; Pohja-Mykrä & Kurki, 2013; Sharmaa, Wright, Joseph, & Desai, 2014; St. John *et al.*, 2012). Economic costs of coexisting with LC have a long history of discussion and but recent reviews have cast doubt on the potency of this explanation as a motivation to poach LCs (Dickman, Marchini, & Manfredo, 2013; Treves & Bruskotter, 2014). For one thing, economic costs may be used to legitimize

Conservation Criminology, First Edition. Edited by Meredith L. Gore.

other motivations to poach LC, testified to by evidence that wealthier individuals are more involved in promoting or implementing poaching of jaguars (Marchini & Macdonald, 2012). Fear may play a role (Flykt *et al.*, 2013), as has resistance to perceived dominant social groups (Browne-Nuñez, Treves, Macfarland, Voyels, & Turng, 2015; Filteau, 2012; von Essen *et al.*, 2015). Personal profit is also a major cause of LC poaching when wildlife parts or live animals have great financial value on international black markets. Overall, however, the attitudes and behavior underlying LC poaching are not as well understood (Browne-Nuñez *et al.*, 2015; St. John *et al.*, 2012).

Poaching warrants more systematic study given that LC poaching is a major source of mortality that has slowed or reversed several population recoveries (Goodrich *et al.*, 2008; Liberg *et al.*, 2012; Treves *et al.*, in pressin press); poaching may also finance illegal activities and insurgents or undermine biodiversity protections (Gavin *et al.*, 2010). LC are generally charismatic and as such their population declines attract widespread media and policy attention (Houston, Bruskotter, & Fan, 2010). The United Nations deemed poaching to be part of a broader global environmental crime crisis in 2015 (Nellemann, Henricksen, Raxter, Ash, & Mrema, 2015). Poaching can cast suspicion on the other opponents of LC conservation who are law-abiding. Thus poaching may also exacerbate sociopolitical conflicts dividing those who coexist with carnivores from those who wish to see LC populations recover. Effective remedies for LC poaching are hampered by our current lack of information about who poaches, where, and the why of conservation crimes more generally (Gavin *et al.*, 2010). Only recently has the conservation community begun to incorporate and synthesize insights from criminology and criminal justice in an effort to test and improve the effectiveness of anti-poaching initiatives. Here we add to that effort by advancing understanding of the proximate mechanisms leading to poaching and the attitudes of various implicated interest groups.

11.1 Understanding Attitudes and Behaviors of Realized and Potential Poachers

In order to predict and prevent poaching, scientists can study its antecedents, both contextual and cognitive, and communicate bidirectionally with law-enforcement agents. The reliability of social science research on poaching behavior is complicated by concealment of the activity and the difficulty of documenting true intentions to poach (St. John *et al.*, 2012) and how and where poachers act (Kahler *et al.*, 2013). Therefore, we turned to criminology and social psychology theories for testable hypotheses to explain poaching opportunity and poaching potential, which we define below. Criminology and social psychology provides theories to link motivations—both impulsive and rational—causally to actions. We turned particularly to rational choice and routine activity theories (Bouhana, 2013; Clarke & Felson, 1993).

Rational choice theory (RTC) tells us people make rational decisions about whether or not to engage in illegal behavior, such as tiger poaching, based on a benefit–cost calculation. A rational choice hypothesis for poaching would suggest the perceived probability of benefiting multiplied by the magnitude of that benefit would be weighed against the perceived probability of punishment multiplied by the severity of punishment. The attitudes and perceptions of would-be poachers are therefore relevant for estimating how they perform this internal, mental calculus or if they do at all (i.e., acting impulsively). Routine activity theory (RAT) tells us crime depends on "a motivated offender with criminal intentions and the ability to act on these inclinations, a suitable victim or target, and the absence of a capable guardian who can prevent the crime" (Review of the Roots of Youth Violence: Literature Reviews, 2013). The estimates of poacher's intentions and inclinations combined with events and circumstances surrounding suitability and guardians would inform conservation and law-enforcement efforts to combat wildlife poaching. However, empirical evidence has cast doubt on at least two major assumptions of these theories that are relevant to LC poaching.

First, efforts to increase arrests or punishments for other sorts of crimes have proven ineffective partly because offenders acted irrationally or impulsively, or for immediate instead of long-term net gain (Exum, 2002; Wright & Brookman 2006; Wright & Rossi, 1983). Perpetrators in those studies reported that they assumed they would not be caught or failed to consider long-term repercussions. When LC poaching results from anger, fear, or impulsive response, irrational poaching may arise from ignoring or discounting the consequences that generate costs. A second challenge to applying RTC to LC poaching may arise when subgroups reward offenders for resisting the broader society. Rewards might manifest as elevated social status after (s)he is caught and punished or inducements such as financial prizes. For example, predator-killing contests have often awarded prizes for the largest coyote killed within wolf range, raising the likelihood of poaching protected wolves "accidentally" (Ketcham, 2014). Organized crime or secret societies may accrue benefits from LC poaching in a different currency than broader society, thereby rewarding criminal acts and offering protection from punishment. The RCT and its simple calculation of benefits- costs seems incomplete when one considers several costs and benefits in different currencies traded within both the broader legal society and the narrower illegal society. For LC poachers, we might expect those associating in an anti-establishment subgroup to calculate the benefits and costs differently so as to ignore the out-group sanctions in favor of their in-group incentives that favor killing a wild animal. Indeed, poachers are sometimes viewed as folk criminals within their communities that tolerate or even encourage poaching because of romantic ideas, (e.g., Robin Hood's daring pursuits in English folk tales and related action films from Hollywood) (Kahler *et al.*, 2013; Marchini & Macdonald, 2012; Pohja-Mykrä & Kurki, 2013). Similarly poachers may believe that they are behaving just like many others in their community, a phenomenon referred to as 'false consensus.' For example poachers perceiving the false consensus may estimate lower risks and costs of punishment, which has been documented in at least one study of LC poaching (St. John *et al.*, 2012). Also poachers may receive intentional or unintentional signals from law enforcement authorities that certain LC have low value to society or that poaching will not be punished, which in turn may promote the behavior (Chapron & Treve, 2016; Pohja-Mykrä & Kurki, 2013; Treves & Bruskotter, 2014). Although RCT may not adequately account for a sub-culture's differential estimation of costs and benefits as described above, the RAT assumptions that inclination, capability, and opportunity can help to predict deviant behavior still deserve attention by those concerned with poaching. Furthermore, these notions complement social psychology's Theory of Planned Behavior, which provides a useful starting point for examining poaching inclinations and their connections to actions.

11.2 Social Psychological Approaches for Understanding the Potential to Poach

The Theory of Planned Behavior (TPB) helps frame the antecedents of a behavioral outcome such as poaching. TPB predicts individual beliefs about actions, social norms, and perceived behavioral control shape individual intentions to act. In Ajzen's (1991) refinement of the TPB, he noted the difference between perceived behavioral control, which is a belief about one's ability to act and succeed, and 'actual control,' which is affected by external events (hereafter 'opportunities') (Ajzen, 1991, p. 191). The distinction between perceived and actual control is particularly relevant for human-wildlife interactions because human behavior interacts with animal agency as well as chance events. For example, animals move deliberately across a landscape and stochastic events affect where they move and when so the vicissitudes of a poacher's own movements combine in complex ways to increase or reduce the number and duration of opportunities to poach. If we consider chance external events and animal behavior jointly as presenting opportunities, or not, for a poacher, then intention might equate to a cognitive readiness if given the opportunity. Intention in this sense resembles 'inclination,' a critical element of RAT (Ajzen, 1991). Likewise, 'capability' in RAT would correspond to perceived behavioral control in TPB. Putting the concepts together in a temporal sequence of cause-and-effect, we might frame the events leading to poaching as follows: a potential poacher starts with a set of attitudes that may produce an intention to act, and if (s)he has the capability when the opportunity arises, then (s)he may manifest poaching behavior (Figure 11.1A). We apply this general framework to a specific case involving wolf-human interactions in the remainder of the chapter using a composite measure of attitudes and intention that we refer to as inclination (Figure 11.1B).

11.3 Case Study on Wolf Poaching

11.3.1 Theoretical Approach and Sampling

We integrated TPB and RAT to understand poaching of a controversial LC—gray wolves. Previously, we investigated attitudes toward wolf policy and individual inclinations to poach wolves in Wisconsin, U.S. (Browne-Nuñez *et al.*, 2015; Hogberg, Treves, Shaw, & Naughton-Treves, 2015; Treves & Martin, 2011; Treves, Naughton-Treves, & Shelley, 2013). We found our estimates of inclination to poach were better predicted by competitiveness by hunters over white-tailed deer than an individual's direct experience with wolf damages or fear for personal safety. We also found that individuals' inclinations to poach increased

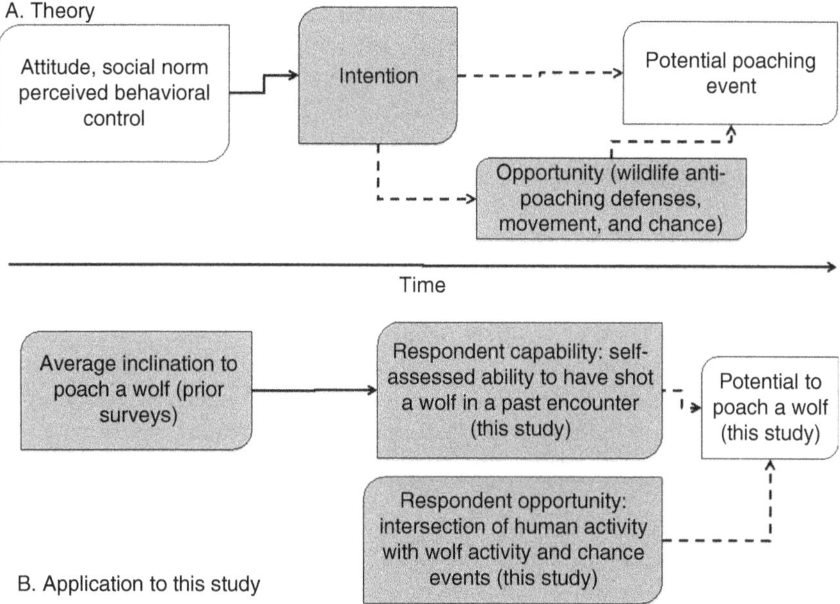

Figure 11.1 (A) Theory for causal connections among a time axis connecting cognitive antecedents preceding the intention to act. And hypothetical (dashed lines) connecting intention to external opportunities and to potential poaching events. External opportunity (the movements and sensory abilities of an animal that bring it into a position or state of vulnerability to poaching) and potential poaching event are probabilistic but influenced by intention in theory. B: We depict a practical application to wolf-poaching. We replace intention with inclination, which is a construct that combines attitude with intention and draw two samples of respondents to examine external opportunity (see Methods). We combine estimates of each to model the potential to poach a wolf among two samples and several classes of respondents. Note the dotted lines indicate hypothetical interaction between intention and opportunity because strong intentions may lead to preparatory behavior that increases opportunity (lower dashed arrow) but intention may be opportunistic in the sense of awaiting chance events (upper dashed arrow).

over time among residents resampled over several years. Many possible causes of this longitudinal change were confounding so we could not elucidate the direct causes of attitude change. However we could rule out that government policies liberalizing wolf-killing did not reverse declining tolerance for wolves. Also a recent study identified themes providing a more nuanced understanding of changing attitudes toward wolves and inclinations to poach them, including fear for personal or family safety, powerlessness to prevent threats, and a lack of trust in the wolf management agency (Browne-Nuñez *et al.*, 2015). Here, we use our attitudinal measures of inclination to poach a wolf as a starting point. However in our region and many others, the motivations and intentions of poachers (i.e., the why) are better understood than the events and behaviors that precede poaching (i.e., the how). Therefore, we integrated information on poaching potential (i.e., probabilities that poaching would manifest) among deer-hunters and among people who had experienced verified, wolf-related threats to personal safety, pets, farm animals (e.g., livestock and farm dogs), or hunting dogs.

A challenge in studying poaching potential is to identify sufficient numbers of incidents in which the opportunity to poach was verified. Without verification, people may claim they saw a wolf but it may have been a coyote or free-running dog. A smaller relative, coyotes can easily be confused for wolves under many field conditions. We interviewed individuals who had experienced verified encounters with wolves. The encounters were verified by a federal agency that examines evidence such as tracks, scat, or other sightings in the vicinity (Treves *et al.*, 2002). Because all of our respondents had actually encountered wolves as verified by the agency, we were able to examine their inclinations and capabilities to poach in a more controlled fashion than the typical self-report of a wolf encounter. Lack of verification plagues many studies of wildlife and poaching. Therefore our work helps to shed light onto how to design, implement, and even evaluate interventions in the face of such data deficiencies. Importantly, our sample was unrepresentative of human-wolf encounters because threats or damages leading to a complaint have been a small minority of all reported encounters with wolves (Treves, Martin, Wydeven, & Weidenhoeft, 2011; Treves *et al.*, 2013). Also our sample was to some extent self-selected in that respondents had reached out to and complained to authorities about the wolves and as far as we know, none of our respondents actually poached a wolf. Therefore, study respondents may differ from those who actually poach wolves. Self-selection is not necessarily considered a source of bias under RAT, because the theory holds anyone has the potential to poach. Regardless, our sample provides the first estimate for the U.S. of the maximum numbers of wolves that might die if people killed a wolf during each type of verified encounter (Backeryd, 2007).

For comparison, we also interviewed randomly sampled respondents who hunted white-tailed deer in wolf range. Deer are a very popular game species is hunted by ~500,000 hunters per year in Wisconsin and the pursuit of deer takes some of the hunters into wolf range with an elevated capability, or readiness, to poach a wolf. In this sample, some respondents reported they had encountered wolves whereas others did not. We were unable to verify either report and recognize such reports may be inaccurate. Nevertheless, the deer-hunter sample allowed us to estimate the frequency of perceived opportunities to kill a coyote or a wolf based on a random sample of people who had been engaged in an activity that involves many hunters each year (Dex, 1995). From this sample we estimated opportunity and capability to poach independent of the likelihood of encounters.

In sum, we had a small sample with verified encounters, where opportunity was equal to 100%, per our definition in Figure 11.2 to estimate self-perceived capability in a rare situation. We also had a large sample with unverified encounters to estimate self-perceived capability and opportunity in a common situation. Although we had no true control, the two samples help us estimate the consequences if policy-makers legalized wolf-killing in different situations (Backeryd, 2007). Comparisons between identity groups such as our subsamples and comparisons between high-risk and lower-risk situations should focus research and prevention efforts more precisely (Clarke & de By, 2013; Haines *et al.*, 2012; Marquez, Vargas, Villafuerte, & Fa, 2013; Treves *et al.*, 2011).

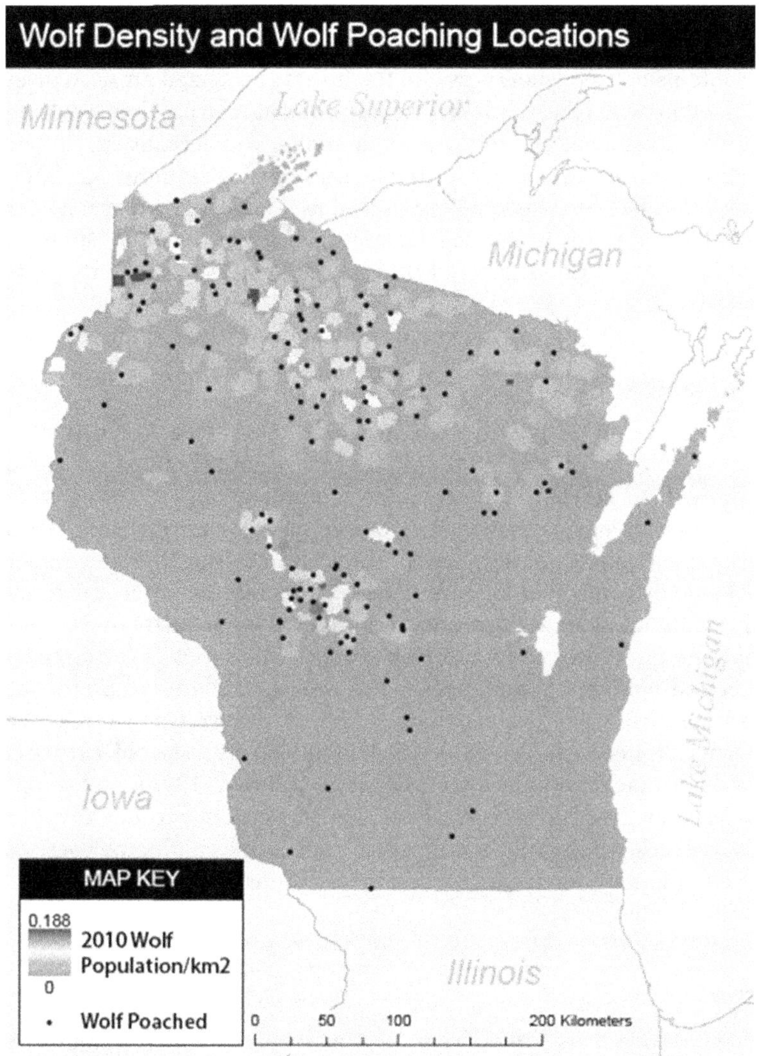

Figure 11.2 Wisconsin, wolf range and population density in 2010, and poaching locations 1979–2011.

11.3.2 Methods

Due to space considerations additional information about methods are presented in a permanent online archive at Treves (2015). The interested reader can review the archive for additional citations, data, and methodological descriptions.

11.3.3 Study Site

Wisconsin extends over 138,644 km^2 with human population density of 41.1 per km$^-$ and 18.7 housing units per km^2. Many private lands and 75% of public lands were open to hunting for at least one season annually during the first decade of the 2000s. These seasons included the autumn white-tailed deer hunt involving approximately 500,000 hunters on public and private lands. Wolf range in Wisconsin contains no vast wilderness and few strictly protected areas. Wolves use areas of the state with relatively less agriculture and human use than expected by chance. Human residents are engaged predominantly in agriculture, timber, rural recreation, and other natural resource uses. In the summer of 2011, Wisconsin's gray wolves were federally protected as an endangered species. At that time, wolves had never been a legal game species and bounties had been discontinued since 1957. Coyotes could be shot on sight in much of the state most of the year.

11.3.4 Study Respondents

We replicated as closely as possible the methods used in Backeryd (2007), achieved human subjects protection program approval and obtained informed consent of individuals at least 18 years of age. Complaints of property loss to wolves were verified; approximately 50% of claims were unverifiable (Ruid *et al.*, 2009). The final respondent sample was drawn from the remainder deemed probable or confirmed and previously estimated the latter error rate in livestock incidents as <9% false positives (Treves *et al.*, 2011). We conducted telephone interviews to record respondents' memories of the circumstances surrounding their experiences with wolves and the respondents' self-reported appraisals of their capability to shoot the wolf or wolves. We sent an advance-notice letter to the complainants so as to avoid surprise, improve the legitimacy of the survey (Salant & Dillman, 1994), and maximize response rates. Deer hunters were reached at random without advance warning by dialing telephone numbers in the same municipalities as the former complainant sample. Questionnaire items analyzed are reproduced verbatim below.

11.3.5 Survey Items

We did not ask respondents if they were inclined to poach a wolf because we were concerned that the telephone interview would not be perceived as confidential enough to assure high rates of truthfulness. We were ultimately interested in respondents' perceived capability to act given the opportunity. After recording respondents' descriptions of the conditions during the encounter with wolves, we asked "Did you see the wolf/wolves immediately before, during, or immediately after the incident?" Of the subset with eyewitness encounters we then determined if they had been armed with a loaded weapon. Then we asked, "Playing the scene back in your memory, do you think you might have been able to shoot the wolf or wolves that you saw immediately before, during, or immediately after this incident?" We assumed respondents, not researchers were the best situated to estimate their own capability to kill the wolf they encountered, taking into account their recollections of their internal condition at the time and external conditions (e.g., light, visual obstructions, distance) at the time of the encounter.

11.3.6 Inclination to Poach

Following methods detailed in the online archive (Treves, 2015), we set the bounds of our respondents' inclinations to poach wolves at 17–29% among deer hunters and 23–43% among bear hunters. We estimated inclination to poach wolves when their domestic animals were threatened among general pet owners and livestock owners as 30-44% and 29-39% respectively. We did not have a questionnaire item relating to threats to health and human safety.

11.3.7 Modeling Potential to Poach

We multiplied the three frequency estimates as in Eq. 11.1 to model the potential to poach a wolf, treating *inclination* and *capability* as independent variables because the former was estimated from our mail-back surveys from 2001–2009, whereas *capability* was estimated from our telephone interview samples of individuals in 2011, both described above. We also treated *opportunity* as independent because it reflected the frequency with which encounters with wolves occurred; they were not necessarily visual and thus as set at 100% for verified complainants but self-reported by the deer hunter sample reporting on visual encounters and taking into account time spent in the field (see Eq. 11.2). Our assumption of independence (multiplying the probabilities) is reasonable given our sources of data but may not hold under other conditions. First, a would-be poacher with strong intentions may seek additional opportunities (e.g., deliberate search for wolves to poach) or those who encounter many opportunities may change their attitudes (e.g., finding wolves more or less valuable as a result of experiences). We discuss the implications of this theoretical non-independence between intention and opportunity below.

To operationalize Eq. 11.1 for our random deer hunters, we used Eq. 11.2, where the first parenthetical product represented capability, and the second parenthetical product represented opportunity. Capability was modeled as the product of A and C. Opportunity for deer hunters was modeled as the product of V and F. We estimated (see also Treves, 2015):

- A using the questions: (1) did you have access to a weapon when you saw the wolf/wolves, (2) if yes, were you carrying it at the time you saw the wolf/wolves, and (3) if yes, was it loaded?
- C using the question: playing the scene back in your memory, do you think you might have been able to shoot the wolf or wolves that you saw immediately before, during, or immediately after this incident?
- V using the question: have you ever seen wolves while deer hunting or preparing your hunting site?
- F using the questions: (1) if yes to V, on how many different days have you seen wolves while you were deer hunting and/or preparing your site, (2) when was this sighting/the most recent sighting, and (3) how many years have you been hunting deer?

The online archive (Treves, 2015) provides the full details for the modeling steps we took to estimate potential to poach following a series of additional equations (i.e., Eq. 11.1–11.5).

11.4 Results

11.4.1 Potential to Poach

We modeled the potential of different stakeholders to poach. Following Eq. 11.2, deer hunters' potential to poach ranged from 5.4–9.2%. Other conditions surrounding the self-reported encounters are reported in Treves (2015). Following Eq. 11.3, 1–1.5% of pet owners with verified wolf complaints had the potential to poach. When asked if they were concerned for their personal safety, 6% responded in the affirmative. Figure 11.3 depicts potential-to-poach by random deer hunters and by pet owners with a verified compliant, with different parameters for the two very different groups. Although a pet owner with a verified encounter had more than twice the opportunity (1.0 vs. 0.45) and a higher inclination to poach a wolf (median 0.37 vs. 0.23) than a random deer hunter by our estimates, the self-reported readiness and capability of the random deer hunters (0.71) so far exceeded the pet owner's self-reported capability (0.035) that the random deer hunters posed a higher potential-to-poach by our model (Fig. 11.3). Many of the respondents with verified encounters self-assessed their capability of shooting a wolf as zero because they did not see the wolves or there were other impediments to action. This substantiated our assertion that opportunity could be separated from capability (Fig. 11.1). Following Eq. 11.4, we predicted 0.01–0.2% of livestock owners with verified wolf complaints had the potential to poach; following Eq. 11.5, we predicted 0.4–0.7% of bear hunters who used hounds and

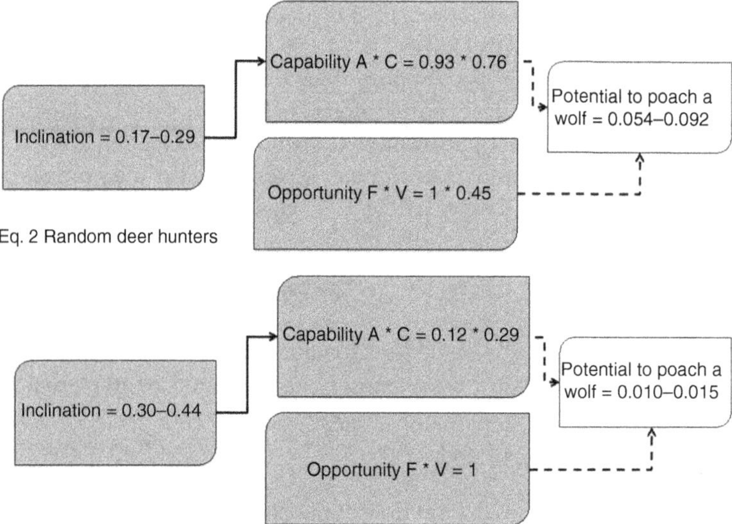

Figure 11.3 Quantifying the potential to poach for two groups of respondents. Random deer hunters were asked to self-report encounters with wolves generating the estimate of opportunity whereas pet owners we interviewed had had verified encounters. In both groups capability was estimated from self-reports of readiness to kill the wolf they encountered. For both groups, inclination was estimated independently from mail-back surveys of much larger samples done in prior studies reported in online archive (Treves, 2015).

had verified wolf complaints had the potential to poach. We did not model potential to poach for those registered as complaining about health or human safety because we did not have an estimate of inclination for such respondents (see Treves, 2015). Other conditions surrounding the verified attacks are presented in Treves (2015).

11.4.2 Effects on Wolf Population

Between 15 March 2007 until 3 October 2011 (the time window we asked complainants to recollect), the State of Wisconsin verified 233 complaints about wolf attacks or threats to farm animals, 72 threats or attacks on hounds, 32 threats or attacks on pets, and 17 health and human safety concerns (WDNR database). If these incidents conformed to our respondents' self-reports, we expect that legalizing the killing of wolves under those complaint situations would result in approximately 1.5 wolves killed every 5 years. That estimate might double if one considered companions of respondents and their capability to poach more than one wolf per incident. These very low rates of mortality resemble those estimated in Sweden under similar hypothetical changes in rules (Backeryd, 2007).

11.4.3 Implications for Theory and Practice

The proximate mechanisms leading to LC poaching remain under-studied. Therefore we know little about encounter rates, the inclination of humans to react lethally to such encounters, and the probabilities that lethal reactions will indeed succeed. As a result, law enforcement actions that enhance guardianship (e.g., direct interventions aimed at preventing harm to wildlife) and actions that identify would-be poachers (e.g., indirect interventions aimed at markets, communications, and routes used by poachers) are entirely reactive. This chapter profiles our work aiming to build understanding for a controversial, endangered LC that is poached without a financial profit motive in a human-dominated ecosystem. By combining estimates of ordinary people's inclinations to poach a wolf with their self-reported capability to do so, and estimated probabilities of encounters with wolves, we were able to estimate relative frequency of wolf-poaching by different categories of people, and estimate a rate of wolf-killing in situations that are common in human-wolf coexistence in Wisconsin, USA. We synthesized social psychology's Theory of Planned Behavior and criminology's RAT to construct our model of potential for wolf-poaching. Our model highlights individual human readiness and self-reported capability to shoot a wolf as more important than inclinations to poach, which we defined as a construct of motivations, attitudes and intentions to poach.

This work may help advance efforts to unify and reconcile different terminologies in the two sets of theories. From a theoretical standpoint, we argued for separation of opportunity to poach into independent components of readiness and capability to poach on the one hand, and the unpredictable movements of a wild animal that avoids people, on the other hand. That argument builds on RAT predicting that potential victims or guardians should act to reduce vulnerability to crime, largely independent of the actions and intentions of the criminal.

Readers are reminded that animal behavior theory is highly advanced in modeling predator-prey encounters, which resemble human-wildlife poaching interactions. Thus, we borrowed from psychological theory to model inclination and capability of a would-be poacher, or intentions and perceived behavioral control respectively, to use Ajzen's (1991) terms. We believe the union of these bodies of theory will improve understanding of poaching. Beyond theory, we provide information we believe will be useful to law enforcement in our region and perhaps beyond; we discuss these implications below.

11.4.4 Deer Hunters

Estimating the potential rate of poaching in various situations is important to conservation, law-enforcement, and organizations interested in preventing illegal activities. Our model of the potential rate of poaching among different groups of people suggests that deer hunters had a more than five times higher relative potential to poach than other categories of respondents in the study. Deer hunters had relatively lower opportunity than other complainants because 100% of the latter had verified encounters (Figure 11.3). By contrast 45% of deer hunters self-reported encounters with a median of one or more species they perceived to be wolves every two years, during deer-hunting or hunting-site preparation. Furthermore, deer hunters had lower inclination to poach wolves as measured in prior surveys of different individuals (Treves *et al.*, 2013). Nevertheless deer hunters had the highest relative potential to poach wolves because of their self-reported capability to shoot a wolf successfully. Those deer-hunters reporting an encounter with animal(s) they perceived to be wolves were usually carrying a loaded weapon in a frame of mind and place conducive to shooting. Yet this potential to poach apparently did not manifest.

Consistent with our model predictions, the plurality of reported poaching, 30%, between 1979–2012 occurred in November, when most permitted deer hunting occurs in Wisconsin (Treves, Langenberg, López-Bao, & Rabenhorst, in press). But does the absolute number of poaching events match our deer hunter respondents' self-reports? In November each year, approximately 500,000 hunters stalk deer in Wisconsin statewide. Even if only 10% of these hunters hunt in the range of the 880 wolves that roamed the state in 2012, and only 5.4% of hunters poached 1 wolf (our study minimum estimate potential-to-poach), every wolf in the state would be poached three times over. Because deer hunters have not done so thus far, one or more of the estimates used in our model must be inflated. Inclination measured might be lower in reality than claimed in our questionnaire surveys, capability to shoot a wolf might be lower than deer hunters claimed in our interviews, or deer hunters who also own livestock or pets they perceive at risk from wolves may be a large proportion of the deer hunter community. Another possibility is that large coyotes are being misperceived as wolves at high rates. Whatever the reason, deer hunters have the potential to poach many more wolves than they have done thus far. Therefore, our estimate of potential-to-poach should not be confused with realized poaching rate nor confused with attempted poaching. Because we do not know how many deer hunters move within wolf pack areas and how accurately they identify wolves or shoot them, we cannot translate our potential-to-poach estimate into a percent of wolves likely to be poached.

One should not read our results so as to blame poached wolves on the average deer hunter. For one, more poaching goes unreported than is reported (Treves *et al.* in pressin press). Also, bear hunters who used hounds had higher inclinations than others in the hunting community. Social media from 2011–2015 have been full of evidence and claims of wolf poaching by bear hunters. Further, the role of deliberate search by a handful of repeat offenders cannot be ruled out. The conservation and law enforcement communities might be able to identify would-be poachers using informants within groups suspected of harboring poachers. Anti-wolf organizations interested in preventing illegal activities might self-police. This study also draws attention to relative differences between categories of people in inclination to poach.

11.4.5 Complainant Sample

Our second sample of complainants (i.e., people with verified complaints of threats to domestic animals) illuminates further the potential to poach. Because the sample of livestock owners, pet owners, and bear hunters who use hounds had verified encounters with wolves, we were able to set opportunity at 100% and focus our analyses on inclination and capability to poach. This complainant sample self-reported lower capabilities to shoot a wolf, partly because loaded weapons were not accessible or the wolves had not been visible during the verified encounter. Therefore, our finding that deer hunters had a higher potential to poach is consistent with predictions of RAT because our respondents had been engaged in activities that either predisposed them to poaching a wolf (e.g., deer hunter sample) or hindered them from poaching a wolf (e.g., complainant sample). Despite complainants having a higher inclination and a verified encounter, they had far lower self-reported capability to poach, resulting in a lower potential to poach.

Among our sample respondents, we estimated pet owners had a higher potential to poach than bear hunters who used hounds. Livestock owners had half the relative potential to poach wolves as did bear hunters. Much of the difference between pet owners, livestock owners, and bear hunters lay in their self-reported capability to poach a wolf. Although bear hunters who used hounds were engaged in a hunting-preparation they reported low capability to poach a wolf because their activity with hounds did not seem compatible with carrying a rifle. By contrast, pet owners rated their capability to shoot a wolf higher than the other two groups. This seemed to reflect a lengthy visual encounter with wolves, perhaps prolonged by the presence of their pet dog, and locations near weapons in some cases. Livestock owners reported the lowest capability, as few had weapons at hand and few saw the wolves. Given the low capability to shoot a wolf among the complainants, we predicted that few wolves would be killed each year if the government legalized a lethal reaction to imminent threats. This finding is consistent with work from Sweden (Backeryd, 2007). However, if the government liberally defined 'imminent threat' or did not enforce its definition, we anticipate future complainants might shoot at wolves that pose no threat, shoot at non-wolves, or otherwise create public safety hazards. Liberalized wildlife harvest has been inferred to increase poaching in some instances (Chapron &

Treves, 2016). Therefore we recommend no change in the current prohibitions on shooting at wildlife of any species.

11.5 Theoretical Considerations on the Causes of Poaching

Theory leads us to expect that poaching requires ability, intent, and opportunity. Intent and opportunity are probably not independent and may interact in important ways. Someone with strong intent can try to make encounters more frequent or more opportune. This would include deliberate search for poaching opportunities. Such deliberate search might arise if the poached animal has high value for its parts or negative value so its destruction brings value to the poacher. Under such circumstances, we predict the rate of poaching would be determined by would-be poachers' search efficiencies and animals' anti-predator efficiencies interacting with the relative abundances of both poachers and animals.

But not all poaching is deliberate search with high motivation. Some poaching may be retaliatory so it is triggered by the actions of the animal. Then deliberate search might ensue where it otherwise would never have arisen. Alternately, the intent to poach might intensify yet rely on chance encounter not retaliatory search. An important difference between retaliation and untriggered poaching is the rate of triggers. We predict the rate of retaliatory poaching would be best predicted the frequency and distribution of triggering events interacting with animals' anti-predator efficiencies rather than the abundances of either poacher or animal directly. Also we might expect the motivation to retaliate might taper off with time or with an initial success in retaliating.

At the other extreme, people with low motivation might be inclined to poach only if the opportunity arises yet make no particular effort to seek out the animal nor require a triggering event other than encounter. Under such conditions, we predict the rate of poaching would depend on the probability of a would-be poacher and animal intersecting in space and time, which would be dictated by their movements and abundances. The three preceding models of poaching make different predictions for the mechanisms and the best predictors of poaching.

In the present paper, we simply assumed no interaction existed between inclination and opportunity. Our efforts to model potential-to-poach were structured so as to treat opportunity as independent from inclination and capability (so we could multiply probabilities rather than treating them as conditional probabilities). In most other studies, the estimates of opportunity, inclination, and capability may all come from the same individuals. In that case, one cannot operationalize the potential to poach by multiplying probabilities because the three probabilities would be statistically dependent. Instead, one has to address whether encounters and reactions result from a random encounter pattern or from a focused, deliberate search pattern by putative poachers. If a substantial number of poachers engage in deliberate search, then potential-to-poach estimates should be based more on inclination than capability or opportunity because would-be poachers would search for opportunities with the capability to act. In sum, the scientific models marshaled to address poaching will differ depending on the motivations of would-be poachers, their search behavior, and the triggering events.

Future researchers should interview confirmed poachers, and test the above causal mechanisms with data on search, opportunistic encounter, and triggering events. Also, we recommend that the designers of anti-poaching interventions consider if poaching occurs by chance encounters, deliberate search, or retaliatory killing. Policy and management interventions that aim to prevent poaching tend to cluster into three types. Those that address the cognition of would-be poachers (e.g., improving attitudes to promote compliance with rules), those that address their behavior (e.g., interdiction and prosecution as a form of deterrence to promote compliance), and those that address the technology involved in poaching or anti-poaching efforts (e.g., firearm controls). Cognitive and behavioral interventions can be combined strategically to address different motivations and inclinations, just as behavioral and technological interventions can be combined to counter different search methods and capabilities of poachers.

The field of conservation has made significant advances in the design of interventions for human-wildlife conflicts (Treves, Wallace, & White, 2009). Some of the lessons learned will be useful to those designing anti-poaching interventions or to conservation criminology generally. For example, conservationists teach that effectiveness should be considered separately and first before cost-efficiency, and the selection of candidate interventions needs to consider unintended consequences such as perverse incentives. For example, cognitive fixes are often touted by policy-makers, but recent empirical evidence about cognitive fixes is consistent, in that inclinations to poach did not change despite policy interventions (lethal control, hunting) that were believed to shape attitudes (Hogberg *et al.*, 2015; Treves *et al.*, 2013). Moreover, the cognitive processes that motivate poaching of controversial species may have little to do with economics and more to do with social norms or symbolism and fear attached to the species (Treves & Bruskotter, 2014). Indeed, tight-knit organizations that foster and conceal specialist poachers might have a widespread effect on sensitive wildlife populations (Lute & Gore, 2014). Scholars have long noted the difficulty of changing attitudes, persuading people to behave differently, and the importance of changing social norms as well as individual ways of thinking (Dunwoody, 2007; Heberlein, 2012; Kinzig *et al.*, 2013; Treves & Bruskotter, 2014). Heberlein hypothesized that structural or technological interventions may be more cost-effective in the long run (Heberlein, 1974, 2012).Others recommend combining structural and cognitive fixes to prevent poaching (St. John *et al.*, 2012). The legalization of wildlife-killing is a commonly promoted combination of a cognitive and structural fix intended to prevent poaching and enhance conservation.

Conferring ownership of wildlife on those who coexist with them, including the right to kill wildlife for profit or other purposes, has commonly been advocated as a way to reduce poaching (reviewed in Di Minin, Bradshaw, & Leader-Williams, 2016). For example, in southern Africa, community-based natural resource management has been a popular method for providing locals with rights to use wildlife populations either non-consumptively (via photographic tourism) or consumptively (via culling, harvest, or trophy hunting). In Namibia and Zambia, for example, such schemes provided benefits to communities by creating income to locals via trophy hunting permits sold. The local community owners of wildlife may then be motivated to protect wildlife on their land because they can obtain income from them (reviewed in Di Minin *et al.*, 2016). Peer-reviewed empirical evidence remains sparse if one scrutinizes the latter study. For example, game surveys suggest this helped Namibian large ungulates, for example, a pre-conservancy report for one area in Namibia (Rodwell, Tagg, & Grobler, 1995). Carnivore-poaching in particular may not abate if profits are focused on ungulates or if properties are small and easily traversed by individual carnivores (Balme, Slotow, & Hunter, 2009; Balme, Slotow, & Hunter, 2010). Moreover, the fundamental idea that liberalizing carnivore-killing will enhance conservation has not found support. In Wisconsin and neighboring Michigan, government policies to legalize wolf-culling as a way to reduce poaching had the opposite result (Chapron & Treves, 2016). We hypothesized that government policy to legalize the killing of problem wolves sent a signal to poachers that wolves were imposing higher costs, or that anti-poaching rules would not be enforced. Therefore, we encourage caution with proposed cognitive fixes especially when no data on psychology or criminology are offered in support of an intervention. Given scientific consensus that both compulsory and voluntary regulatory mechanisms are needed to prevent or limit illegal resource use (Kinzig *et al.*, 2013; May, 2005), we recommend renewed study and investment in both. We made recommendations for research above. As for interventions, we recommend the hunting community self-police with third-party verification as a first step to preventing poaching. We recommend policy-makers set legal lower quotas for wildlife killing; lower by the amount of all other sources of mortality, especially poaching measured transparently and scientifically. Then we recommend deploying effective anti-poaching interventions that incorporate the modern tools of criminology and policing.

References

Ajzen, I. (1991). The theory of planned behavior. *Organizational Behavior and Human Decision Processes*, 50, 179–211.

Backeryd, J. (2007). Wolf attacks on dogs in Scandinavia 1995-2005. Masters Thesis. Swedish University of Agricultural Sciences, Grimso.

Balme, G., Slotow, R., & Hunter, L. T. B. (2009). Impact of conservation interventions on the dynamics and persistence of a persecuted leopard (Panthera pardus) population. *Biological Conservation*, 142, 2681–2690.

Balme, G., Slotow, R., & Hunter, L. T. B. (2010). Edge effects and the impact of non- protected areas in carnivore conservation: leopards in the Phinda-Mkhuze Complex, South Africa. *Animal Conservation*, 13, 315–323.

Banse, T. (2011). Wolf foes turn to Congress and Legislatures. Retrieved from http://www.opb.org/news/article/wolf-foes-turn-congress-and-legislatures/

Bouhana, N. (2013). The reasoning criminal vs. Homer Simpson: Conceptual challenges for crime science. *Frontiers in Human Neuroscience*, 7, 1–6.

Browne-Nuñez, C., Treves, A., Macfarland, D., Voyles, Z., & Turng, C. (2015). Evaluating the potential for legalized lethal control of wolves to reduce illegal take: A mixed- methods examination of attitudes and behavioral inclinations. *Biological Conservation*, 189, 59–71.

Bruskotter, J. T., & Wilson, R. S. (2014). Determining where the wild things will be: using Psychological theory to find tolerance for large carnivores. *Conservation Letters*, 7, 158–165.

Chapron, G., & Treves, A. (2016). Blood does not buy goodwill: allowing culling increases poaching of a large carnivore. *Proceedings of the Royal Society B: Biological Sciences*, 283, 20152939.

Clarke, R. V., & de By, R. A. (2013). Poaching, habitat loss and the decline of Neotropical parrots: A comparative spatial analysis. *Journal of Experimental Criminology*, 9, 333–353.

Clarke, R. V., & Felson, M. (1993). Introduction: Criminology, routine activity, and rational choice. In Clarke, R. V., & Felson, M. (Eds.). *Routine activity and rational choice*. New Brunswick, NJ: Transaction Publishers.

Dex, S. (1995). The reliability of recall data: A literature review. *Bulletin de Methodologie Sociologique*, 49, 58–80.

Di Minin, E., Bradshaw, C., & Leader-Williams, N. (2016). Banning trophy hunting will exacerbate biodiversity loss. *Trends in Ecology and Evolution*, 31, 99–102.

Dickman, A., Marchini, S., & Manfredo, M. (2013). The human dimension in addressing conflict with large carnivores. In Macdonald, D., & Willis, K. J. (Eds.). *Key topics in conservation biology*. London: John Wiley & Sons.

Dunwoody, S. (2007). The challenge of trying to make a difference using media messages. In Moser, S. C., & Dilling, L. (Eds.). *Creating a climate for change*. Cambridge, United Kingdom: Cambridge University Press.

Epstein, Y. (2013). *Governing ecologies: Species protection in overlapping and contiguous legal regimes*. Uppsala, Sweden: Acta Universitatis Upsaliensis 91.

Exum, M. L. (2002). *The effects of alcohol intoxication and anger on violent decision-making in men*. Dissertation Abstracts International: The Humanities and Social Sciences, 62, 3195- A.

Filteau, M. R. (2012). Deterring defiance: Don't give a poacher a reason to poach. *International Journal of Rural Criminology*, 1, 236–255.

Flykt, A., Johansson, M., Karlsson, J., Lindeberg, S., & Lipp, O. (2013). Fear of wolves and bears – physiological responses and negative associations. A Swedish sample. *Human Dimensions of Wildlife*, 18, 416–434.

Gavin, M. C., Solomon, J. N., & Blank, S. G. (2010). Measuring and monitoring illegal use of natural resources. *Conservation Biology*, 24, 89–100.

Goodrich, J. M., Kerley, L. L., Smirnov, E. N., Miquelle, D. G., McDonald, L., Quigley, H. B.,...McDonald, T. (2008). Survival rates and causes of mortality of Amur tigers on and near the Sikhote-Alin Biosphere Zapovednik. *Journal of Zoology*, 276, 323–329.

Haines, A. M., Elledge, D., Wilsing, L. K., Grabe, M., Barske, M. D., Burke, N., & Webb, S. L. (2012). Spatially explicit analysis of poaching activity as a conservation management tool. *Wildlife Society Bulletin*, 36, 685–692.

Heberlein, T. A. (1974). The three fixes: technological, cognitive and structural. In Field, D., Barren, J. C., & Long, B. F. (Eds.). *Water and community development: Social and economic perspectives*. Ann Arbor, MI: Ann Arbor Science.

Heberlein, T. A. (2012). *Navigating environmental attitudes*. Oxford, United Kingdom: Oxford University Press.

Hogberg, J., Treves, A., Shaw, B., & Naughton-Treves, L. (2015). Changes in attitudes toward wolves before and after an inaugural public hunting and trapping season: early evidence from Wisconsin's wolf range. *Environmental Conservation*, 43, 45–55.

Houston, M., Bruskotter, J. T., & Fan, D. P. (2010). Attitudes toward wolves in the United States and Canada: A content analysis of the print news media, 1999-2008. *Human Dimensions of Wildlife*, 15, 389–403.

Kahler, J. S., & Gore, M. L. (2012). Beyond the cooking pot and pocket book: factors influencing noncompliance with wildlife poaching rules. *International Journal of Comparative and Applied Criminal Justice*, 36, 103–120.

Kahler, J. S., Roloff, G. J., & Gore, M. L. (2013). Poaching risks in community-based natural resource management. *Conservation Biology*, 27, 177–186.

Ketcham, C. (2014). How to kill a wolf: An undercover report from the Idaho coyote and wolf derby. Retrieved from http://www.vice.com/read/how-to-kill-a-wolf-0000259-v21n3

Kinzig, A. P., Ehrlich, P. R., Alston, L. J., Arrow, K., Barrett, S., Buchman, T. G., &... Saari, D. (2013). Social norms and global environmental challenges: The complex interaction of behaviors, values, and policy. *Bioscience*, 63, 164–175.

Knight, J. (2003). *Waiting for wolves in Japan*. Oxford: Oxford University Press.

Liberg, O., Chapron, G., Wabakken, P., Pedersen, H. C., Hobbs, N. T., & Sand, H. k. (2012). Shoot, shovel and shut up: cryptic poaching slows restoration of a large carnivore in Europe. *Proceedings of the Royal Society of London Series B*, 270, 91–98.

Lute, M. L., & Gore, M. L. (2014). Stewardship as a path to cooperation? Exploring the role of identity in intergroup conflict among Michigan wolf stakeholders. *Human Dimensions of Wildlife*, 19, 267–279.

Marchini, S., & Macdonald, D. W. (2012). Predicting ranchers' intention to kill jaguars: Case studies in Amazonia and Pantanal. *Biological Conservation*, 147, 213–221.

Marquez, C., Vargas, J. M., Villafuerte, R., & Fa, J. E. (2013). Risk mapping of illegal poisoning of avian and mammalian predators. *Journal of Wildlife Management*, 77, 75- 83.

May, P. J. (2005). Regulation and compliance motivations: examining difference approaches *Public Administration Review*, 65, 31–44.

Muth, R. M. (1998). The persistence of poaching in advanced industrial society: Meanings and motivations—An introductory comment. *Society & Natural Resources*, 11, 5–7.

Muth, R. M., & Bowe Jr., J. F. (1998). Illegal harvest of renewable natural resources in North America: Toward a typology of the motivations for poaching. *Society & Natural Resources*, 11, 9–24.

Nellemann, C., Henriksen, R., Raxter, P., Ash, N., & Mrema, E. (2014). The Environmental Crime Crisis: Threats to Sustainable Development from Illegal Exploitation and Trade in Wildlife and Forest Resources. Geneva: United Nations Environment Program. http://www.unep.org/unea/docs/RRAcrimecrisis.pdf (retrieved 14 November 2016).

Nie, M. (2003). *Beyond wolves: The politics of wolf recovery and management*. Minneapolis, MN: University of Minnesota Press.

Pohja-Mykrä, M. K., & Kurki, S. (2013). Large carnivore poaching and strong community support to it challenges the legitimacy of current population management. *Helsingin Yliopiston Ruralia-Instituutin Raportteja*, 98, 44.

Review of the Roots of Youth Violence: Literature Reviews. (2013). Retrieved from http://www.children.gov.on.ca/htdocs/English/topics/youthandthelaw/roots/volume5/chapter03_rational_choice.aspx - foot2,

Rodwell, T. C., Tagg, J., & Grobler, M. (1995). Wildlife resources in the Caprivi, Namibia: The results of an aerial census in 1994 and comparisons with past surveys. Retrieved from http://www.drfn.info:85/pdf/RDP09.pdf

Ruid, D. B., Paul, W. J., Roell, B. J., Wideven, A. P., Willging, R. C., Jurewicz, R. L., & Lonsway, D. H. (2009). Wolf–human conflicts and management in Minnesota, Wisconsin, and Michigan. In Wydeven, A. P., Van Deelen, T. R., & Heske, E. J. (Eds.). *Recovery of Gray Wolves in the Great Lakes Region of the United States: An endangered species success story*. New York, NY: Springer.

Salant, P., & Dillman, D. A. (1994). *How to conduct your own survey*. New York: John Wiley and Sons.

Sharmaa, K., Wright, B., Joseph, T., & Desai, N. (2014). Tiger poaching and trafficking in India: Estimating rates of occurrence and detection over four decades. *Biological Conservation*, 179, 33–39.

St. John, F. A. V., Keane, A. M., Edwards-Jones, G., Jones, L., Yarnell, R. W., & Jones, J. P. (2012). Identifying indicators of illegal behavior: carnivore killing in human-managed landscapes. *Proceedings of the Royal Society B-Biological Sciences*, 279, 804–812.

Stewart, K. (1996). Mountain gorillas killed by poachers. *Gorilla Conservation News*, 10, 17.

Treves, A. (2015). Data Archives. Retrieved from http://faculty.nelson.wisc.edu/treves/data_archives/

Treves, A., & Bruskotter, J. T. (2014). Tolerance for predatory wildlife. *Science*, 344, 476–477.

Treves, A., Chapron, G., López-Bao, J. V., Shoemaker, C., Goeckner, A., & Bruskotter, J. T. (2015). Predators and the public trust. *Biological Reviews*. Retrieved from http://onlinelibrary.wiley.com/doi/10.1111/brv.12227/epdf

Treves, A., Jurewicz, R. L., Naughton-Treves, L., Rose, R. A., Willging, R. C., & Wydeven, A. P. (2002). Wolf depredation on domestic animals: control and compensation in Wisconsin, 1976-2000. *Wildlife Society Bulletin*, 30, 231–241.

Treves, A., Langenberg, J. A., López-Bao, J. V., & Rabenhorst, M. F. (in press). Gray wolf mortality patterns in Wisconsin from 1979 to 2012. Journal of Mammalogy.

Treves, A., & Martin, K. A. (2011). Hunters as stewards of wolves in Wisconsin and the Northern Rocky Mountains, USA. *Society & Natural Resources*, 24, 984–994.

Treves, A., Martin, K. A., Wydeven, A. P., & Wiedenhoeft, J. E. (2011). Forecasting environmental hazards and the application of risk maps to predator attacks on livestock. *Bioscience*, 61, 451–458.

Treves, A., Naughton-Treves, L., & Shelley, V. S. (2013). Longitudinal analysis of attitudes toward wolves. *Conservation Biology*, 27, 315–323.

Treves, A., Wallace, R. B., & White, S. (2009). Participatory planning of interventions to mitigate human-wildlife conflicts. *Conservation Biology*, 23, 1577–1587.

von Essen, E., Hansen, H. P., Kallstrom, H. N., Peterson, M. N., & Peterson, T. R. (2015). The radicalisation of rural resistance: How hunting counterpublics in the Nordic countries contribute to illegal hunting. *Journal of Rural Studies*, 39, 199–209.

Wright, J., & Rossi, P. (1983). *Armed and considered dangerous: A survey of felons and their firearms*. New York: Hawthorn.

Wright, R., Brookman, F., & T., B. (2006). Foreground dynamics of street robbery in Britain. *British Journal of Criminology*, 46, 1–15.

Index

Locators in *italics* denote figures; locators in **bold** denote tables.

Conservation Criminology, First Edition. Edited by Meredith L. Gore.

d

n

o

p

CPSIA information can be obtained
at www.ICGtesting.com
Printed in the USA
LVHW101930161220
674340LV00009B/409